We Were
YOUNG and
AT WAR

We Were
YOUNG and
AT WAR

The first-hand story of young lives
lived and lost in World War II

Sarah Wallis & Svetlana Palmer

Collins

This paperback edition published in 2010

First published in 2009 by Collins
A division of HarperCollins Publishers
77–85 Fulham Palace Road
London W6 8JB

www.harpercollins.co.uk

Collins is a registered trademark of
HarperCollins Publishers Ltd

ISBN 978-0-00-730357-1

Typeset in Great Britain by G&M Designs Limited,
Raunds, Northamptonshire

Printed and bound in Great Britain by
Clays Ltd, St Ives plc

Mixed Sources
Product group from well-managed
forests and other controlled sources
www.fsc.org Cert no. SW-COC-001806
© 1996 Forest Stewardship Council

Collins uses papers that are natural, renewable and recyclable products
made from wood grown in sustainable forests. The manufacturing processes
conform to the environmental regulations of the country of origin.

Contents

To Miriam, Claude and Hilda

To Ben, Eleanor, Joel, Lukas, Sergei and Tristan

Preface

*W*hile the diary of Anne Frank remains the most famous child's diary the world over, other young people's accounts that survived the Second World War have been largely forgotten, or remain unknown outside their own countries. Yet, written in private, concealed from parental gaze or enemy capture, these faded notebooks and singed papers tell us so much of what it was like to grow up in that war. Intimate and often more direct than those of adults, these diaries were a place to confide and to question, to preserve one's dignity, or maintain independence of spirit and thought.

The diaries and correspondence that follow have been chosen for the uniqueness of the personal narrative and the quality of the writing. Though we initially set out to find diaries that followed the authors through adolescence to the end of the war, we soon realized that, unlike fiction, real diaries couldn't always be made to fit. While some span the entire conflict, others start later, or contain large gaps; a few end abruptly, all too often a measure of the author's short life. Parts of some diaries are missing; it is a miracle some have survived at all. Where we have included letters, many are telling by their omissions, as well as the writer's tone.

Though ordered chronologically, this book does not set out to be a history of the war. Instead, it is driven by the stories of the contributors, framed by historical events and interwoven to bring out the often unexpected parallels and collisions of thoughts, ideas and emotions of those caught up in historic events, sometimes on opposite sides of the conflict, or thousands of miles apart. None of the diarists can be said to be representative of their nation: some succumbed to the ideas they were fed by adults around them *or by the state, others confound our expectations; many of them perhaps shed light on why it is that wars are fought by the young.*

After years of gathering, translating and researching these stories, we feel very close to our diarists. This is due not only to the length of time we have spent with them but also to the nature of their testimonies, so candid and so often courageous; they tackle the unpalatable, and reveal so much of themselves.

Svetlana Palmer and Sarah Wallis, London, 2009

Part One

Part One

CHAPTER ONE

The German Invasion of Poland

September–October 1939

'We'll see what will happen to me …'

Edward
Niesobski in
1939.

Dawid Sierakowiak
with his class in 1941.
Disputed only
surviving
photograph.

*T*hroughout the summer of 1939 governments across Europe hoped war could be prevented, or at least delayed. Though France and Britain did not respond when Hitler annexed Austria in March 1938 and Czech Sudetenland in September, they drew a line at Hitler's claims on Poland. Hoping their alliance would serve as a deterrent, the two countries promised to come to Poland's aid if Germany invaded. Their calculation was proved wrong. At 4.45 a.m. on 1 September 1939, 1.5 million German soldiers and 2,700 tanks began to cross Polish borders.

Having regained its independence at the end of the First World War, Poland was a lasting symbol of Germany's humiliating defeat and territorial losses incurred as a result of the 1919 Versailles Peace Treaty. For nearly twenty years Poland had been home to 700,000 ethnic Germans, but animosity was rife, intensified when thousands of Germans were forcibly moved inland in the run up to the war, lest they assist the invader. Now Hitler urged his commanders to liberate their fellow 'Aryans' and send 'every man, woman and child of Polish descent and language to their deaths, without pity or remorse'. Once conquered, Poland would be depopulated and resettled with the 'pure Aryan master race'.

A country made up of many ethnic minorities, Poland was also home to 3 million Jews, the largest Jewish community in Europe. On receiving news of the German invasion, thousands fled their homes, aware of Hitler's threats to 'annihilate the Jewish race in Europe'. While his neighbours fled, fifteen-year-old Polish Jewish teenager Dawid Sierakowiak and his family decided to stay put in their home town of Łódź in central Poland. With no *savings to pay for any means of escape, and unsure which way to go, they decided to face their fate in the city.*

Sixteen-year-old Polish teenager Edward Niesobski, from the small border town of Ostrów in western Poland, knew war was imminent. As a member of the Polish Scout Movement, which promoted the nation's independent spirit among the young, Edward had been undergoing regular paramilitary training for months, expecting to defend his country when the time came.

Dawid Sierakowiak recorded his thoughts and experiences in a diary he had started earlier that summer, but Edward Niesobski began to write only on the day of the German invasion itself. While waiting for instructions from his scout leader on the plan of action and his own role, Edward recorded the stark contrast between his romantic image of war and the actual events on the day.

1 September 1939

We've been expecting something big to happen all week. People have been gathering in groups all over town, talking; reservists have been called up; soldiers have been confiscating horses and cars. We are not going to let the enemy take us without a fight. Our scout group has been on full alert too. On Wednesday afternoon posters were put up, warning citizens to make sure they're fully prepared. Mobilization began on Thursday. My mother and siblings have already left the city, but I'm staying here with my dad. A siren went off at about 5 a.m. this morning; then came the air raids. It has started. The greedy German crusaders are reaching out with their empty claws. They want to take all our dearest places away from us: Poznań province, Silesia and Pomerania. The whole country is rising up as one today to fight them.

German planes are circling in the sky like black hawks. Their drone is the voice of death. This morning I saw large groups of people crossing over from the other side of the border. They said they'd been attacked last night by their German neighbours! That's why they left their homes and came over to our side of the border, some of them only half-dressed. Some are on bikes, others on horses and carts loaded with their most precious possessions. I'm not all that surprised some people who live along the border are now declaring that they are German. Everyone has the right to say who they are, and if you're German, you're German. But the thing is, these are the same Germans who've been eating our bread for the past 20 years, who have lived in our country all this time. They tried to stop us from rebuilding Poland after the last war, and now they're aiming guns at our chests, guns that they've kept hidden all this time. Well we, the Polish people, are not going to forgive them. They must have had so much anger inside. But I'm not afraid of war because I believe we are going to win and I believe that after a thousand years of fighting with our worst Western enemy we are going to destroy them, once and for all. *'The Germans won't spit in our face, and they won't make our children German,'* as the song goes. No longer shall our brothers on the other side of the border live in pain under the German yoke. So I am actually very happy.

The entire Ostrów administration has been evacuated by train. Most people have left too. Our army is moving to new positions. It looks like Ostrów is going to be surrendered without a fight. I'm not really worried about it though, I am sure it must be part of our military plan …

It's the afternoon now and I have packed most of my things, just in case. I didn't want to leave the city at first, but as soon as Dad got back he got all his stuff together, even his fishing rod, and convinced me that we should catch the last train.

I know we'll never give up, however hard things get. Even so, what happened next made me wonder. In the evening, people were no longer just leaving, they were running for their lives. Around 11 p.m. all remaining soldiers started to retreat, blowing up every bridge behind them. People are fleeing with no idea where they are going. We're told to run away, but where to, and why? ...

... We made it onto the last train. From the last carriage, they destroyed the tracks behind us. People are shocked by the amount of guns and ammunition the ethnic Germans had on them. Where did they hide them all? How come our military hadn't spotted them? We were looking for little clues, but missed the big ones, it seems. And now we see the results of our carelessness. The sky behind us is red. We can hear shooting in the distance, and we are nearly in Czekanow. And here we stay until 3 a.m.

As German land and air forces attacked simultaneously from the south, west and north, Edward and his father fled east, in the direction of Warsaw.

2 September 1939

In the morning we pull into Kalisz, but everyone's being evacuated from there as well. Our train is chased by German planes all day long. I wasn't scared of them until I saw what they could do. I saw charred skeletons in burned-out trains – they were people once. I saw people with no arms and legs, I saw a head roll into a ditch, I saw human insides hanging off telephone wires. When you hear the moans of the dying, and children crying, and then just moments later you see a plane right above you drop its bombs, well all you can do is wait for death. You no longer care about the dying, or the orphans. It's them today, but it might be your turn tomorrow. I got very sad thinking I might have to die far away from the people I love. That was the only thing I cared about.

There have been funny scenes today too. Every time we got bombed this young couple jumped off the train and ran into the potato fields, because someone had apparently told them to get at least 300 metres away from the train when there's a raid. So every time the train started moving again, they had to run as fast as they could to get back on. We stayed the night in Sieradz.

3 September 1939

Queues of carts pulled by oxen in the streets, everyone is running from the Germans, the villagers are more afraid of them than of the devil himself, or just as much. In any case, the devil is always dressed up as a German in all the pictures they see. Where are all these people headed? They have no idea. How many will come back to find their family home in ruins?

At a station after Sieradz our train took on the first wounded. These people covered in blood are the first crop of the harvest of war – and to think, all of it caused by just one person, Hitler. When you cut wood, there are always splinters, as the saying goes.

Our train stops on the approach to Łódź. People look up to see if they can spot the bearers of death in the skies, coming to turn our carriages into coffins. And then, there they are. First we hear their engines, then we see them, like black hawks. They are flying towards Łódź airport, it seems. We can see three of our Polish silver birds chasing them. The heavy hawks rise up and up, slowly. There are nine of them. Our birds approach from the sides, two of them sit on the German tails. After a while, two of the German planes fall with smoke pouring out; the rest fly away. We all feel very happy. Hope fills our hearts again as we see what our silver birds can do to their hawks. The train begins to move, but just as we get to Łódź station, we're under attack once again. We run for cover. From our shelter underground we can hear the din of anti-aircraft guns, the sound of airplanes and explosions. This might be our grave, we'll be buried alive if it collapses on our heads. This could be the end.

We hear a radio announcement that England has declared war on Germany, but the news comes as a terrible shock – why only now? The Germans have already crossed the Varta river, thousands of cities have been bombed, thousands of German planes are hovering over the whole of our country. You were supposed to come and help Poland right from the start! The sky is bright red in the north, where the spirit factory is on fire. We sleep at the train station.

A few blocks away from Łódź railway station, fifteen-year-old Dawid Sierakowiak was also sheltering from the German air raid.

3 September 1939

Half past midnight, an air-raid siren. I curse like a trooper. It's cold, dark and horrible outside. In the shelter we mess around a bit, but as usual the women shriek at us, 'This is war, you know – it's not a party!' We go out onto the street. We'd rather face the cold and the bombs than be with those old hags! Long live humour, down with hysteria!

The siren stops, we go to bed, but at five in the morning another one goes off. I grope for some clothes (it's cold, I'm half asleep) and bolt for the fire point. All quiet until nine, the siren has stopped. After that I'm on duty. It warms up. People everywhere are making piles of earth around their cellars. They're trampling all over the grass, digging it up with spades. The liaisons from our building get together, we chat, tell stupid jokes, then we all chip in. Three of us go out searching and come back with 300 grams of seeds. We share them out equally, offering some to the girls and any small children who are around. Suddenly, a siren sounds. We go downstairs for cover, I read out my comedy sketches. It gets stuffy so we go up to the third floor. Suddenly there's good news. It's reported on the radio that England has declared war on Germany. We shout for joy and run out to share the good news, in spite of the siren. The radio broadcasts 'God save the King', 'The Marseillaise' and 'Poland is not yet lost' [Polish National Anthem]. It feels good.

After dinner – another siren. The first big air raid on Łódź. Twelve planes in triangles of three have broken through the defence lines and are bombing the city. We stand in front of the entrance to our block of

Page from Dawid's diary, September 1939.

flats and watch the battle. Little clouds of smoke appear around the planes from the shots fired by our anti-aircraft artillery. The squadron manages to evade them, then we see clouds of smoke coming from somewhere in the town centre. Incendiary bombs! Soon we can see smoke in other parts too. All of a sudden we see the planes coming towards us. Terrified, fighting the urge to watch, we take cover on the staircase, then come out again, repeating this about twenty times in five minutes. Three planes fly overhead, it looks like we're about to be bombed, but no. We breathe a sigh of relief. The next three pass over and leave us in peace too. The rest of the planes disappear. The danger is over, for now at least. We tell the terrified, distressed women in the shelter what has happened. Some of them are holding small children in their arms. It's a truly moving scene. Suddenly, a neighbourhood liaison in a gas mask runs in and reports that gas has been thrown in several places in the city. Panic sets in. The lucky owners of gas masks put them on, others take out their gauze pads. Outside it gets cold and windy. We beat the gong as an alarm. Tumult, fear, commotion. At last everything calms down. The gas warning turns out to be a false alarm.

This evening's news is as welcome as this morning's – France and Australia have joined the war! And the Polish soldiers on Westerplatte are still holding on, not letting the Krauts advance a step further, even though there are many more of them. And the station in Zbszyń has been taken back from the Germans! We say goodnight and go to bed full of joy.

4 September 1939

Two sirens during the night. It was bitterly cold. We crowded together in the shelter, warming one another as we slept. This whole war business is starting to get tiring and boring. This morning I slept until ten. It was nice and sunny, after the cold night. After the third siren we got some shocking but good news. The Germans torpedoed an English passenger ship carrying several hundred rich and influential American citizens. Eight hundred people were killed! Roosevelt has already said that the United States will not stay neutral in the war, even before this. What will he say now? All the air raid sirens today were false alarms. I have nothing to do. We sit and talk, we flirt with the girls … School on Monday, at last!

Expecting further news of Allied assistance, Dawid remained in Łódź. However, President Roosevelt responded by reassuring his citizens that America would remain neutral, despite the attack. The next day, Edward Niesobski tried to locate the rest of his family.

4 September 1939

This morning I started looking for my mum. There are twelve villages in the Mazev district, so I have asked around to try and find her address. My dad took a train back to Łódź to join the army. There are checkpoints at every bridge. I couldn't get any information at the first place I was sent. The town hall is struggling to cope with the numbers of refugees who need housing, and they're not working very hard at it either. There was a big poster at the town hall, calling on soldiers to join up. It said our eternal enemy was threatening our right to life and to freedom, and called upon everyone to fight. It made me feel sure we are going to win.

My search for my mum brought no results today. She wasn't in any of the villages I've been to so far, so I decided to stay the night at the fifth one. I am starting to lose all hope of ever seeing her again.

5 September 1939

I went back to Mazev this morning to look for Mum. There were only four villages left to search. In the afternoon I borrowed a bike and cycled towards Leczyca to look for her. I must have been going for about 5 miles when I suddenly heard someone calling my name. I turned around – and there was my mum!!! My search is over at last. How lucky to have found each other again!

Two hours later we got back to Osendowice, where Mum's been staying. The first thing I did was scrub myself clean. I hadn't had a proper wash since September 1st! It was already dark when I heard a voice, not just any voice, it was my dad!!!! He came looking for us, all the way from Łódź, and finally we are all back together again. My sister Krysia was happiest of all. She must have thought the Germans had eaten us all up. She was wrong of course, because Germans wouldn't eat lean meat like ours.

As the German army approached Łódź, the Polish government ordered all fit men between the ages of sixteen and sixty to march to Warsaw's defence. Fifteen-year-old Dawid, just a year too young to be mobilized, stayed behind on air-raid duty.

6 September 1939

God! What's going on! Panic, mass exodus, defeatism. The city has been deserted by police and other state institutions and is just waiting in terror for the entry of German troops. What's happened to people? They just can't stay put, running around in fear and confusion, pointlessly shifting worn out pieces of furniture. My duty ends at one in the morning. I go and wake up Rysiek for the next shift. He's in a pessimistic mood, it's from him I hear the so-called plans to evacuate the city. He says that in the office where his father works everything is packed up and that they'll be leaving Łódź any moment. But how? I'm told the Germans are going to take the city any moment now.

Run, run away, further and further away, step by step, wade, cry, forget – anything to be as far as possible from the danger. My dear, oversensitive mother is showing self-control. She comforts Mrs Grodzieńska and talks her out of her crazy plan to run away, gradually calming down the mass psychosis of a crowd about to be slaughtered. Father's losing his mind, he doesn't know what to do. Other Jewish neighbours come to talk. They talk about the order given to all those fit to carry arms to leave the city so as not be sent by the enemy to labour camps. They don't know what to do. They deliberate, then decide to stay put. People are leaving all the time: hordes of men are walking to a rallying point in Brzeziny. Reservists and conscripts are leaving the city. Behind them, women with bedding, clothing and food in bundles on their backs. There are small children with them. All our commanding officers have left the city and their posts, so we appointed ourselves as a joke and kept up the pretence until noon.

8 September 1939

Łódź has been occupied. It's been quiet all day today, too quiet. This afternoon I'm sitting in the park drawing a portrait of one of the girls when suddenly there's terrifying news. Łódź has surrendered! German patrols are in Piotrkowska Street. Fear, surprise ... surrendered without a fight? Perhaps it's just a tactical manoeuvre. We'll see. In the meantime all talk has stopped, the streets are empty, faces and hearts have hardened into stern severity and hatred. Mr Grabiński comes back from town and describes how the local Germans have been greeting their compatriots. The Grand Hotel, where the generals are to stay, is bedecked with garlands of flowers. Civilians – boys and girls – are jumping into military cars with the joyous cry 'Heil Hitler!', speaking German loudly in the streets. People who used to be quiet, patriotic and civil are now showing their true faces. The street lamps have been switched back on in the evening. No danger of air raids now.

That night, as German troops were welcomed with fireworks and dancing in Łódź, hundreds of Jews were burnt to death in a Bedzin synagogue, just over 100 miles south of the city. Dozens of Polish towns were in flames, but despite German 'cleansing measures' against thousands of Poles and Jews, Britain and France ruled out coming to Poland's immediate assistance, themselves under pressure to mobilize for war.

9 September 1939

In the morning an announcement was posted in Polish and German (German first!) calling for calm when the German troops enter the city. Signed: Citizens' Committee of Łódź. Later, I went a bit further out to watch the troops arrive. Lots of cars, the soldiers look quite ordinary, their uniforms different from the Polish ones though – they are steel green. Their faces are self-confident, swashbuckling. The conquerors! A car full of high-ranking officers with severe faces passes by, quick as lightning. People are quiet, they look on impassively. Hush! We go back to our blocks and sit around on benches, talking and joking. What the heck!

13 September 1939

Rosh Hashanah holiday [the day before Jewish New Year] is sad, drab, same as any other day. The same dry bread with a small piece of herring (only the herring makes it different from any other day). The order came today that the shops are to be open tomorrow. For Jews, this is the worst blow for a long time – the shops open on Rosh Hashanah! And the synagogues are to stay closed. Nowhere to pray together for mercy, nothing. All our basic freedoms are being taken away from us. I'm not a traditionalist and I always thought it was liberating to duck out of prayers, but these orders are painful to Jewish people. Now I understand what faith gives to believers – they are at peace, serene. To take away a man's only consolation, his faith, and to forbid a life-affirming religion, it's an unforgivable crime. The Jewish people won't let Hitler get away with it. Our revenge will be terrible.

15 September 1939

This is the first time mum went to buy bread and came back without. She gets up at five a.m. and stands in the queue until seven, when the bakery opens and gives out one-kilo loaves. That's how it's been for a week now. Today there was no more bread when it was her turn. Maybe one has to start queuing at one in the morning. In town, Hitler's agents take Jewish people out of the food queues, so that poor Jews who have no [Polish] maid are condemned to death from starvation. Twentieth-century German humanitarianism! The Rabinowiczes and their neighbours came back today from their wanderings. They look terrible. Their two sons were on another cart and they haven't come back. Nobody knows where they are. They talk of exchanges of fire, searching for places to sleep, going on foot for miles, dangers and so on. It makes my flesh creep. There are funny moments too. Humour can be found anywhere. Laughter in the midst of calamity.

With Warsaw itself under continuous artillery fire and merciless aerial bombing, after two weeks on the road Edward's family decided to head home. Coming across a quiet village south of the capital, they stopped for a few days of rest.

15 September 1939

Last night the Germans occupied all the places we have abandoned. They sent their cars in first, which moved pretty fast along the pavements so as to avoid the sand we put on the roads to slow them down.

They've set up camp next to the forest, surrounded by machine guns and cars. Their uniforms are made out of a greyish-green material. Their helmets are very smooth. They wear swastikas and eagles and they are in black and white, the German national colours.

People in the local villages have changed sides quick as a flash; they've turned German overnight. They bow when they see a German officer in the street. The Germans look down on them with scorn, but they don't seem to mind. German soldiers go round asking for cigarettes and tobacco, and the village girls flirt with them, dressed up in their Sunday best. I try to avoid seeing any of this, so I sleep in the stables.

17 September 1939

We went to bed in our clothes but couldn't sleep because of the shooting. By the morning German planes had pushed our infantry back into the forest. They shot at our soldiers and civilians shot at them too. It's all a complete mess. In the evening I decided I had to get some sleep. I was too tired to care about what might happen.

While Edward missed the events of that day, in Łódź, Dawid recorded what news he could, but admitted to being confused.

17 September 1939

It turned out today that our gymnasium has actually been disbanded. Gymnasium Number 1 is being merged with the girls' school. The buildings have been occupied. I feel despair overtaking me. In the afternoon I was out walking with [my friend] Jadzia when Marek ran up to us with strange, terrifying news. Russia has broken the non-aggression pact with Poland and has occupied our eastern areas. We still don't have the details. I couldn't understand anything at first. Later on, German, Soviet, English and Polish radio gradually clarified the situation. The Soviet government has mobilized its troops as it felt threatened (so much for their non-aggression pact with the Germans). Since there is no Polish government in Warsaw any more, Russia feels obliged to defend Belarus and the Ukraine against Germany. The Polish High Command has declared that it will not fight with Russia (so this act of aggression is clearly convenient in spite of everything) but will concentrate all its forces against the Germans. And the English radio commented that evidently the Russian army will cooperate with the Polish army. So what's going on? Could it be that Russia has remembered that Nazism is its worst enemy, after all?

Contrary to Dawid's hopes, Soviet troops began to occupy eastern Poland in accordance with the secret addendum to the German-Soviet Non-Aggression Pact signed in August 1939. As Poland was split into two spheres of influence, all the Polish Army's hopes of regrouping in the east for another offensive were dashed. In occupied Łódź, Dawid enjoyed the return of at least some signs of normality.

19 September 1939

I went to school by tram in a clean uniform (I had to walk back, and will have to walk tomorrow, no money for the tram). There are fifteen girls and eighteen boys – from both gymnasia. We had three lessons, same as yesterday. Revision, mostly. We didn't get any reports. There were a few new teachers, not many. We don't know if we are going to be taught with the girls or separately, because it's a squeeze. If separately, we'll probably be the afternoon shift.

At five in the afternoon, I listened to Hitler on the radio. He spoke from '*die befreite Stadt Danzig*' [German, 'the liberated city of Danzig', or Gdańsk in Polish] after an ovation from the crowd. That speech showed he doesn't deserve his reputation as a great statesman. He threw himself around, screamed, insulted, pleaded, buttered people up, but most of all he lied and lied. He lied that Poland had started the war, he lied about the persecution of Germans in Poland ('*Barbaren!*'). He lied about his good peaceful intentions, etc. Then he came out with a string of insults directed at the Polish authorities, Churchill, Cooper (Duff) and Eden. He talked about his desire for a deal with England and France. He talked about the injustice of the Treaty of Versailles, saying that Poland will never exist in the borders decided by the Treaty. He said that the English effort to overthrow the ruling German government would never succeed – the best proof we've heard that the English are seriously attempting such a thing. At the end, he talked about his good relations with Russia (? …) and the impossibility of a German–Russian conflict. He ended his speech with a few phrases, full of pathos, about Gdańsk.

Three days later, Edward once again passed through Łódź, this time on his way home.

22 September 1939

The city doesn't look like there is a war on; it's back to normal. Schools have been open again since 11 September. There are lots of German posters on the walls and Hitler's flags all over. I feel like a stranger in my own country. There's not much food in Łódź and people spend hours queuing for potatoes. We walk across Łódź to Kalisz train station.

23 September 1939

We spend the night at the train station with 300 other people, waiting for a train which never comes. It finally arrives at about 3 p.m. It moves very slowly and I can see the wrecks of burned-out trains, and some freshly repaired bridges. We reach Kalisz at 8 p.m., where we wait for an hour. From there, we go straight on to Ostrów. At 3.30 a.m., after three weeks on the move, I am back at home. Everything is just as we left it, because our aunt lived there while we were away. The first thing we do is have a bath. You can imagine what we looked like at the end of our 'adventure'!

Edward's diary breaks off here. Within days, Poland surrendered and his home town of Ostrów was annexed into the Third Reich. As Polish language and culture were banned, all Polish citizens were subject to an intensive programme of Germanization. While the fate of Łódź and its 250,000-strong Jewish community remained undecided, Dawid described the immediate changes in the life of his neighbourhood.

3 October 1939

Though it is just about possible for most clerks, workers and shopkeepers to go back to their work, it's harder for Jews. Business people, shop owners, middlemen, merchants, etc., all are too afraid to go out in case they are picked up for forced labour and so lose their livelihood. They try selling things door-to-door, like most of our neighbours do – stockings, bread, sugar, knitted clothes, etc. Everyone has something to sell, the goods pass though the hands of dozens of middlemen, wholesalers and traders, but none of this can save the Jewish people from a rapid slide into poverty. My father has no work, he is just suffocating at home. We have no money either. A total fiasco!

4 October 1939

Unfortunately, I haven't managed to avoid the miserable fate of other Jewish people – forced labour. Some older people talked me into going to school along Wólczańska Street – a shorter route, and I went that way yesterday: there were swastikas on all the houses, lots of German cars, masses of soldiers and local Germans wearing swastikas. I managed to get through it yesterday, and today, emboldened, I went the same way. Near Andrzeja Street a German pupil ran up to me with a big stick in his hands and shouted; '*Komm arbeiten! In die Schule darfst du nicht gehen!*' [Come to work! You can't go to school!]. I didn't protest – I knew that a student card wouldn't help. He took me to a square where some Jews had been put to work picking leaves off the ground. The sadist wanted to force me to climb some 2-metre high fence, but seeing that I wouldn't do it, he went away. The work in the square was supervised by a soldier, who also had a big stick, and crudely ordered me to fill puddles with sand. I've never been so humiliated, I saw the smiling mugs of passers-by laughing, enjoying the misfortune of others. The stupid, abysmally stupid louts! It's they who should be ashamed, our tormentors. Humiliation inflicted by force is not humiliation! But anger, a helpless rage boils inside anyone forced to do this stupid work while being taunted. There is only one answer: revenge! After half an hour's work, the soldier called all the Jews (some of whom had their caps turned back to front 'for fun'), lined us up, ordered one of us to take back the spades and the rest to go home. Playing at being magnanimous!

I arrived at school in the middle of the first lesson, late for the first time in my entire school career. The teachers can't do anything about it: 'for reasons outside the Jews' control'. I went home the old way, through Kilinski Street. At home mum was frightened to hear how I'd been forced to work. In the evening we found out that one of the Germans living in our street 'keeps an eye' on the Jews in our block of flats. This really upset my poor nervous parents. Meanwhile, at school, they've announced that pupils who don't pay a sum of money will be barred. What's going to happen to me?

CHAPTER TWO

The German Invasion of Western Europe

April–September 1940

'Please send me a map of France, Belgium and Southern England'

Brian Poole in
February 1945; insert
is of Trudie Lach.

Micheline Singer's
school ID card, 1940.

Herbert Veigel
(centre) in February
1941 with brothers
Gerhard and Fritz.

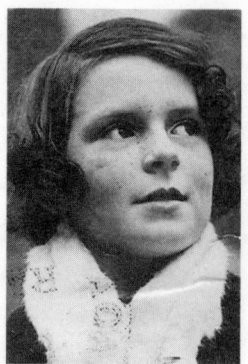

*F*rom September 1939, Britain and France had been preparing to defend themselves against Germany's Blitzkrieg, or 'lightning war', which had defeated Poland so quickly. Britain had no conscript army and spent the opening months of the war building up its manpower, while sending the five existing regular divisions of the British Expeditionary Force (BEF) across the Channel to France in December. France called up all 101 divisions of its army, still haunted by the experience of the First World War. Many soldiers were deployed to the Maginot Line, concrete defences built along the border with Germany, which the French hoped was inviolable and would prevent a surprise attack. By the spring, Hitler had already postponed his invasion of Western Europe twice, once because of the autumn mud and the second time after an intelligence breach.

To the majority of people in Britain and France in the winter of 1939–40, the war hardly seemed real. Aside from the absence of enlisted fathers, sons and brothers, nothing much seemed to happen. In London and Paris, cafés and restaurants were full; theatres and cinemas opened as usual. In Britain the period became known as 'the phoney war', in France 'la drôle de guerre', the funny or odd war. Many of the British children evacuated from the cities in September 1939, in anticipation of devastating German bombing raids, returned home. By April 1940 the German generals had drawn up a new strategy and were now waiting for a period of favourable weather to launch their offensive in the West.

Seventeen-year-old Herbert Veigel, from the provincial town of Heilbronn in southern Germany, had just completed his training in radio communication with the Luftwaffe. On the outbreak of war he had signed up as a volunteer, lying about his age and forging his father's signature. Six years in the Hitler Youth had groomed him as a soldier and prepared him for the 'unavoidable war' to win new German 'living space' in foreign lands. Soldiering also offered him an escape from his pious parents and the tedium of school. The youngest boy of seven siblings, Herbert had often felt overshadowed by his elder brothers' academic and sporting successes. Now that three of his brothers, all devout Nazis, were fighting for Germany, one already decorated for his part in the invasion of Poland, Herbert was determined not to be left behind.

Thirteen-year-old Parisian Micheline Singer's main experience of the war so far was the flattering attention she received from British Expeditionary Force troops stationed in France. When war was declared the previous September, Micheline and her family had been staying with relatives in the Normandy town of Verneuil. Her father enlisted immediately, while the rest of the family stayed on in Normandy rather than return home to Paris, the more likely target of a German attack. Micheline's mother struggled on her own to rein in her increasingly independent-minded daughter.

In England, sixteen-year-old grammar school boy Brian Poole could not wait for the war to speed up. He was impatient to leave the Boy Scouts and enlist in the armed forces. An only child, Brian lived in the Cheshire village of Lostock Gralam, an hour's bus ride from Manchester. A year earlier Brian had signed up for a penpal scheme, and he and New Jersey schoolgirl, Trudie Lach, now also sixteen, had been exchanging regular letters across the Atlantic. Brian had initially introduced himself, describing his hobbies as 'stamp collecting, model aeroplane building, keeping birds, cycling' and scouting. When Brian wrote to Trudie that April, almost exactly a year into their friendship, they were still getting to know each other.

5 April 1940

Dear Trudie,

Thanks for the mags. You want a snap of me, do you? Why to look at my face? Wouldn't it be better if you did not? I am afraid you might stop writing to me, and that would never do. Anyhow I have not got any good ones so I will get one taken. Have you a new one of yourself?

Seven months of war and nothing has happened, it's very depressing you know. Dad and I think Chamberlain's an old woman. We want more men like Churchill.

I am sure your new dress looks very sweet, so let me add another compliment to your collection. What colour is it? No the boys don't take much interest in girls clothes here, but we would not dream of taking a girl out who was not smart.

I am looking forward to the time when we will meet. It certainly would be fine.

We have a lovely pine forest only 6 miles from home. We went through it two weeks ago and it nearly broke Mother's heart to see that they were chopping lots of the trees down for war purposes. One of the damnations of war.

Our district is getting more war-minded. Wincham Hall only ¾ of a mile away from home has been turned into a training centre for troops. The first batch of men arrived last Wednesday. Real raw recruits marched from the station by a sergeant.

I have got a German helmet that father brought home from the last war. I have decided to paint it with red, white and blue stripes and wear it if air raids come. Mother is ashamed of me for touching it.

I went to the end of term dance last Thursday, the first one for about two months. I and the boys arrived a little late and the best girls had been picked up and some chaps weren't letting them go. So the only dances we could enjoy were foxtrots and general excuse-me dances. So being, I and the boys went home by ourselves. We decided to sing and make a noise until a policeman arrived and told us to shut up.

I am enclosing two newspaper cuttings one about Jitterbugs and the other a picture of our top-score fighter pilot. Don't you think he's a fine chap?

Yours,

Brian

Trudie Lach in 1939.

Though in Britain it still seemed as if nothing much was happening, by the spring five newly created divisions of the British Expeditionary Force were ready for combat and had joined the troops already stationed in France. In Normandy, Micheline and her mother were having increasingly frequent rows. After one, in which she was accused of being selfish, Micheline decided she needed a new confidante and began to keep a diary.

6 April 1940

I met an English soldier this afternoon. He was very young, very handsome and distinguished, and unusually for an Englishman, he had magnificent teeth. Another one joined us, he was nice too, and then another one with glasses, who took the first two away with him. They all had motorbikes.

Our Latin teacher wasn't there and I think our laughter could be heard from 20km away.

24 April 1940

Yesterday I spent all day talking with two very nice English soldiers, laughing the whole time. Two lorries arrived at 5 o'clock this afternoon and I went to talk to them too (the four soldiers in them, not the lorries).

Oh I'd better finish off writing about yesterday. We had so much fun ... I did something terrible, I hardly dare confess ... I skipped school. It's amazing how easy it is! I was so happy to miss Latin! I was sad when the soldiers left. But today's ones! The first thing they did was invite me to come and sleep with them in their lorry and to go for a walk that night ... To which I replied: 'Don't be stupid.' They called me 'Sweetheart', etc. Luckily all the English soldiers are not like that, if they were I wouldn't be able to enjoy my one source of entertainment in Verneuil.

25 April 1940

Lots more English soldiers passed through. Some of them asked for my address. I hope they write to me. They behaved much better than yesterday's lot! Besides, they didn't have too bad a time. They offered me a cigarette, which I smoked in the street! If the people of Verneuil don't like it, I don't care. Another one asked for my address. I gave it to him. Will he write to me? Will he write to me? That is the question!

Page from Micheline's notebook, 1939.

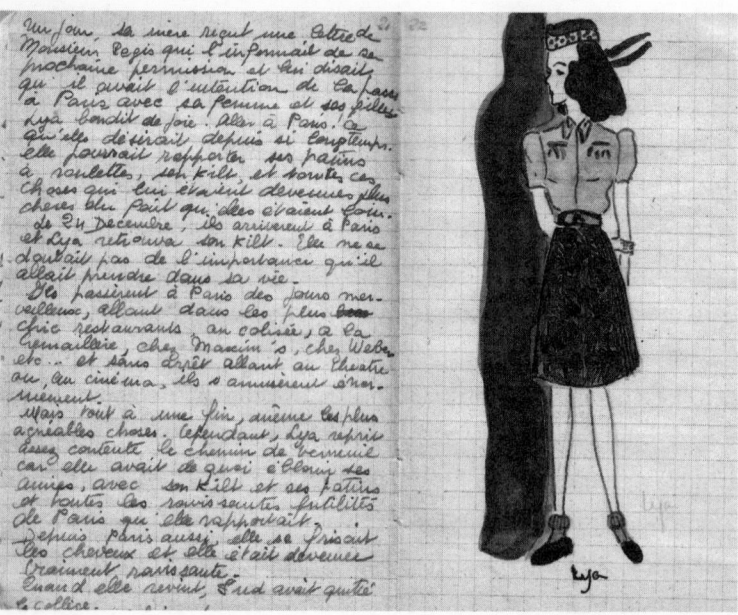

I love watching the English go by! ... My one source of pleasure is talking to them. I think I'm going to get told off by the Latin teacher for missing my lesson last Tuesday, but I don't care!

On 10 May, a week of good weather was forecast and Hitler launched 'Operation Yellow'. One hundred and thirty-six German divisions attacked Holland and Belgium. Within days Holland capitulated and German troops made the first breach in the French defences. Flieger (Aircraftman) Herbert Veigel was serving as a radio operator with the staff of the Supreme Command of 2nd Army Corps behind the German lines. He wrote home to his family from an area already conquered by the front-line troops, just over a mile away from the French border.

19 May 1940

My dear family,

We crossed the border into Belgium yesterday, and after we did, the first villages we came to had been destroyed, their bridges blown up. They'd been abandoned. Cows ran around in the fields, mooing because they hadn't been milked for days. Everywhere we went we saw the same thing, endless columns marching along ruined streets, passing bombed-out villages, every now and then a wooden cross with a steel helmet next to it. There are Belgian tanks and lorries in the ditches. And our Stukas 9 and Jaeger constantly overhead. If it weren't for the sound of the artillery day and night, you wouldn't know there was a war on. Who would have thought that I would be here!

Fondest hellos to you all, from your loving Herbert

22 May 1940

Dear family,

I just wanted to write a quick note, to let you know I'm still alive. What with eating, drinking, sleeping and **** [self censorship] duties there's hardly any time for writing. The day before yesterday our whole division advanced by 90km. The retreating troops can't get away from our front-line troops. Prisoners stream in the other direction, all different and jumbled up: French, Belgians, Negroes, Indians, Chinese, etc. They look so terribly dejected. In most of the towns there are only a few houses still standing, the rest shot to bits and burnt down.

The way we live needs to be described. All the villages have been cleared, so all the houses are at our disposal. We ended up in an outwardly unremarkable house, which is quite magic inside. Ten of us have moved in, we each have a bed; there are two in each room. And we have everything we need. There's a lovely kitchen with beautiful crockery and an unbelievable stock of food. The cellar is full of wine and champagne. The cupboards are full of valuable things. It is such a shame we can't take anything with us. There's a piano here too and we've been playing and singing. We are living like 'Gods in France'. When you

Herbert's letter, 6 June 1940.

see a scene like this you can truly say: our greatest victory so far is that the war has not been fought in our own country. Please send me a map of France, Belgium and Southern England.

Send my greetings to everyone, with a Heil Hitler!

Your Herbert

3 June 1940

My dear Parents,

We're off again tomorrow. I can't tell you where to. Fifty letters have been opened [by the censor] and I might get into big trouble. Please don't tell anyone about what I wrote in my last letter. Our lodgings are still excellent. We always seem to find the best houses: there's even a bath, which we have all been using, of course. It's the first house we've found with running water. These people must have had lots of money to be able to afford all this. If we want coffee, we have only the finest coffee beans. There are kilos of it. It's such a shame I have no room in my rucksack. Otherwise, Mummy dearest, I would bring you a few pounds. And such fantastic wine! If it were not for the scenes of war all around, if you just looked at our lifestyle in this house you'd never know there was a war going on. We all think it will be over by the summer. And we must come to terms with the number of losses. Victories like this always cost a lot of blood. We only hope that our own families don't have to sacrifice too much.

Please send my greetings to my siblings,

All my love from your Herbert

*By the time Herbert sent this letter, optimistic officials in Berlin were
already drafting memos on the post-war strategy for the European countries under German control.*

*In Britain, the War Cabinet, under new Prime Minister Winston
Churchill, held a meeting to assess Britain's ability to withstand an invasion
were France to fall and Germany commit its full forces across the Channel.
Much of Britain's arms and ammunition had been left behind in northern
France when 300,000 BEF soldiers escaped across the Channel from Dunkirk.*

*From Cheshire, Brian wrote to Trudie about his own small contribution
in the aftermath of Dunkirk.*

5 June 1940

Dear Trudie,

Please excuse my writing as I have broken my finger, the one next to
my little finger on my right hand. We were camping and the scout master
woke us up at five in the morning to say that 2,500 of the BEF were arriv-
ing that morning [from Dunkirk] at a certain place 5 miles away. Of
course, we were only too glad to put up tents, 400 in number. It was misty
and we raced down the road, a steep hill with a bend in it, I did not pull
out quick enough, hit the curb, did a headlong dive over my [bicycle]
handlebars and crashed.

I'll never forget those men all my life. All smiling not a grumble, some
had only the clothes they stood up in. I talked to some of them. I am
enclosing a French coin which was in a soldier's pocket in the most
successful retreat in history.

We are all now resolved to give the Germans Hell!!! And we'll fight
like that too. I'm feeling okay at present. I've just heard from a friend
who was in Belgium. I was getting very worried about him.

Your letter arrived today. The snaps are very good. You look very good in your new frock. I'll get my snap done quickly.

Food. I like plenty. I am very fond of fried potatoes, so have plenty.

MENU

	Breakfast	Lunch	Tea
Monday	Kellogg's' Corn Flakes, egg, bacon, fried bread	cold beef, potatoes, cabbage, carrots, gravy	fruit, jelly, cream
Tuesday		fried fish and potatoes	eggs boiled
Wednesday		fried potatoes, steak and kidney pie	salmon, salad
Thursday		fried liver, bacon, gravy	cold meat pie
Friday		stew, potatoes	Welsh rarebit
Saturday		sausage and cheese	Cornish pasties

We all dine together on Sunday. This is bumper day:

Breakfast	Lunch	Tea
grapefruit eggs, bacon, toast	beef or mutton, roast potatoes cabbage, cauliflower, peas	salad, cold ham or tongue fruit trifle, cream, rice pudding

That's a typical week with the war on. I might add Mother is a fine hand at making steak and kidney pie. She likes baking. What do you eat?

I'm same as you, much immune from love. I once thought I was but afterwards I realized I wasn't. Certainly when I saw her, my heart went boom-boom. How old was your dentist?

You're certainly going to have a holiday. I don't know whether I shall have a holiday this year. Dad thinks it's not fair to go enjoying ourselves when men are fighting for our lives.

Do you let the chaps chase you or do you chase the chaps?

How do you like your men?

Do you like fishing?

You and yours keep well.

Yours,

Brian

It's a lovely boiling hot day so I'm going to sit in the sun by the river and do a little fishing.

Across the Channel the Germans used that day's good weather to launch their biggest attack on France yet. Many civilians abandoned their homes in a panicked exodus south. By the end of the week one sixth of the population of France was on the move. In Verneuil, just 100km west of Paris, Micheline, her mother and sister, Nicole, were caught up in the chaos and a week went by before Micheline was able to record the events in her diary.

9 June 1940

Everything's gone wrong. The Bosches are everywhere, every day they make terrible gains. Daddy says he is going to send a message to Aunt Laura, asking if we can go to hers. Between Sunday evening and Monday morning Evreux was bombed six or seven times. It's in ruins.

10 June 1940

Verneuil was bombed at 1.30. There was a train full of soldiers at the station. It is always so stupid to leave the trains sitting there like that. A bomb dropped on it: 30 dead and 100 wounded. I watched the bombs fall. I wasn't afraid, I don't know why. I just thought it was disgusting to attack such a small town. It's funny a plane on a bombing raid looks a bit like a big bird. During the bombardment we prayed with the little boy from downstairs, who said: 'The animals! The pigs! The bastards!' He and Nicole were very frightened. The Krauts made a big racket. All three of us were breathless. Weird …

We can't stay in Verneuil. All the shopkeepers have fled. As the RAF troops went past in convoy we asked if they could take us with them. But none of them could.

For dinner we have rotten hard-boiled eggs.

11 June 1940

Morning: I am really sick! It must have been the hard-boiled eggs … I threw up twice but then I felt better afterwards. In the afternoon we left by bus with Brunetier the dentist and his daughter, wife, cousin and his horrible other daughter. We all just about managed to fit in. Mummy asks why my case is so heavy, but it's not surprising as I have my diary in it and the first five volumes of my novel. Result: I have only the one dress, and I forgot my handbag.

We have a dog with us, Mme Bissell's, she abandoned it. The bus had barely set off when it was sick, all over Nicole's new skirt. The smell was so bad that three officers sitting behind us put on their gas masks. We reach La Loupe. There's a bomb alert.

We were lucky to get a place on a livestock truck. Hot and dusty and very dirty! The bombing carries on the whole way. I squash my bag in half sitting on it, and I'm bathed in sweat. We stop for four hours on the track, 1km from Le Mans. We are dying of thirst and Brunetier's cousin gives her daughter something to drink without offering us any.

11 June 1940

Evening: We reach Le Mans at last. I like the town immediately. Mostly because it is stuffed full of English soldiers. It's an English town. Maybe Bill and Sinclair are here!

We're having dinner. It's 9 p.m. Air-raid warning! No electricity. We go out and it's pouring with rain. We sit down against the wall. I have my new hat on – completely ruined. Mummy is covered in mud from head to toe; the rain spreads it everywhere. There's a terrible smell. We find a shelter and stay till 1 a.m. It's warm and dark, good for sleeping. People move around from time to time, children cry out. The pot of honey came open in my bag and everything is covered in it! … I open my eyes and then I go back to sleep.

Darak, the dog, is a darling. He never whimpers, even if someone steps on his paws. The station guard moved us from the shelter. We spent the rest of the night on the station platform, where we couldn't sleep. At every sound, Mummy woke me, saying, 'Is that an air-raid warning?' English officers and soldiers go past sometimes. There's a lieutenant with glasses and an ugly girl who are getting to know each other and I bet they will love each other madly as soon as we are gone.

At 4 in the morning we take the train to Angers. We lost the Brunetiers in the shelter, but met up with them again in Rennes. We change trains in Angers and I take the opportunity to wash the honey out of my bag.

13 June 1940

We are resting. I couldn't put my hair in curlers in the train or at the station in Le Mans, so I look hideous.

Terribly tired.

14 June 1940

Very tired but things are getting better. Marie-France, my cousin, has cheered me up. She is very nice. If only there were Tommies here, then I really would be happy! There are no more air raids and I miss them because we are constantly just waiting for them to arrive, and I hate waiting.

Yesterday Paris was declared an open city; today the Bosches are fighting all around it. Our troops are pulling out. It's crazy how many men they have! The situation is hopeless but I'm sure we'll win. They put up their stupid posters: 'We will win because we are stronger.' But that's not true. We will win because it's not possible that God will allow the killers of small children to win control.

That day, 14 June, a month after first breaking through the French defences, German troops entered Paris without a fight. The government had fled, declaring the capital an 'open city' to prevent it being reduced to ruins. The first German soldiers to reach the city centre planted Swastika flags on the Arc de Triomphe and the Eiffel Tower. As Herbert Veigel's division advanced further across France, he was able to write letters home during brief rest periods.

15 June 1940

My dear family,

It's unbelievable how fast we are advancing, right on schedule too. Today we heard the news that our troops have marched into Paris. By the time you get this letter, France might have capitulated. And the war should be over in a few weeks after that! All this will hopefully mean that every last German will have faith in our Führer from now on. We have known for a long time that he is the greatest German of all time.

Fondest greetings from your Herbert

17 June 1940

Dearest family,

We are in pursuit of the defeated enemy at an incredible pace. We will soon have the last of them surrounded. I am writing to you again for a very particular reason. Last night we discovered a hosiery factory and we made off with as many socks as we could, ladies' and men's. When I was packing early this morning I noticed that in the dark I had grabbed lots of odd pairs, mismatched in size and colour. I put them together as best I could, and now I'm worried that they'll all be too big. But you can make them smaller, can't you? The factory was already on fire when we went in and now it's nothing but a heap of ashes.

With fondest love,

Your Herbert

21 June 1940

Dear Parents,

We're now heading for the south of France. All along the roads you see signs of frantic retreat by the French. There's equipment and all kinds of things lying around everywhere. If it wasn't essential they just dropped it. We see thousands of prisoners every day, with very few guards. They're not putting up any kind of defence. Whole units seek out the prisoner-of-war camps and give themselves up. That's how shattered they are by the strength of the German army. I am shocked again and again by what I see of the streams of refugees. Mothers come and beg us for bread! They are all moved by the honourable behaviour of the German soldiers, they had imagined them to be barbarians.

Fondest thoughts from your Herbert

Four days earlier, the French head of state, Marshal Pétain, urged his coun-trymen to lay down their arms; and over half the total of French soldiers taken prisoner during the course of the war surrendered in the week that followed. But not everyone complied. Micheline, her mother and Nicole were staying with their relatives, just 150 miles south of Paris, as they antic-ipated their first encounter with German troops.

18 June 1940

We have been sent to a farm in the countryside because the soldiers are going to try and defend L'Ile Bouchard.

Before we left we had a long discussion. Cousin Jules said that the Germans do not rape women 'because they are decent'. Uncle Fritz, who spends his days sucking his false teeth, never intervenes in conversations. But at this point he adjusted his dentures and said: 'That's not why, oh no! It's because they don't have the temperament.'

We are staying in a room infested with spiders, ants, dead flies, etc.

21 June 1940

The Bosches are in L'Ile Bouchard. They are very disciplined and well behaved and pay for everything they buy. We are discussing an armistice. We are going to let the English carry on alone.

Today, Saturday, they positioned themselves near us. In the evening 'they' came. They wanted to dance with us, with Louise, her three sisters and me. We said we weren't feeling well and they didn't press the point. Luckily, Mummy said to them:

'Young girls, headache.'

And one of them said: 'Ah yes! France headache.'

23 June 1940

It's never ending. They have stolen all the bicycles. All their lorries are French or English and they have pinched loads of things sent to us by the Americans.

In the afternoon Louise, Nicole and I went up to the windmill to get some peace and quiet, because the soldiers come by all the time to wash or just visit. The farmers are unbelievable. They are terrified of the Bosches and give them all their wine, eggs, etc., and bow and scrape to them. With the result that some of them think they can get away with anything. We came down from the windmill and were going to lie on a blanket on the grass. Two Bosches arrived and sat down right next to us; as we got up, they picked up this notebook and opened it. Luckily they don't speak French so they couldn't understand a word. But my diary has been soiled by Bosche hands. They left dirty fingerprints on these pages. It's my first defeat, my first humiliation.

We thought France was sure to win, and one month later everything's ruined. But there's still England, and we'll see what happens … In any case France and Britain are more united than ever.

26 June 1940

What a lot has happened today!

The Armistice was signed, for a start. The conditions are very tough, they include demobilizing the army but we haven't been told much yet. French troops are going to England en masse to carry on the fight and the RAF is bombing continuously.

Yesterday I talked with two German soldiers. They spoke excellent French and English, which they learnt at some university or other. I was up a tree and they were down below. I saw one of them again today, in the street, and he said hello to me. I was unsure what to do, whether to speak to him in front of people or not. He was with a whole group of soldiers. I nodded my head slightly and walked on. Suddenly I heard a click, and then another. I turned round – another click. It was a real ambush. Two of them were taking pictures of me. I was furious. As they went past another said to me, in French, of course:

'You are very pretty, mademoiselle.'

Grr … Grrr … The Bosches, they have no right to say that to me!

Later I was sitting on the kitchen windowsill with Marie-France, Hedwige [the maid] and Nicole and we were laughing. Suddenly some-one came up silently and put an arm round me. I thought it was Papa! Marie-France, Hedwige and Nicole started laughing like idiots. I turned round and saw it was a Bosche! I ran away as fast as I could, while those idiots just carried on laughing.

When I calmed down, I had a look at him and decided I had reacted like a little girl. He didn't do anything terrible. Frankly, I wish he were English because he's really quite good looking. And he's got brown hair and I vowed when I was nine that I'd never marry anyone blond.

So now that's two men who have taken me in their arms – this one and Sinclair, the Scot. But Sinclair wanted to show me the inside of his lorry.

1 July 1940

There is apparently a big battle going on between the English and the Bosches in the north of France. Good.

We went with Hedwige – who is from Alsace and speaks German – to ask the Bosches to lend us a ball and they came and played with us. We had fun but it was even more fun seeing the looks on Aunt Louise and Uncle Fritz's faces, they looked so protective, especially whenever a German came close to one of us. Uncle Fritz said: 'Ah! Who'd have thought they'd ever play with German soldiers.' And we enjoyed riling them. They are so annoying, going on at us all day long, trying to have a word with us, always wanting us to listen, always bossing us around.

4 July 1940

The Bosches who arrived on the 28th have left again. It's so lovely and quiet. They were real brutes, and there were industrial quantities of them. The commander often walked around in nothing but his boots, his monocle and his riding whip.

We are waiting for another division of Bosches to arrive, any day now. What fun!

With France under German control, Italy declared its allegiance to Germany. Now fighting alone, Britain seemed to be facing the imminent threat of invasion. Churchill was determined to 'fight for every inch', as he told the nation over the radio: 'Whatever has happened in France makes no difference to our actions and purpose.' Inspired by Churchill's resolve, From Cheshire Brian shared his own with Trudie.

20 June 1940

Dear Trudie,

Now for it, we're expecting it any time now. Bombs, parachutists anything. We're fighting with our backs to the wall, only us left to defend democracy. Any invader who sets foot on British soil is for it, instant death, no mercy. Any Italian pigs, especially. Only they daren't come out to fight! I can't see how you Americans stand by and watch, it's as much your fault as ours. You helped to make the Versailles Treaty. You and us stopped France from knocking hell out of Germany in 1919. And you think you're too far away to be troubled but if our fleet goes you're doomed. I admit the material help you are giving is welcome but I don't think it is enough. Your air force is small but the quality of men and material are I believe first rate. This thrown into the war would I'm sure turn the tables. Okay. It's off my chest. Please don't think me rude.

None of your letters have been censored only your mags. Nothing crossed out at all.

Just now our country is very beautiful. The trees are greener, the flowers prettier and even the birds seem to be singing sweeter. It makes us realize that these are the things we are fighting for. I and my friends are fully prepared to die fighting rather than let the Germans take all these things from us.

After great consideration I have decided to send a snap. It is three months old though. I'll send you a better one as soon as possible. This isn't a good one, you will notice also I've spilt rubber lubricant on my trousers.

Remember me to your people tell them not to worry we'll win if it takes a hundred years.

Yours,

Brian

A month later Brian turned seventeen and was now old enough to join his father in the 1 million strong volunteer army created in May 1940 to help defend Britain from invasion.

4 August 1940

Dear Trudie,

The best news yet, I am in the Home Guard. I've had three rifle drills up to now and I do my first duty from 9 p.m. to 6 a.m. on Wednesday, three hours duty, the rest asleep on the floor ready for action. What we want is not to shoot the Bosche but to bayonet him. That which the Germans don't like, cold steel. The General in command said our motto shall be: 'Kill the Bosche' and shoot to kill. Done a fine bit of work today, cleaned 20 rifles with Dad. No so bad, eh? Our house is simply littered with field dressings, supplies of uniforms, steel helmets, ammunition and I don't know what.

You have a sensible choice of your ideal man. Most girls have soft ideas such as having a chap with his hair parted in the centre.

By jingo I'm looking forward to receiving the record of your voice. If it's unbreakable you can send it at once, can't you?

The Royal Air Force are distinctly puzzled. For years they have had no rivalry – met no serious competitors in matters of the fair sex. But now the Poles. No one quite knows what it is about the Poles. The girls are not very helpful about it. They just make silly cooing noises and go all goofy when you ask them. 'Ooh! They're too wonderful!' is all you get. It is all very mysterious and galling for the Don Juans of the RAF. Also it's impossible to tell a Pole who had just pinched your girl what you think of him. It is a waste of words, and you cannot very well hit a brave ally over a little thing like that.

Last night and the night before we were in the dugout but no bombs were dropped. A week ago three bombs were dropped 2 miles away. All three failed to explode.

I read some more articles about the Americans who think we are starving. They have offered to send food here. Do not believe it we have plenty. I am eating more than ever.

I am going to stay in bed if they come over tonight and get up if the bombs begin to fall.

Why are you not asking me questions? I've run dry because I've no questions to answer!

Questions:

What is your attitude to the idea of compulsory military training?

Are you doing any sunbathing?

How do you wear your hair?

Hoping you're okay and having a fine time.

Yours,

Brian

Before the German troops could cross the Channel, the Luftwaffe needed to establish air superiority. Herbert was now stationed on the northern coast of France, near Calais, as 11 August, the date set for the Luftwaffe to intensify its daylight raids on Britain, drew closer.

7 August 1940

My dear family,

We have been relieved of lifeguard duty, just as the great strike against England is imminent. I think we are going to really experience something now, and we won't have much longer to wait. I can't tell you where we are. We are living the real outdoor life, like we used to in the Hitler Youth.

It's a shame about the beautiful material and the white suit, but maybe we can get a better, cheaper one in England. Six planes flew over today but they were forced to turn back in a hurry. They don't have far to go, it only takes about 10 minutes from here. All day long they flew overhead, sometimes 50 or more fighter planes.

Your Herbert

14 August 1940

My dears,

I just got Mother's lovely letter from Freudenstadt. I am so glad all is well at home.

I hope all this camping will finish soon. We are getting filthy, as there's very little water and we're in the same clothes for days on end. Tommy has discovered us and bombs us every night. But he is normally turned away by our anti-aircraft guns before he can strike. He never hits anything though. Last Saturday a Bristol Blenheim flew over at eight in the morning and was about to drop a bomb when our guns returned fire and after about ten shots he was on fire. A few seconds later he crashed near us. There was a huge explosion and bits flew everywhere. There was wreckage spread around for about 60 metres and you could hardly believe it was once a proud bomber of the Royal Air Force; all three crew were dead of course; when we arrived the bodies were still burning. But you can't feel any sympathy for them because they were trying to kill us.

Warmest hello from your Herbert

The next day the Luftwaffe launched its biggest assault on Britain so far. In France, in response to Pétain's call for the millions of refugees who had fled south to come home, Micheline and her family returned to their own flat in occupied Paris.

12 August 1940

The Lycée Racine reopened today and I have signed up for some summer courses. It won't be like this for long but it's quite shocking: no notebooks, no textbooks, no homework. Great or what! Lessons are from 9 till 11 in the morning, nothing in the afternoon. I can go up from the 5th to the 4th form without taking any exams because the head teacher ran away from the college at Verneuil and the Germans who've settled in there have taken everything. I found all this out from Yvette. She's back too, I was so pleased to see her again. She told me that Mademoiselle Brachuet, the Latin teacher, was so scared during the bombing of Verneuil that she wet her pants. She was out for a walk with the weekly boarders and Yvette saw it all. I would have loved to have been there! It would have been revenge for everything she put me through.

There are 2,000 Germans in Verneuil as well as 9,000 French prisoners, 40 Scots and a few English. Everything's been looted by those who stayed and by refugees passing through. The Germans have requisitioned most of the houses. The Flercks have a huge villa and they have four of them staying, which suits them fine as they get sent to do the shopping – the Germans don't like to queue. The only annoying thing is that when the Germans are drunk, they sometimes go to the wrong room. Oh to be a fly on the wall! …

The Germans have launched a massive attack on the English from the sea. The English threw tonnes of oil and petrol onto the water and when their planes bombed the Channel it all burst into flames, along with the Bosches. Hip, hip, hip, hurray! At least the English know how to defend themselves! They won't let their country be invaded while they're busy making fine speeches, like spineless old Pétain.

The incident in the Channel was part of a deception tactic to make it appear that the shores of Britain were protected by a wall of fire, and as invincible to the Germans as Micheline hoped.

By 20 August, the RAF's aerial defence of Britain was still keeping the invasion at bay. On that day Brian wrote to Trudie about his part in the events of the previous week.

20 August 1940

Dear Trudie,

The Battle for Britain has begun. But we are prepared for them. I have had 3 bombs dropped within 300 yards of me. We were out on duty with the Home Guard when we heard the aeroplane overhead, the scream of bombs, thuds and flashes of flame. By the time this letter reaches you I bet I'll have had some dropped nearer than that. The Home Guard brought its first Nazi bomber down on Sunday with rifle fire. I tried to machine-gun them but it did not come off. I am practising bomb throwing every night now. We are to fight guerrilla warfare and will be tougher now to kill a sentry without making any noise and such as that. Oh Boy. What fun!!!!! The thing I am dreading most is the army boots, big hefty things with studs in the bottom, Oh oh!!!!

What do you think about our Air Force, grand work, what? A friend of mine saw an anti-aircraft gun shoot a bomber clean in two only 16 miles away from home.

Yes I did make the plane in my picture. It is only 30-inch wingspan. I did make them 60- and 70-inch wingspan. But now the war's to be taken seriously it's no time for a boy old enough to fight to go flying model planes.

I went to a dance last Saturday night and they had a fine new dance called the kiss waltz. It's a waltz as you may have guessed and every time the lights go out you kiss your partner. It's good, fine, delicious. Do you have anything like this?

You still don't ask me any questions in your letters. When I write I have to think out all my own stuff. Write plenty. You don't know how I look forward to your letters they buck me up fine. So don't forget write plenty.

I suppose you are basking in the sun as I write this letter. I bet you are as brown as a berry.

I read in one of today's papers that conscription may be reduced from 20 years to 18, that means if it is true I'll be in it next year ready for when we invade Europe.

Have any of your letters from me been censored?

I don't like to think some old faggot in the censor reads our letters do you?

Hoping you are well and in the best of health.

Yours,

Brian

20 September 1940

Dear Trudie,

All's well. Still alive and kicking. But greatly enraged at the brutal bombing by our swinish enemy of London. If they destroy the Tower of London, the Houses of Parliament or any building like that I shall go raving mad.

We have been on manoeuvres all this afternoon with the Home Guard. First Day in my army boots. Oh!! Each one weighs about a ton.

It's very exciting learning how to advance in short rushes, bayonet charging. We have had grand instruction on bayonets from Dad. Where to stick it, in the throat, in the lungs or in the stomach giving it a twist as you pull it out. Things like this I would never have done before the war. But now nothing would give me greater pleasure than to cut a Hun's throat.

In answer to your question what is 'fish 'n chips'. This is Britain's favourite meal. You creep home to eat them, or now in the black-out you lower your dignity and eat them going home. If you come to England after the war you must have 12 cents worth for our first supper.

We don't know whether Adolf is still going to invade us but the RAF are giving him a belting every night.

You might think these letters stale, with nothing but war to talk about. You see, we are now all concerned with seeing it through and have little time for films, etc. But it will take more than Hitler to stop our little timetable, won't it?

Yours,

Brian

CHAPTER THREE

Under German Occupation

January–June 1941

'Don't leave us under the barbarian's yoke'

*B*y January 1941, 290 million Europeans were living under Nazi rule, with Hitler declaring that within 'a hundred years' the German language would be 'the language of Europe'. Britain and its Empire now fought alone to prevent Germany's complete domination of Europe west of the Soviet border. Churchill was determined to 'aid and stir the people of every conquered country to resistance and revolt', and planned to be ready to launch a land attack by 1942, having received the 'tools ... necessary for victory' from the United States, under the Lend-Lease scheme.

Inside the countries of German-occupied Europe people were treated according to Nazi racial policy. Even the daily food rations were allocated according to race, with Jewish Poles clearly intended to starve on 184 calories a day compared to the French on a ration of 1,300. In France there was an element of 'cooperation', albeit on unequal terms: France would be plundered but not completely exploited. While the Germans expropriated coal, food and works of art, a French administration continued to exist, universities and schools remained open and the south of the country remained nominally French. In the east, Poland had ceased to exist as an independent country and its lands were taken over as extra 'living space' and resettled by Germans. Schools and universities were shut down and the German language imposed. The country's 3 million Jews were taken from their homes and enclosed in medieval-style ghettos, where they were forced to work for the German authorities.

Dawid Sierakowiak and his family were evicted from their home in Łódź in May 1940 and moved into a ghetto created in the city's slum area. A perimeter fence sealed in Łódź's Jewish inhabitants, separating them from the rest of the city, renamed 'Litzmannstadt', which was then renovated and resettled with Germans. With no school to attend, at sixteen Dawid was confined to a narrow, perpetually hungry existence in which he and his family struggled to keep their dignity.

In England, Brian Poole had spent the remainder of 1940 enduring the Blitz. A raid on Manchester, in December, had destroyed his father's office and much of the city centre. Apart from a few gaps in their correspondence, which they put down to shipping losses, Brian and Trudie continued to share details of their lives on either side of the Atlantic.

By the end of July Micheline Singer and her family had moved back into their flat in the fashionable eighth district of Paris, just off the Champs-Élysées. The occupying Germans transformed the area around Micheline's home: the hotel opposite was requisitioned for high-ranking administrators, the Wehrmacht took over the ministry next door and the Gestapo based themselves just around the corner. Some things continued as before: Micheline and her best friend, Yvette, were back at their old girls' school, the Lycée Racine, where normal lessons resumed, though they now had to learn German.

After six months under German occupation, Micheline remained passionately Anglophile.

11 January 1941

I haven't made any good New Year's resolutions this year except to fight ferociously if we get the chance to revolt against the Bosches. I know how to fight! Last year a boy misbehaved with me and I broke three of his teeth.

I think the thing I love most about England is the Royal Air Force. I am mad about it and I would like a member of the RAF because he would be English and a pilot. That's one of the reasons why I want the English to win. But I am devastated because I looked at myself in the mirror with my skirt that's too short and my curls and realized that though I feel grown up because I have read loads and have quite a lot of experience, I don't look it. I would so like to look like a young woman on victory day, because ... oh, what a lot of nonsense I write!

15 January 1941

I keep trying to persuade myself that swedes and margarine are delicious.

The day before yesterday Yvette was listening to the radio when she heard a new song:

Hitler ... I can't bear the name ... he's a pig, he smells, he is finished ...
Unfortunately the signal went and she didn't hear the rest.

Here's another joke: What is the smallest meadow in the world? A Bosche's uniform because there's always a cow [slang for police] in it.

17 January 1941

I was weighed on Tuesday and I've lost 2 ½ kilos since October. Rations! I've nicked a pot of jam. I hid it behind my bookshelf. I am ashamed of doing such things because I know I will have to confess them to you, my dear diary. I would never have stolen jam before, I don't even like it, but now we eat so badly that I am always hungry. Today, for example, we had four lambs' kidneys, 5 francs each. They weren't on the ration card, they were very fatty though, and only as big as your thumb. And aside from the food, the gas doesn't heat up properly (since the Bosches came it's been useless). At twenty-five to one we still hadn't had lunch and we had to leave [for school again] at twenty to. So I started with pudding, then ate some potatoes and swede (which still wasn't cooked, so I left it) and finally left, munching on my minuscule kidney.

19 January 1941

I am in mourning for my silk stockings! They are completely ruined. I first wore them two years ago in Verneuil! So they have done me well. Luckily, Mummy has lots more in the same colour, so she won't notice if I take some!

I've finished the pot of jam.

22 January 1941

A friend of Yvette's was imprisoned, aged 16, for putting up a poster. He was locked in a cell for three months and when his father went to fetch him he had to take him home in an ambulance because he couldn't walk. He is very ill after eating nothing but swedes.

We are wondering, with growing anxiety, how this month is going to end. Probably with us eating swedes.

25 January 1941

The weather is wonderful! It makes me miss Verneuil.

I so miss Verneuil and all the English soldiers, I miss our mad parties, the clean air, the trees, the river. I miss my first love, my freedom, bunking off school, the countryside.

Could it be that the first year of the war was the best year of my life? It was the case for too many French people, but we are paying for it now. Despite all my arguments with Mummy, I was happy and I didn't realize it. I just wanted to be twenty, or a few years older anyway.

A fourteen-year-old's soul is very complicated. I am depressed because I got a four in English, I didn't do well in the German test and my class made fun of the portrait I did today. No one really understands me, except maybe Yvette. People treat me like a big baby! But I have a woman's soul. I know I am pretty, I have big eyes and a beautiful mouth. I love looking at the curve of my eyebrows, I find it soothing. And I know that there are days when I am particularly attractive; on those days I can sense a magnetic attraction. I hate feeling ugly or badly dressed. Are these the thoughts of a 'big baby'? A baby who knows when someone has looked at her and knows the words, 'You are pretty, mademoiselle,' are meant for her.

It's ten-thirty and I have to turn the light out, good-bye.

Though Britain was still fighting alone, Lend-Lease signalled the end of US neutrality. As if to reflect the shift in relations between their two countries, Brian had decided that 'yours' was too formal a way of closing his letters to Trudie and in his last letter he had asked her to come up with an alternative ending.

21 March 1941

Dear Trudie,

If I remember rightly we have been writing to each other for 2 years now. That's fine I hope we keep it up. We weren't quite 16 years old when we started and now you will be 18 by the time this letter reaches you. So I wish you all the best.

You will notice I have enclosed two 'photographs'!!! They are neither good nor flattering ... They will do to be going on with. I hope!!

What does the dog do in a raid? Well she goes under the table and pants something awful. We're more concerned about the dog than the bombs.

We are really grateful for what President Roosevelt has done for us and what the factories of America are going to produce for us. But the folks I know aren't in agreement with all this 'fussing' of America that our government is doing. After all it's our flesh and blood that is bearing the brunt and keeping American youth out of it.

I've often wondered what they will call this war. I should use one of these; both are my suggestions: 'Second German War' or 'The War of Liberation'. What do you think?

We've got a big weekend off next week with the Home Guard.

Brian's letter, 21 March 1941.

The RAF will dive-bomb and machine-gun us and it has been said our own 'parachutists' may take part. It is to test the training of the Home Guard in the past nine months and will be as near to invasion as possible.

Well I want a bath before it goes dark, it wouldn't do to be caught in the blitz while in the bath, would it now?

Here's to the best for you and your people.

… ?????

Brian

P.S. I could suggest lots of endings but would they suit you, eh??

6 April 1941

Dear Trudie,

'Aya Toots?' as they say in the States. How's things?

Being Sunday morning I listened to the 9 a.m. news in bed (lout!) to hear that Hitler had declared war on Yugoslavia. What a world we live in!

The 20th Feb letter has been lost with a snap of you in it (tears!!). I'll bet the fishes are admiring you at the bottom of the Atlantic. So remember you owe me one now. So send one pronto d'ye hear?

My patience won't allow me to wait until the end of the war to have a little part of our debate now. You can make a reply to what I'm going to say and then when we've explained each other's point of view we will say no more. Agreed? Remember we're great friends and what we say about each other's country has nothing to do with our own friendship. Okay. I'll fire away.

Your statesmen have admitted time and time again that we are fighting America's battle. Why then, should we who are going a little hungry, standing the strain of air-bombardment, watching our cities destroyed and our own flesh and blood killed in cold blood while America sits tightly, says the bloom of her youth will not die on Europe's battlefields but we will send you the tackle and your youth can die for us. Remember, America's population is three times as large as ours. Admitted it has a great moral effect, that we can get equipment elsewhere. Remember all this is my personal opinion. I hope you don't think I'm rude but one of the things we are fighting for is freedom of speech. I hope you're not vexed with me, you are not, are you?

By the way, I might say I admire your country greatly, life is much pleasanter there but give me good Old England any day.

Well, I'll close now with my suggestion. Keep well.

Lots of love

Brian

That spring, while the Luftwaffe continued to bomb Britain's cities, the Axis powers pushed ahead with their campaign in the Balkans. In Paris, Micheline followed the news closely and kept to her New Year's resolution of fighting the 'Bosche' whenever she could.

23 March 1941

I have discovered a new way of listening to the English radio, without having to go anywhere: I put it up the chimney. There's been a notice about people holding on to nickel coins and not handing them over to Hitler. So we're going to keep them all and if the Germans demand we hand them in, I'll throw them in the Seine.

26 March 1941

The walls of Paris are covered with 'V's', I wonder why. The English radio asked people to write a 'V' for victory, and you find them everywhere: on shop windows, blackboards, tables, everywhere. There's a new sign too: a 'V' made from two pins in a buttonhole. Yvette and I counted seventy-five in five minutes.

28 March 1941

On our way back from school today it was raining and Yvette and I stopped several times to shelter from the rain, each time we wrote a 'V'. On Rue D'Astorg, I wrote a 'V' on a German car. I heard the sound of boots behind me and I made off in a hurry. The Bosche approached, looked at the sign on the car and just gave Yvette a big beaming smile. God! We've done hundreds of 'V's'. I never thought it would be that easy in daylight.

31 March 1941

Yvette and I went to look for German propaganda leaflets at a shop on Rue de la Ville-l'Éveque, they'd been told to distribute them. The woman gave us all she had left, saying: 'Take the lot. Thanks for getting them out of my sight.' We threw them in the sewer opposite the Bosches. (When I told Mummy this story she said they might well search the sewer, etc.). I did another 'V' on a German car. If they knew about it I would have been arrested long ago.

8 April 1941

Since the beginning of the month we have bought four loaves of bread, 2 kilos each – and I managed to get three of them without giving up a coupon because I ran away without handing it over.

I went to the swimming pool on my own for the first time. I played ball with the Germans, they were very nice, I must admit. They are more fun than the French, because you can't play with a Frenchman for five minutes before he starts flirting with you and I hate that. With the Bosches you can just have fun without having to think about anything else.

9 April 1941

The Germans have taken Thessalonika and the Greek army has capitulated. God help them, and us. God help the whole world! Don't leave us under the barbarian's yoke. Take pity on France. Still, the English are advancing in Africa.

10 April 1941

Nicole and I went to the pool. A Bosche took my arm and amused himself by walking onto the diving board, still clinging on to me. I pushed him into the water to get rid of him. After that, I caught another one, who was sitting in the water waiting to catch a ball, I grabbed him by the head and made him do a back flip. But that's not the main thing. I don't know what I should think, or if Mummy would say I did anything wrong. Should I regret it? I don't know. Anyway, we were playing ball when a Bosche took our ball from us. He didn't want to give it back and

I didn't dare demand it back in German. But Nicole insisted that he return it. He put his hand on his face and told her she was a fool. Then he asked me to have a coffee with him; I refused, of course.

He looked sad, but didn't say anything. Then I told him he would never reach England, that England was invincible and that everyone who had ever attacked her had been defeated. I gave Napoleon as an example and said the same thing would happen to Hitler.

But the worst thing was: he waited for us to get dressed, then he took my comb and used it to comb his hair! Then he walked out into the street with us (I was ashamed to see the way people looked at us). He was going our way, on the metro (the Bosches don't have to pay), and he got into the same carriage. He asked if I would go for a walk with him. I said no. Then he asked when we were next going to the pool. Nicole said she was going on Saturday, so I'll go then too. If Daddy knew, he would be furious! Would he be wrong to be? I suppose people will treat me the way I treat women who go out with Bosches, and in their eyes I am … Oh! I don't want to think of it. What excuses me, in my eyes at least, is that I was direct with him and told him exactly what I thought! (He is tall, blond, twenty-five years old, and he thinks Paris is the most beautiful city in the world.)

12 April 1941

My Birthday!

I am fifteen years old! Age matters a lot in life. I am no longer a little girl now and I had my first date with a Bosche!

He came, but also today I made a new friend, Janine. (I don't know her last name.) We became good friends in just one day. She was at the pool and is really very charming. It's incredible what we two dared to say to the Bosche. At first he wanted to throw Janine in the water, but then he let her go. He asked if I smoked; I can't bear smoking, but I said, I only smoke English cigarettes, German cigarettes stink. But I said it in such a way that he couldn't get angry. He offered us sweets, oranges and biscuits. We didn't like the biscuits, so he suggested we take them home for Darak (we told Daddy I found them in my cubicle). Then Janine went to get changed and I explained to Walter I couldn't go out with him 'because French people won't like it'. He understood and said sadly, 'Enemy.'

The oranges were exquisite.

15 April 1941

Met Walter and Janine at the pool again. Walter is a musician and he skipped his concert today, pretending he had a dentist's appointment, so he could come and join us. I got him to correct my Bosche homework. I hope I get a good mark. He found twenty mistakes.

27 April 1941

Yugoslavia has been defeated and the Germans are at the gates of Athens. What can I say? I have never lost hope, my only hope is in England. England isn't Yugoslavia or Greece; it's not possible that such magnificent people could be defeated, and leave us enslaved under the barbarian's yoke.

I haven't seen Walter again but he caused me quite a lot of trouble. Monique, Yvette, Nicole and Mummy accuse me of falling in love with him. Me, love a Bosche! What a terrible thought! He is very nice but he is and always will be a Bosche. I told Mummy that I should never have spoken about Walter to anyone. She told me I should never have spoken to Walter, full stop.

And she's right. Since I was a child, I have always considered the Bosche to be cruel barbarians. They're the enemy: I have been brought up to hate them, and I did, without knowing any of them personally, because of their past crimes. And now that my country is under the boot of the oppressor, I realize I should never have spoken to a Bosche, out of respect for the past ... The worst thing was when Denise said to me: 'When the English are here, you love the English, and when the Bosches are here, if you can use them, then you use them' (she never forgave me for that German homework).

What can I say?

Then Monique said to me that she thought there was nothing dishonourable about liking a Bosche and that she wouldn't stop being my friend because of it. So I will just carry on as before.

After almost a year incarcerated in the Łódź ghetto, Dawid's diary entries focused less on the Germans and more on the authority figure he could see – the 'Jewish Chairman', Chaim Rumkowski, who had been nominated by the Nazis to run the ghetto from within and who had decided to cooperate in the hope that he could save some of his community. Dawid's notebooks covering 1940 and early 1941 were lost later in the war; his existing diary resumes in April.

22 April 1941

Rumkowski has had a great idea about how to prevent workers at the bread cooperatives from eating all the bread. As of tomorrow each person will be issued with a two-kilogram loaf of bread every five days, so doing away with the weighing, cutting and eating of bread in cooperatives. Commissars in bakeries will be responsible for weighing the bread. What's more, the private sale of wood stolen from fences, privies – any timber structures in the ghetto, in fact, that have not yet been torn down – is now prohibited. No one knows what's going to happen, there's been no coal ration for months, and the last time Rumkowski issued wood was at the beginning of February. So we have to make do with soup once a day, from the community kitchen we're registered with, and even though there are extra potato rations, there is no way to cook them. There is more than one way to skin a cat! Starving to death is becoming a real possibility.

I registered at the school on Dworska Street today. There's supposed to be some food at school, we won't know exactly what until Friday. So I will be going to school again – if I don't have a job, of course. I'd almost given up on it anyway. This will put an end to my aimlessness and also, I hope, to the philosophizing and depression which go with it.

I didn't have any work today, but I ran to the shop every hour to see if the swedes had come.

24 April 1941

The swedes have finally arrived. Worked all day today, but we still haven't finished distributing them. I got my coupon at last, so I could take my portion before they were all gone.

25 April 1941

At last we've finished with the swedes, but this also means that my job has ended. Now they tell us that we're not getting paid per number of days worked but for the total amount of swedes issued. So I can't count on more than ten to twelve Reichsmark for more than two weeks of running around. And we won't be getting it until next week.

27 April 1941

First day of school today. Marysin is quite a long way away, and what's worse, it's very muddy because of the non-stop rain. The shoes I got at school are starting to wear out and there's no way to repair them. We'll be walking to school barefoot before long. The school is in a small building, there is hardly enough space for benches. There is no other school equipment (not even a blackboard). We sit in the classroom in our coats because there is no cloakroom.

We had six lessons today. During the last lesson we had a visit from Rumkowski and other ghetto 'dignitaries'. Rumkowski inspected the kitchen, tasted the soup (maybe that's why it was so good) and spoke to us. He talked about the problems with opening the school and said he'll try to get more for us. He told us to be diligent, clean and well behaved. So now to study, study and study some more.

28 April 1941

German victories come one after another. In Yugoslavia and Greece, the fighting is almost over. The English are losing in Africa. There is talk of tension in German–Soviet relations and these rumours are some kind of consolation. But we've been cursed too much for anything good to happen any time soon. We're sure to have to suffer some more.

Somehow Dawid and his friends managed to get hold of the local German newspaper, which, though full of propaganda, still gave them some idea of the war's progress.

 In Britain over the following week, the Luftwaffe bombed Liverpool's docks for seven nights in a row, part of a general increase in the campaign against Britain. Brian, who had yet to encounter a German in the flesh, wrote to Trudie later than usual, missing his virtually sacred letter-writing date by two days.

7 May 1941

Dear Trudie,

 Your letter of March 23rd arrived today. It's taken over six weeks, what a time! It certainly is a very short one and you haven't asked me one question. Tut, tut! I have had no proper sleep for six successive nights and I am going to bed early tonight.

 We are in the news. Last Saturday night when Liverpool was having its biggest 'Blitz' one of our 'Defiant' night fighters chased a Junkers 88 from Liverpool and shot it down over Lostock Gralam. The plane was dashing about out of control. I heard it coming. I was in the house, I shouted 'Look out Mother!' as I heard the plane roaring towards the house, it roared past and Dad and I rushed out. People who were outside said it was marvellous that it hadn't crashed into the row of five houses of which ours is one.

We jumped into the car and followed it until it crashed and burst into flames. We were amongst the first to arrive there and we helped put the flames out. What a Godsend it had crashed in a field of oats. We found no bodies in the machine. So we began to search then news came through that two had escaped by parachute, one had been captured by soldiers and the other by members of our Home Guard platoon. That left two to find. We spread out and Dad found another parachute, open, and the harness undone. So he called me and three others to search. We were going to turn past a stream when someone shined his torch in the water, and there was a body lying face upward in the water. He was dead. I've never felt like being sick in all my days as at that moment. I turned away and someone said to me: 'I shouldn't be sorry for him if I were you, he's killed lots of women and children tonight.' I said 'true'. And my heart hardened and I turned towards him. He had been badly shot, and how he found the effort to crawl from the parachute to the water nobody knows. He was an NCO about twenty-three years of age and very broad and well built. The other man, the pilot, was found by a dog, his parachute had failed to open. These two are to be buried with full military honours tomorrow, by the men of the squadron that shot him down.

Well things have not gone too grand in Greece and we realize our heavy lack of equipment. Mere courage is no good alone. We are relying on America to send us tackle. And I think it should be conveyed by you. We can't fight Hitler with all the resources of Europe in his hands, alone. I don't see now why your men can't participate in the war. Enough of this war. Lets talk about 'somat' else.

Talking about carrots, I like raw ones over grated, but have not the slightest idea what pea-nut butter is. What is it? Did you know our night-fighter pilots eat carrots to give them keen eyesight?

Well must get some shut-eye before Jerry arrives tonight. You and yours keep well ....

Lots of love!!!!

Brian

In Łódź, Dawid would have come across the dead and the dying regularly. In May 1941 alone almost 1,000 ghetto inhabitants died from starvation and disease. Over the following two months, Chairman Rumkowski clamped down on any signs of dissent, which threatened the smooth running of the ghetto, targeting strike leaders in the workshops and Communists. Dawid had been a committed Communist since pre-war days.

16 May 1941

I was examined by a doctor today and she was terrified at how thin I was. She's sending me for some X-rays. Maybe I could get double soup at school. Five portions wouldn't hurt but two would still be good. One isn't enough, for sure. But the check-up left me frightened and worried. Lung disease is the latest craze in the ghetto. It wipes people out, just like dysentery or typhus. And the food situation is getting worse. There haven't been any potatoes for a week and there won't be any for a long time.

Today Niutek Radzyner came to me with an unusual proposal. He and some of the best members of our organization have formed a close-knit group, a commune almost, to study theory together (they have Marx's *Capital* and Lenin's works) and work for the organization in general. Niutek asked me to join them, which would mean personal contact of the kind I'm not used to. I agreed, but I wonder what will come of it. Anyway, it's an interesting initiative and I'm sure I'll gain a lot from it.

24 May 1941

I've been catching up with schoolwork all day today. I am hungry as hell, not a crumb left of the bread which was meant to last till Tuesday. I console myself that I am not the only one. It is hard to control myself, I feel so weak that I just have to eat and so the bread disappears. Then I suffer even more. But there's nothing to be done. And so we dig our own graves.

25 May 1941

At last it feels like May, and although emaciated and famished people (like me, for example) still can't wear summer clothes yet, the winter coats have been put away. It's dry everywhere, and the smell in Marysin reminds me of life before the war and makes my heart pang. If these were normal times we'd be three weeks away from our exams [after four years of secondary school] and looking forward to the summer holidays. Some school outing, then youth camp or a trip to the countryside. It makes me want to cry, just thinking about it. To hell with everything!

26 May 1941

At school everything seems normal. No tests so far but we're working
our way through the course. We're doing Cicero's famous speech against
Cataline; in maths we're on quadratic equations. We're behind in most
other subjects, except German. School soups are quite good, and my
extra-curricular soup is much appreciated. But five portions wouldn't
be too much.

A school gazette is being set up. I contributed some caricatures and
they might include one of my Jewish articles. All the ones I've written
so far turned out to be unpublishable – even the ghetto has its bourgeois
ideology, clearly formulated and defined.

Things are not too good at home, but Mum has a job now. She leaves
at seven in the morning and comes home at nine in the evening. Father
goes out to day shift from eight to eight. All the housework is on [my
sister] Nadzia's shoulders, she does all the queuing, cleaning and so on
– all this on just one soup a day with 300g of bread (she and Mum each
give Father 100g of bread, but he is very ungrateful and treats them as
badly as he does me – it just shows how selfish he is). As she works in
the kitchen, Mum gets one extra portion of good soup – the same as
every worker in the ghetto. We don't cook at home any more – there's
nothing *to* cook. It's getting harder and harder to find food. There are
no potatoes or barley, bread has 8 per cent chestnut flour added and its
daily ration won't increase. There is a real food crisis. And it's only the
second year of war!

27 May 1941

Everyone is impatient to hear Roosevelt's speech, which is supposed to be today. People are pointing out it was the 27th May 1917 that the United States declared war on Germany, and they hope they will do so again on the same day. I have no textbook to check the date but, even if it's correct, I don't think that America will enter the war today. I hope I'm proved wrong. Everyone is teasing me for my pessimism. But, sadly, they usually have to admit that I was right. And that kills me …

28 May 1941

Sure enough, he didn't say anything special. We have to wait, and wait, and wait – it's enough to make a person mad, listening to this empty blabber. Here, the statistics are showing an incredible increase in the numbers of children and young people with TB but, over there, they wait and see. To hell with them!

15 June 1941

This sadist, this moron, Rumkowski, is doing terrible things. He sacked two Communist teachers. The stated reason: they were organizing a teachers' protest. The likely real reason: alleged Communist activities at school. We are keeping a low profile and taking our leaders' advice not to organize any meetings for a week or two. There's a risk of expulsion, they might even shut the school down.

28 June 1941

A very difficult problem today, it has upset me a lot. Niutek Radzyner told me that, since all the Party's work in the ghetto has been suspended, a core group will meet in great secrecy, consisting of people dedicated to the cause, body and soul, to the exclusion of everything else. They are to be at the disposal of the party for any action. There are to be five members, chosen after long consideration. I am among the candidates and Niutek openly asked me what I thought about it. I was so surprised and worried that I couldn't give him an answer today. I put it off till tomorrow. After thinking it over I've come to the following conclusion: although I am absolutely certain of my views and ideals, a professional, extreme revolutionary activity is not my goal in life and I wouldn't be capable of taking part in something like 'death battalions'. For my reply, I've decided to say that in the case of a specific action I am ready to take an active part at the decisive moment, but that regular, professional activity, being constantly in danger – excluding all other goals, ideals and concerns – is out of the question.

29 June 1941

I told Niutek about my decision at school today. He himself is taking a different course, but he understood and accepted my explanation.

Today was the funeral of a girl from our school, killed in a storm last Thursday. There is absolutely no safety in the ghetto. The devil only knows what else will happen to us.

CHAPTER FOUR

The Invasion of Russia

June 1941–January 1942

*'I dream of bread, butter,
pies and potatoes …'*

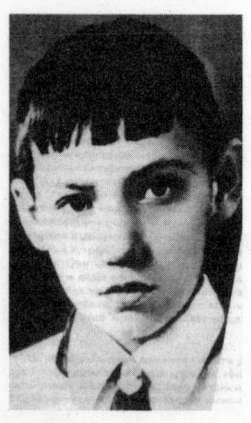

Yura Ryabinkin in
1939.

Herbert Veigel in
Russia, winter 1941.

*I*n December 1940, Hitler announced to a closed gathering of his army commanders that 'hegemony over Europe will be decided in a battle against Russia'. That winter, while the Luftwaffe and the RAF battled in the skies over Britain, trainloads of German troops were sent east in preparation for the campaign. 'Operation Barbarossa' was planned as a swift summer offensive, aimed at capturing the Soviet Union's major cities and securing its vast oil reserves and mineral riches. Ideology, however, was as much of a driving force. Insisting on taking 'the Bolshevik breeding grounds' of Leningrad and Stalingrad first, Hitler proclaimed the new campaign as a 'merciless and fanatical struggle' against Bolshevism and promised to secure extensive 'living space' for the 'Aryan race' in the east. Once the Soviet Union was defeated, Hitler expected to bring Britain to its knees.

Stalin refused to believe war with Hitler was imminent and dismissed warnings of the German attack as 'disinformation'. He hoped the 1939 Non-Aggression Pact would hold out long enough to advance the Soviet Union's military preparations, and wanted to ensure nothing provoked Germany into action ahead of time. In May 1941, after a top Soviet spy pinpointed the date of the German invasion to between 20 and 22 June 1941, Red Army reserves were finally ordered to move west with such urgency that neither armaments nor equipment could be taken along.

Radio operator Herbert Veigel, now eighteen, received his orders in the first days of June 1941. Having spent nearly a year on a quiet posting in Holland, he was excited to be on the move again. His company travelled across Poland to join over 3 million soldiers of the Wehrmacht gathered *along the Soviet Union's western borders. Having been told the Red Army was made up of 'swamp people' – 'primitive Ivans' who were no match for the 'sophisticated Aryan troops', Herbert, like most German soldiers, expected the Russian campaign to be over before the summer was out.*

On the night of 21 June 1941, fifteen-year-old Russian schoolboy Yura Ryabinkin struggled to get to sleep at his home in Leningrad. On the longest 'white night' of the year – when night is as light as day – thousands of school leavers were out celebrating the end of exams, singing in the streets until the early hours. But it was not this that was keeping Yura awake, but a 'strange humming noise'. Outside Leningrad, at Kronstadt naval base, the authorities had declared a state of full alert after spotting suspicious German air activity.

Yura lived in a three-roomed flat in the city centre with his mother, a librarian at the Union of Industrial Construction Workers, and eight-year-old sister, Ira. The children barely knew their father, who had left the family years earlier and later became an 'unmentionable', a victim of Stalin's Great Purges in the 1930s. Replacing him as the man of the family, Yura was often on household duty after school but spent all his free time at the Palace of Young Pioneers, a haven of children's clubs and activities. Like thousands of Leningrad boys brought up in 'the cradle of the Russian Revolution', Yura worshipped Russia's war heroes and dreamt of becoming a 'Red Sailor'. With his keen interest in history, the day Germany invaded the Soviet Union Yura began to keep a diary, in an unused school exercise book.

22 June 1941

I couldn't sleep last night because of a strange humming noise. I saw searchlights out of my window and it was dawn before I finally managed to get to sleep. I woke up at eleven, got dressed, had breakfast and went to the Palace of Young Pioneers, because I wanted to get a grade in chess this summer.

As I left home, I noticed the street sweeper was wearing a gas mask and a red band on his arm. There were militiamen on every street corner. They were wearing gas masks too, which was odd. There were only two chess players at the Palace of Young Pioneers, and as I was lining up my pieces I noticed a group of boys gathered around another boy. When I heard what he was saying, I froze on the spot.

He said that the German bombers had attacked Kiev, Zhitomir and Sevastopol at four in the morning and Molotov went on the radio to announce we were at war with Germany!

I had to sit down. What news! I never imagined such a thing was possible. Germany! Germany is at war with us! So that's why everyone was wearing gas masks. My head was spinning. I couldn't think straight, but I stayed on to play three games of chess. I won all three. What a weird creature I am!

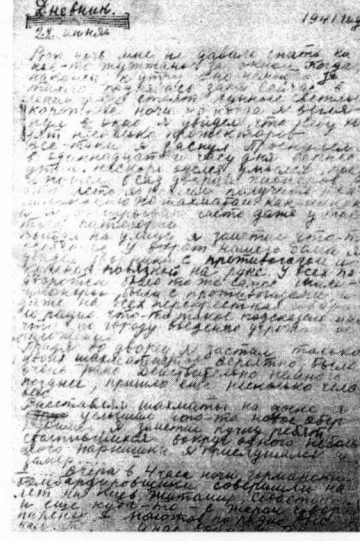

Page from Yura's diary, 22 June 1941.

It is half past eleven at night now, and the day is coming to an end. The decisive struggle has begun. The struggle between two incompatible ways of life, between fascism and socialism! The future of all humanity will depend on the outcome of this great historic struggle!

29 June 1941

I helped build an air-raid shelter at the Palace of Young Pioneers today, and before that I was helping to unload sand in the Arts Square. There wasn't really much to do, so some kids made a model of Hitler's head out of sand and started hitting it with spades. I joined in, of course.

As soon as I got home, my sister Ira ran up to me shouting, 'Look, look what Mummy bought for me! None of it's yours! It's all mine!' I saw Ira's new doll and sailor's outfit laid out on the sofa, and her new boots too, sitting on the dining-room table.

There was something for me. Mama pushed a folded note into my hands. I opened it without a thought. It was a letter addressed to the District Military Committee written on behalf of us both, saying we were volunteering to join the Red Army.

It turned out there was a Communist Party meeting at my mother's office today, where all the party members had agreed to join the Red Army. Not one single person had refused. I felt proud at first, then a little scared, but eventually pride won over fear.

30 June 1941

This morning I went to the Palace of Young Pioneers. I played pool for half an hour, then I helped with the air-raid shelter till about seven.

More news – I might not be accepted into the army after all, because I'm too young and I suffer from pleurisy. So I'll probably be excused from work at the Palace and sent to a summer camp instead.

There would be no children's holiday camps that year, as the Wehrmacht, having taken the Soviet forces by surprise, swiftly advanced into the heart of Russia. After a week on the move in a reconnaissance tank, Herbert Veigel sent his first letter home.

1 July 1941

Dear Parents,

I've got some time to myself at last, so I can finally write and let you know I'm doing fine. This is the first chance we've had to send any letters. We are advancing so fast, non-stop! The day before yesterday we were in Minsk.

As you probably guessed I was right in the thick of it when it all started on June 22nd. We were about 10km from the border, near Brest-Litovsk. When the Führer's orders were read out the night before, we finally knew for definite what we had been wondering about for weeks. At 3.15 in the morning, when the artillery and the dive-bombers set about their destructive work, I was already at my radio, monitoring communications. We crossed the border at the Bug. There was heavy fighting in the outskirts of Brest-Litovsk when we drove through. I saw my first dead bodies, loads of them in fact. It sent a shiver down my spine, but I am getting used to it now, this war business. I'm sure you've heard the reports on the radio, so you know what's going on. I only need tell you we are advancing extremely quickly.

There are Russians in huge numbers in all the forested areas. They keep trying to break through, but we push them back ferociously, every time. There are lots of snipers, some of them are women, too, but we show them no mercy. I get the strong impression that the Russians have enormous numbers of troops at their disposal. But we will still beat them. You will have to wait till I'm back for all the details; for now you'll have to content yourself with the news that I'm well. I wear the same clothes for days on end and get hardly any sleep, but that's war for you. We have more than enough to eat. The Russians' enormous food reserves have come in very handy. We've plundered a lot of equipment and clothing as well. But things are very different here compared to the war in France.

Yours, Herbert

6 July 1941

Dear Parents,

We've advanced a little, but not as fast as we did at the start, because we now have to clear up all the areas we take. We rely heavily on the fact that the Russians can be subverted very easily. We think their army is on the brink of total collapse, they are in retreat and they seem to be panicking, leaving everything behind, tanks and cars, planes even. The stragglers hiding out in the forests are keeping us busy. Three days ago the signal communication platoon of a regiment half an hour ahead of us was ambushed, and seventeen men were killed in the most brutal way. We arrived not long after; they had all been mutilated. One of them had

had his heart cut out; there it was lying on his body. Others had their faces cut up and their skin peeled off, the sort of thing we've heard went on in the Polish campaign. Our fighter pilots took revenge; they obliterated the village these Russians had come from.

We are now 600km from Moscow. This is the first decent road since Minsk; till now they have been terrible, and so dusty we could hardly see a thing. But now we are on asphalt, all the way to Moscow.

Yours, Herbert

Despite the initial chaos and disarray, the Red Army rallied to offer bitter resistance. However, by the end of the summer German forces were just 30 miles outside Leningrad, where Yura described the day he turned sixteen.

2 September 1941

Nothing interesting happened on my birthday.

Mum gave me 5 roubles to spend in the canteen. I bought a chess textbook to cheer myself up, but by the time I got to the canteen there was no cheap food left. Then Mum brought me two pies after work, and we made some soup, too. So now I'm full, and happy!

Every newspaper headline screams out: We will never surrender Leningrad! We will defend it to the last drop of blood! We must strengthen our tank defences! But our army is not winning, I don't know why, maybe because it hasn't got enough decent weapons. The militiamen in the street, the volunteers and even the Red Army soldiers are all armed with ancient-looking guns and pistols. The Germans are advancing on us in tanks, and we're expected to fight back with grenades and glass bottles filled with fuel. It makes you wonder.

8 September 1941

A day of alerts, worries and problems. There was an air-raid warning. I looked out into the street, then up, and then I saw ... twelve Junkers! Then there were these deafening explosions, one after another, though actually not loud enough to make the windows rattle. It seems the bombs fell far away, but they must have been incredibly devastating. The damage from the fascist bombing was horrendous. Half the sky was filled with smoke. The harbour and the Kirov factory were bombed. When night fell it looked like a sea of fire where the Kirov factory used to be. Little by little the flames died down, but the smoke has got into absolutely everything, everywhere. Even now I can smell it, this bitter stench, pinching my throat.

This was the first air attack on Leningrad.

It will be night soon. What will it bring?

That night German troops severed the last land connection between Leningrad and the rest of Russia. Hitler ordered the besieged city to be erased from the face of the earth. Stalin, in turn, ordered Leningrad's defenders not to give up the city, whatever the cost. Nearly 2.5 million people, the majority of them civilians, women and children, were left trapped inside.

With the onset of autumn, Herbert Veigel warned his parents not to expect him home any time soon.

18 September 1941

My dears,

The rolls were delicious, just like they tasted at home! And I am very grateful for the cigarettes too: you can hardly imagine what it is like when a company has had no cigarettes for days on end – a single one goes for a huge price. It's a bit late for the papers, as there's no tobacco left; what there was we rolled up in typewriter paper. You wouldn't think that smoking would play such a big role, but we have no other pleasures and even the most disgusting food tastes okay if you can have a cigarette afterwards. And, of course, I was really pleased to get the sweets. Also, quite a lot of wine and champagne was delivered yesterday, but the officers took most of it and we were lucky to get anything.

It's impossible to tell how things will turn out for us here in the east. I really don't think we will conquer Russia this year. But I hope that doesn't mean we are condemned to spend the winter here. That would be tough. Whatever happens, we have no doubt in our ultimate victory, however long it takes. And the home front must hold out too.

Yours, Herbert

6 October 1941

Dear Parents,

We were part of the latest and hopefully the last big offensive, right from the start. I was in a reconnaissance vehicle with the advance party of a tank division. Our job is to guide in the attacks by the Stukas, the bombers and the fighter planes, at the very front line.

We came across pretty strong resistance as we broke through the Russian line. They were very shocked to see us so far into their own territory and most of them fled in total panic. Amazingly, we managed to take an airfield where lots of planes were lined up ready to take off. Everyone had run away.

The next day we advanced 117km! What little resistance there was, usually on the bridges, was easily overcome. In the village where we spent the night, the ovens were still warm and there was food on the stove, so we enjoyed ourselves. We'd already taken lots of food from their military.

The next day we attacked Orel. It was hell. We were under fire from fighter planes, day and night. Luckily the showers of bullets raining down on us couldn't penetrate our armour. The fighter planes didn't arrive till the evening but when they did they shot down ten planes and destroyed twenty-seven on the ground. That's a few more to add to my score.

There was fierce resistance on the edge of the city but we were among the first tanks to reach the centre. We broke into a few shops and by the light of the fires outside we 'cleaned up'. There was so much to be had. If there'd been room for all of it in the tank I would have come away a rich man.

It is hard to describe, but it really is a fantastic feeling being master of a place only just captured from the enemy. We took a few prisoners and moved into the biggest and best hotel in town. There were the finest roast meats and fish fillets in the kitchen, and lots more delights. We had a feast by candlelight (there was even good port) and lay down to sleep in freshly made hotel beds. It was all a bit spooky, but after a while you stop worrying.

We'll be on the move again tomorrow. We'll soon be in Moscow if we carry on like this! Then this campaign will be over.

Don't worry about me, I've been spared thus far and I don't think anything will happen to me now. There's only so much you can get across in a letter. The details will have to wait till later, if you still want to hear them. But I can already imagine that after the war is over I won't want to think about any of it again. No doubt about it though, the Russians are well and truly beaten.

Yours, Herbert

Trapped inside besieged Leningrad, under daily bombardment and artillery fire, Yura spent most of his nights on air-raid duty on the roof of his school.

13 October 1941

These endless nights of terror will be etched in my memory forever. The darkness, the 'bat' in the bucket [to extinguish fire], the murky stairwell with its small window, the din of the anti-aircraft guns. Your ears prick up every time you hear a noise, your heart beats faster every time you hear the whistling of a bomb, or the howling of a German plane. The window lights up with every explosion, the staircase shakes, the whole house shakes when a bomb goes off nearby. And this is all happening every single night. All you want to do is sleep, eat and forget yourself. But then the whistling starts again and you just press yourself against the wall, curl up into a ball until it dies down.

David and I went up on the roof last night. There was a short whistle, then an explosion right over our heads. It was brighter than day. David knew what it was before I did. He grabbed a spade and started trying to put it out and I joined in; we worked as fast as we could, but the thick acrid smoke caught in our throats, pinching and crawling inside our lungs. We were sweating, but we kept going. A woman at the next post was shouting, 'A bomb! A bomb! Put it out!' She started throwing fistfuls of sand at it.

I grabbed a spade and covered the burning pieces with sand. The bright light turned into thick darkness. I looked across at the other roof, there were a dozen people dashing about. When the alarm was over I went to sleep. We woke up to bad news on the radio – the town of Viazma has fallen. The German advance goes on.

Later on I heard that a total of twenty-three bombs landed on our school that night. (I put out two myself and helped with a third one.)

As the German troops approached Moscow, panic broke out in the Soviet capital and the government was urgently evacuated. Stalin himself decided to stay put at the last minute, ordering all able-bodied civilians over sixteen to be mobilized for the city's defence.

In besieged Leningrad, Yura's mother sought in vain for permission to evacuate her children by air; workers and factory equipment were deemed higher priority for the war effort. Amidst acute food shortages, the family agreed to let a city official and his wife move into one of the rooms in their flat, on a vague promise of access to a special canteen reserved for the higher ranks.

29 October 1941

So weak I can barely move. Climbing up a set of stairs is a huge effort. Mum says my face has begun to swell up. And all because of the lack of food.

I don't know how I am supposed to study. The other day I wanted to do some algebra, but all I could think about was bread.

I don't look after myself very well. I sleep in my clothes, I rinse my face a little in the morning, I no longer wash my hands with soap, I don't change my clothes. Our flat is cold and dark, we now spend our evenings in candlelight.

But what bothers me most is this: here I am, living in hunger and cold, with fleas, while right next door life is so completely different. They always have bread and *kasha*, meat and sweets. Our new neighbour's room is warm and cosy, brightly lit by a kerosene lamp ... Envy. All I feel towards our neighbour Anfisa is envy, and I can't stop myself.

9–10 November 1941

Every night I go to sleep and dream about bread, butter, pies and potatoes. And when I'm going to sleep, all I can think about is that when the night is over, in twelve hours, I'll get my bread ration.

For some reason, my whole character has completely changed. I've got weaker, my hand trembles as I write. My knees are so weak I can't take a step without falling over.

Even so, I could most definitely say that if it wasn't for those well-fed people next door, I could get used to it. But when I look in their kitchen and see leftovers in the pans, breakfasts left unfinished on the plates, lunches and suppers that Anfisa leaves, I feel ... I feel torn to pieces. And the smell of their bread, pancakes and *kasha* tickle my nostrils as if to say: 'You see! You see! But you, you are not allowed, you have to go hungry.' I can get used to the shooting and the bombing, but not this. I just can't!

I can hear Anfisa laughing, all jolly. My mum borrowed a lump of sugar from her yesterday. We've not been able to buy the rations our family is entitled to for the quarter: 400g of grain, 615g of butter, 100g of flour. The food is just nowhere to be found, and when there is a delivery, there are hundreds of people waiting outside in the cold. There is usually only enough for 80 or maybe 100 people. So people queue, freeze and then leave with nothing. You get up at 4 a.m., queue till 9 p.m. and leave with nothing. It hurts but there is nothing you can do. Hunger forces you to join the human feeding frenzy in the icy cold ... After weeks of this, I have no feelings left, only cold, dumb indifference to everything. I don't get enough to eat, I sleep badly and, on top of this, I have to study. But I can't. What does the evening hold in store for me? Mum and Ira return home hungry, cold and tired. There's no food or firewood, but what there is a lot of is shouting, because one of our neighbours managed to get hold of some meat and grain somewhere, but I – I haven't. They say there's meat in the shops, but I couldn't find it. My mum pulls a face and sighs: she is at work all day, she can't get to the shops. So off I go again, back into the queues. And I come back empty-handed, again. I know I'm the only one who can get hold of food, I'm the only one that can bring all three of us back to life, but I haven't got the strength. If only I had felt boots. But I don't!

I decided swelling up is better than this. I will drink as much water as I can. Only my cheeks are swollen at the moment, but in a week, in a month, if I don't get hit by a bomb, my whole body will swell up by New Year.

I sit and cry ... I'm only 16 years old! The bastards who started this war ... Goodbye, my childhood dreams! You will never return. I wish the past would just disappear to hell, I wish I'd never known what bread and sausage were! I wish the memories of past happiness didn't keep coming back to me. Happiness! That's the only word for all of my past life ... I used to feel secure about my future!!! I will never feel the same again ...

Tonight, once the sirens stopped, I managed to get to a shop. I fought my way through a huge crowd. There was such a stampede that the grown-ups were screaming, moaning and crying, but I managed to get through. I got to the front and was given 190g of butter and 500g of horse-meat sausage with soya. When I got home, I felt sharp pains in my chest, just like I had two years ago. There are only two cures for pleurisy: 1) good food, 2) dry, clean and warm air. And neither of these is available.

I forgot to say that my mother's legs have swollen up and gone hard as stone.

Hitler's orders were quoted in the newspaper. They are to finish off Bolshevik Moscow at any price.

I have to get up to be in the queue by 5 a.m. We're all stressed and tense. My mother is never calm any more; all you get from her is endless shouting and hysterics. The reason: hunger, and the fact that we live in constant fear. There are only three of us in our family, but we're always arguing and fighting. When Mum is dividing up food, Ira and I watch her every move to make sure she's being fair. I feel very uneasy even writing this down.

By mid-November 1941 there were hardly any cats, dogs or birds left in Leningrad, and one of the first cases of cannibalism was registered when a desperate woman was arrested for suffocating her six-week-old baby to feed her three older children. The dire situation in the city was kept secret from the rest of the country; all mail was rigorously censored.

German censors, too, had to stay extra vigilant, as discontent spread among their troops, unprepared for the extreme weather conditions. While some of Herbert's mail was now slower, the all-important food parcels continued to arrive intact, and on time.

18 November 1941

Dear Parents,

We got our mail the day before yesterday, just before our division was ordered on the attack again. The rusks came in very handy this morning, as there was no bread left. Our scout car couldn't be fixed, so we have to wait until someone comes with more tools. But we're not sorry about that. The two of us, my driver and I, are living a really peaceful life, and we literally don't notice the hours passing. We live in two rooms (or at least what passes for a room here in Russia). It's quick and easy to make a bed out of a bit of straw. Every day, the only things we have to worry about are: water, wood and – not least – food. There's always something for us to do, which keeps us warm in this rotten freezing weather.

Yesterday I took the radio out of the tank so now we can listen to beautiful music from back home, for as long as the batteries hold out. Unfortunately it's too dark to write by the light of the paraffin lamp, so the only way to be with our dear families back home is in our thoughts. The evenings are really long, so we go to bed early. After all the stresses and strains of the past few months this kind of rest is doubly good. If you can ignore the miserable surroundings and the daily bombardments, you can almost believe there isn't a war on. But then you get this longing for normal life, all the little things you just took for granted back home, and you get really homesick. All we live for is the hope of going home and for holidays, or, rather, we carry on living because we still have this hope left. I really want to be home for Christmas. That would be so wonderful! You can't allow yourself to think it's definite, but you can hope, so that's what I do.

In besieged Leningrad, bread rations were reduced for the third time that November. Up to half of the carefully measured soggy dark mass that Yura queued up for every morning consisted of chaff and sawdust.

28 November 1941

I've lost all hope that we'll get evacuated. It's all talk. I am going to stop going to school – I read but it just doesn't go into my head. How could it? At home, there is hunger, cold, shouting and crying, and the well-fed neighbours. Every day is so incredibly similar to the one before. Horrible, grey weather, low grey clouds, snow in the yard and such dull, grey thoughts. Thoughts of food, warmth and comfort. There's not a scrap of bread at home (we now get 125 grams a day), not a crumb, nothing edible at all.

When Mum returns home tonight, she is going to take Ira's bread ration card away from me. Oh well, I'll sacrifice myself for Ira. Let her survive at least, and escape from this hell … I wish I could get out of here. How selfish I am! I've become so hard! What is happening to me? Am I even the person I was three months ago? The day before yesterday I took food from our neighbour's saucepan with my spoon. I secretly stole from our hidden supplies of butter and cabbage that are meant to be for the next 10 days. I watch greedily as my mum divides one little sweet into tiny pieces … I argue and shout about every tiny crumb of food. What have I become? The only way I could be myself again, like I was before, is if I could still believe that tomorrow, or the day after tomorrow, I might be evacuated with my family. That's all it would take, but it's not going to happen. And still I have this secret glimmer of hope, deep inside my soul. If it weren't for that, I would fall into stealing and robbing. There is only one thing I wouldn't do: I could

never betray anyone. That much I know for sure. As for the rest, I can't
write, my hand is too cold …

10 December 1941

No news about evacuation. This is so painful! I can feel my strength
draining away, I am on the road to death, a hungry death. The longer
this goes on, the nearer I get to a slow death. I heard one woman in a
queue yesterday saying five people have already died of starvation in our
block of flats …

They say a person shows their true character in a crisis, but this hasn't
made me stronger, it's turned me into a weakling. It turns out I'm very
selfish. But right now there is nothing I can do to change my character.
If I could at least try! Then tomorrow, if I manage to buy any biscuits, I
would bring them all home. But I know I won't be able to, I'll eat at least
a quarter of one. That's how my selfishness shows itself. But I will try to
bring back everything I get. Everything! Everything!!! Everything!!!

I no longer get excited about news from the front, where a massive
new offensive has begun. It's New Year's Eve in twenty days. What will
happen to us before then? This New Year's Eve, we're not going to have
a tree. We'll remember our previous celebrations as if it had all been a
dream, the fir tree with lit candles, the special supper we used to have,
with all the starters, all the little delicacies and sweet things! …

*With Christmas approaching, Herbert also tried to suppress nostalgic
memories of past celebrations back home, but asked his family to join him
in prayer.*

11 December 1941

Dear Parents,

This is my Christmas letter. There is no chance I'll be celebrating with you this year. We should be grateful for the relatively good life we have right now. And at some point, there must be some holiday leave coming, when we can see each other. We can all look forward to it.

We are still under the influence of the great speech by our Führer, about this decisive phase of the war. We should really feel a sense of satisfaction. And for the sake of all those who have already perished in this war, we should not weaken for one moment, or doubt the end result. We know that the war will be tough and may last a long time, but that should not lessen our resolve. We want to ask our Maker to bless our forthcoming battles and to protect our Führer and let him make the right decisions. And then our personal sacrifices will never seem too great or too harsh.

And so, my dear family, you must celebrate Christmas without me. But however far we are from each other, the Christmas trees and the crib make us feel part of the family circle, they bind us all together. We can be together in spirit, standing quietly before the child in the manger. All worry and pain forgotten, we can all pray together: 'Glory to God, Peace on Earth and Goodwill to all Men!'

We must have faith and be happy this Christmas, and great things will happen.

Yours, Herbert

Within days of this letter, Herbert and all of his reconnaissance crew succumbed to severe frostbite. Herbert nearly lost both his legs but wrote nothing of this at the time. Years later he recalled being saved by a Russian woman who spent three days rubbing his feet. With thousands of German soldiers debilitated by frost and disease that December, Soviet troops were able not only to win the battle for Moscow, but also to begin pushing the German forces back across central Russia. In besieged Leningrad, Yura was oblivious to all but the all-consuming hunger.

15 December 1941

Every new day takes me closer to suicide. There really is no escape. What horrific hunger! If someone offered me deadly poison, that could kill me without making me suffer, I would take it. I want to live, but I can't live like this! So what am I going to do?

This is it. I have no honesty any more, I don't believe in it. Two days ago I was sent to buy sweets. Apart from the fact that I bought cocoa powder mixed with sugar instead of sweets, hoping Ira wouldn't eat that, and so my share would be bigger, I also stole half of it. We were allocated 600g for the next 10 days, but I invented a story about how someone snatched three of the packets right out of my hands. I acted it all out at home, complete with tears. I gave my mum my word, I swore on my Young Pioneer's Oath that I hadn't taken any of it for myself. And then, even after seeing my mother's tears and her misery, I sneakily ate the cocoa on the sly, and I felt no guilt, nothing. Today, coming back from the bakery, I stole again. I took an extra bit of bread from Mama and Ira, about 25 grams, and ate that in secret, too.

I have fallen into an abyss. You can probably call it a complete absence of decency, a total lack of shame or honour. I am not a worthy son to my mother, I am not a worthy brother to my sister. I'm a selfish human being, because in these hard times I no longer care about the people meant to be my nearest and dearest. Meanwhile my mother, despite her swollen legs and sick heart, and without a morsel of bread to eat, is running around all the institutions, rushing around the icy streets in a pair of light shoes, trying to get us out of here. I've lost all hope of any evacuation. My whole world has disappeared, there is only food.

I am finished. My life is over, and what lies ahead of me is not life. I'd only like two things now: to die this minute, and for my mother to read this diary. Let her curse me as a dirty, hypocritical animal devoid of all feelings. Let her disown me, because I have fallen too far.

What's going to happen next? Will death not take me? I want it to be quick, not this drawn-out starving death looming in front of me like a bloody ghost. I am so unhappy, so ashamed. I can't bear to look at Ira.

Will I kill myself, could I do it?

Food! Food!

For eight long days, Yura abandoned his diary. Then on 24 December 1941, an increase in bread rations was announced, raising the miniscule 125 grams (8 oz) a day to a meagre 200 grams (10.5 oz) a day.

24 December 1941

I haven't written anything for a long time.

My character has changed for the better. I think it was when I lost Ira's sugar ration card. I'd been behaving so badly towards Mum and Ira but then I lost my concentration in the shop just for one second, and lost our entitlement to 200g of sugar, 100g of chocolate for Ira and 150g of sweets. I want to change. I want to become a different person. However, I do feel that if I am to lead a new life of total honesty, I need Mum's and Ira's full support. For the first time in weeks, I brought home all the sweets I managed to get at the canteen. I've been sharing bread with Ira and Mum, though I do still steal a crumb from them from time to time. Yet today I felt such warmth from them, when they shared their sweets with me: Mum gave me a quarter of hers (but took it back later) and Ira gave me half of hers as a thank you, because I went to get some biscuits and some wheat pancakes from the canteen. I nearly burst into tears. These are the two people I've been lying to! And now they know all about my lies! What miracles can happen to a person when he is treated well. But then ... then that same Mum took a biscuit from me, and that same Ira cried when Mum gave us a sweet each. And she did have more than me. And today, I have committed another sin. I hid a biscuit. Yes, it was bad of me.

My mum has been promised we'll be evacuated on the 28th. She went to the District Party Committee about it, because if our evacuation is put off until January 1st we're dead.

Silent sorrow is weighing me down, it's hard and painful. I remember the days and evenings we used to spend in our flat. You can still see glimpses of our pre-war life in the kitchen. There is a map of Europe on the wall, an open book on the table, a clock ticking on the wall and it's warm when the stove is lit. But I'd like to be able to walk around our whole apartment. I'd like to put on my hat, coat and mittens and open the door into the corridor. It's frosty out there. I breathe out thick clouds of steam. I shiver as the cold goes right through my clothes. The corridor is empty. We used to have three rooms but now we only have the two. Now the neighbours have the one by the kitchen. What can I say about them? A cheerful little stove heats up their room; delicious smells come from under their door. Their faces are lit up with the nice feeling that comes from having a full stomach. And right next to their room, there is an empty room with a smashed window, covered in brown wallpaper. Cold wind blows in from the street. An empty oak desk stands by the wall, there's an empty bookshelf in the corner. Dust and spider webs cover the walls. That used to be our dining room, and there was once a sofa there, a chest of drawers and chairs. It all seems such a long time ago. There'd be the remains of lunch on the table, and books in the bookcase. It was here I used to read *The Three Musketeers*, munching on a bun with butter and cheese, or chocolate. It was warm, and there were games, books, chess, magazines ... I often used to skip lunch, choosing to play volleyball or hang out with friends. It is so hard to remember the Leningrad Palace of Young Pioneers: the chess club, parties, the library, games, the history club, puddings in the canteen, concerts, the balls we used to have ... That was happiness! And I didn't even realize it. Happiness to live in the USSR in peaceful times, happiness to have a mother to care for you, happiness to know no one is going to take your future away from you. That's what happiness is.

This room used to be filled with happy laughter. There would be a gramophone record playing and a Christmas tree all the way up to the ceiling, with dozens of gingerbread biscuits hanging on it – and no one would touch them. Now our entire life takes place in the kitchen; it's where we sleep, eat if there's anything to eat, and keep ourselves warm if we have any firewood.

Our whole flat is empty and quiet, as if it has turned into a block of ice, which will only melt in the spring ...

By the end of December 1941, Soviet troops had secured a gap in the German encirclement linking the city to the mainland with an ice road across the frozen Ladoga Lake. That month alone, over 53,000 people died in Leningrad; many more were unaccounted for, as relatives hid their dead to live off their meagre rations, supplemented by boiled strips of shoe leather, wallpaper glue, or soil dug out from under the snow. Evacuation was the only hope, but just a few trucks made it in and out of the city across the frozen lake under continuous bombardment.

3 January 1942

This may be my last entry. I'm afraid I won't get to finish my diary and write *The End* on the last page. Someone else will write 'death', in their handwriting. But I so want to live, to believe, to feel! The evacuation won't be happening until spring, when the trains start running again on the Northern Railway. I won't survive till then. I've swollen up completely. Every cell in my body has too much water in it. All my internal organs must be swollen. I am too tired to move, to get off a chair, even to speak. This is because I have had too much water, and so little food. Everything is water water water.

Mama and Ira have split from me. They're going to leave me behind. Mama is suffering from terrible nervous exhaustion, she is forgetting herself … Every single day she says she and Ira will get out of here, but not me. What use am I as a worker? As a student? I might survive for a week, only to stretch my legs later … Is this the way it's going to be? Death, Death is staring me in the face. There's no escaping it. What can I do? Go to the hospital? But I'm covered in lice … what am I going to do, dear God? I'm going to die, I'm going to die, but I so want to live, get away from here and live, live! … At least Ira will survive, maybe. I feel so awful. My mum is so rude to me these days. She hits me sometimes, and shouts at me all the time. But I'm not cross with her, I know I'm a parasite, a parasite around her neck and Ira's neck. Yes, death, death is ahead. There's no hope, only the fear that my dear mother and sister are going to die too.

6 January 1942

I can barely walk or do any work. I have no energy left. Mama can barely walk too. She often hits me and tells me off and shouts at me. She has huge wild nervous fits, she can't bear to look at me, this weak, starving and exhausted person who is always getting in the way, who can barely move, who is 'pretending' to be sick and listless. But I'm not pretending! I'm not! This is not acting. All my energy is leaving me, leaving, swimming away ... And time is dragging on and on, for so long, so long. Oh my God what is happening to me?

And now I I I

These are Yura's last words, scrawled repeatedly across a page as his strength deserted him. Some hours later, Yura's mother and sister left him alone in the flat, having finally received a permit required for evacuation. Yura could no longer walk; his mother was too weak to carry him. On crossing the frozen lake in a truck, Yura's mother and sister were taken to the town of Vologda in the far north of Russia. Issued with a loaf of bread on arrival, Yura's mother died within minutes of eating. Eight-year-old Ira recovered from acute dystrophy and survived the war in an orphanage. Yura Ryabinkin perished in Leningrad, one of an estimated 650,000 civilians who died during the 900-day siege, the longest in modern history.

CHAPTER FIVE

The War Goes Global

September 1941–July 1942

'A Hero's Death'

Hachiro Sasaki in 1940 (left), with best friend Hirasawa.

Ina Konstantinova c. 1941.

David Kogan c. 1950.

D espite warning signs picked up by American intelligence, the Japanese attack on the Pacific Fleet at Pearl Harbor on the morning of Sunday 7 December 1941 came as a complete shock to the nation. As Congress gathered for an emergency vote, American and British outposts in the Pacific, on Guam and Wake Island, and the Philippines, were also caught off guard.

On learning of the Japanese success, Hitler proclaimed 'it was now impossible to lose the war'. With the battle for Moscow lost and his troops pushed back across central Russia, on 11 December 1941 Hitler declared war on the United States, three days after America's declaration of war on Japan. With America now at war on opposite sides of the world, the war went global.

News that America was now a fully-fledged ally in the fight against the Axis powers raised hopes across Europe, but it would be another two and a half years before American troops would land on European soil. That winter, on the Eastern Front, the Red Army continued to reclaim ground and embarked on a new and decisive tactic, sending partisan groups behind enemy lines to harass enemy troops and disrupt their lines of communications and supply. Made up of Communist Party members, Red Army officers and civilians from occupied territories – including children as young as ten – these small mobile detachments successfully diverted significant numbers of front-line forces.

Amongst those moved to the German rear to deal with the partisan warfare was Private Herbert Veigel, now nineteen. Having recovered from *frostbite and still holding out without the long-promised home leave, Herbert was beginning to wonder if there was any way he could get out of Russia.*

Seventeen-year-old Russian schoolgirl, Ina Konstantinova, from Kashin, a provincial town 60 miles north of Moscow, had wanted to volunteer for the front as soon as her country was invaded. Yet as the German troops approached the Soviet capital, her father sent Ina, her mother and younger sister Rena away while he stayed behind to set up partisan resistance. A Komsomol (Young Communist League) member, Ina was brought up to believe Soviet girls were equal to boys in every way and was determined to ensure her turn to fight would come.

Eighteen-year-old Japanese teenager Hachiro Sasaki, a high-achieving student from Tokyo's elite First High School, was less sure about fighting for his country. Even though Japan's education system aimed to create a 'uniform national character', dedicated to serving the Emperor, Hachiro maintained a will of his own. Having trained his 'mind, body and spirit' for a higher cause, Hachiro regarded himself as a socialist and a pacifist. In December 1941, his views, recorded in a private diary, were in direct conflict with the prevailing mood in Japan.

Thousands of miles away, twelve-year-old New Yorker David Kogan had begun to keep a diary in July 1941. A studious only child of first-generation Jewish-American parents, David wrote little about the distant European war or the threat of an escalating conflict between America and Japan. After his family's recent move to South Yonkers, an industrial New York suburb on the eastern banks of the Hudson River, David was preoccupied with making friends in his new neighbourhood.

On the first day of the autumn term at his new high school, David wrote in his diary about the 'ASC', a local Athletics and Social Club for boys:

1 September 1941

The playing situation in our section: On Sherman Avenue where we lived before, the Jews played together with everybody. They were 5 per cent of the kid population. Around here in South Yonkers, the Jews are 35 per cent of the population: the other kids do not play with them. For years the Jewish kids sat at home, got fat and weak. Last year a club was formed. It draws the Jews closer together.

27 September 1941

In the morning I met Bob Gordon. He told me I got voted into the club. After lunch I had to return some books to the library. Then I went to the stamp man and bought some US stamps. Coming home on a trolley, a queer man came on and almost sat on my lap. He kept on praising Lindbergh. Then he asked my name. Then he asked if I were Jewish. Then he asked if I were going into the second-hand clothing business. After this he asked me about *gefilte* fish. When I left he yelled 'shit-boy'. He kept waving while I walked up Rockledge.

18 November 1941

I took a cigarette from Mom's case and smoked three quarters of it this morning. I inhaled and exhaled through my nose. My imagination got the best of me. I told a boy that my Mom will let me smoke a cig a day for 20 years. It is all over the school. I gave my talk on the *NY Daily News*. The teacher said it was swell. I went to the doctor's for my medical examination for school. Am in good condition.

24 November 1941

Uncle Bill called up and said Dad's cousin Sam Sterlin from Paris is coming at 2.00 p.m. When we arrived the boat was docking. Finally they came out. He is very small, thin, and weak. She is small, but plump. That night they told the story of their adventures, the most interesting I have ever heard.

The Sterlins were in Paris when Hitler marched in. A friend of theirs who made believe he played ball with the Nazis helped them to escape to unoccupied France. For days they had to hide in a monastery. Finally, after great hardship, they passed through Spain and Portugal to Lisbon. There they embarked for the United States. They spoke in Yiddish, a language understood by all, including myself.

7 December 1941

Jack and I had our lesson this morning. The two hours were spent on the Bible. We finished the first six days of the Creation of the World. I can read them fluently and translate them into Yiddish and English. After lunch Janeta came home from a walk excited over the news of some attack, and suggested we turn on the radio. The Japs attacked Hawaii and Manila, and declared war on the United States and Britain.

8 December 1941

This morning I thought everyone in the classes would be talking about war. Pupils and teachers were silent. Before lunch it was announced we should go to the auditorium and hear Roosevelt's speech. He wanted the

American Congress to recognize the state of war between Japan and the US. It was an impressive sight, 1,400 strong, listening with reverence to our great President.

That day in Tokyo, thirteen time zones east of New York, an imperial radio announcement asked all citizens to 'join hands and rise for the nation'. The city's walls were hastily pasted with a new slogan: 'One Hundred Million, Now the Enemy is America and Britain. Slaughter them!' Hachiro Sasaki's diary entry that day was uncharacteristically brief.

8 December 1941

War declared on Britain and America.

9 December 1941

I find I can no longer feel blissfully happy about life, like I used to. I can't help it. Things worry me. What will it be like after the war? [My friends] Yanagida and Taga said they weren't worried now that the war had started good and proper. I can't share their feelings. I began to feel quite guilty about it. I thought perhaps I am not as pure as they are, but then I found out [our teacher] Mr Abe was also having doubts. I must not do myself down. I have time to think things through.

11 December 1941

I feel like smashing my own head in, I just don't seem to be able to feel
genuinely happy about our victories. Even after I listened to Hitler's
speech about the conclusion of the Tripartite Pact, my head still
wouldn't let me join in the ecstatic national celebrations. I want to
smash it up.

12 December 1941

I am stubbornly resisting this euphoria that has taken hold of the country. Mustn't give in. Is it real? Is it the true voice of the nation? How could
anyone have doubts, have any negative feelings about it all?

I don't want to be sceptical. I want to be emotional with them. I want
to rage against our enemies. But even the phrase 'enemy states' makes
no sense to me. Bell and Morris [British teachers at school] are fellow
human beings. We don't have any animosity towards each other. It's just
states and their systems that are at war. If I went to war, I'd carry out my
duty as well as I could without complaining. But is it all genuine, all that?
I am not certain. Curse this pathetic head of mine!

15 December 1941

Nothing is more idiotic than pouring all one's energy into war. Human
spiritual power manifested in times of war is certainly impressive, but
why not use that energy for something else? It would be unthinkable to
start a war over economic matters. At present, under his majesty's benev-
olence, I am enjoying an enriched life in his Empire, and if his majesty
ordered me to go and fight I would not refuse, because I believe my mind

is not so fragile that it would be crushed by war. However, I would resolutely speak my mind as a pacifist. I shall do everything I can to stop this war.

In Britain, America's entry into the war was greeted with a surge of optimism. Brian Poole volunteered to join the RAF as soon as he turned eighteen. With no vacancies to join as aircrew he served as a member of the service police and waited for opportunities to receive technical training. Writing from an RAF base in Longtown, he shared the latest news with his American penpal, Trudie.

22 December 1941

Dear Trudie,

Greetings, fellow comrade in arms. Since my last letter Japan has attacked America and now right is completely ranged against wrong, we either sink or swim together. We are both in the same boat – you were unprepared at Hawaii and it seems we are unprepared in Malaya. Such a pity we are both having reverses when the Germans are on the run in Russia and Libya. We have certainly underestimated the little bow-legged yellow man.

I see in our pantry is a tin of 'Treet', that tinned meat of yours. For many years now I've been looking at these luscious dishes in colour on the back of magazines, now with lease and lend they are coming here, but Alas! They are rationed.

You asked whether I flew the plane myself. I did handle the controls for a while, but I only flew straight. Talking about the Air Forces, I've had to remaster whether I wanted to or not. The electricians are urgently required and if we remastered we would get our course within a month. Anyhow it's not so bad, the officer told us younger chaps that if we did well on our course we would be allowed to go as flight electricians. All these big new bombers, four-engine ones, carry a flight engineer, flight rigger and flight electricians. So all being well we will be on operations in about 6 months, boy! Oh boy that will be the day.

Gerch! I'm no ladies man. Perhaps you won't believe me but I've only had two dates since I've been in the RAF.

I'm still in the police. Two of us told some chaps off and they got rough so as you may guess we had a fight. I got a thick lip but blacked my opponent's eye and made his nose bleed. Not a bad show because I'm not a habitual fighter. I only do so when the occasion merits it.

I shall have a quiet Christmas this time but shall spend it at home. I hope you get my Christmas card. Remember me to your folks. You keep well too, hang on and all will be well.

Love

Brian …

PS. What about that Photograph??????

In Tokyo, as Japanese propaganda portrayed Roosevelt and Churchill as the greedy banker and the plundering pirate, Hachiro Sasaki knew no Japanese citizen was permitted to regard his private life 'as the subject of one's will, and thereby to lead a selfish life'.

1 January 1942

Fine day. Mount Fuji is looking splendid.

To be honest, I'm living in a chaotic world, full of doubts and suspicions. I tell myself: Don't rely so much on other people. Stand by your decisions, don't regret them like a girl. Be confident, believe in yourself … But I have not rid myself of my dishonesty, cowardice, vanity, self-absorption, sentimentality, false courage … My thoughts are confused, as much as anything. It's pitiful, but I'll get over it. This hardship will be the making of me, and I shall reveal my true greatness one day. My compatriots, endowed with their happy-go-lucky nature and belief in their superiority, should learn that the ultimate victory will belong to the great ones who have struggled.

We are not machines. We are not merely intellectual.

22 January 1942

It is so hypocritical to carry on with this barbaric war while at the same time envying America's high standards of living. Fundamental human energy should not be wasted on contemptible things like war and the accumulation of wealth. Human qualities are worth most when used for the happiness of the human society.

The sinking of our hospital ship *Harbin* has provoked fierce criticism, they say it's an act of inhumanity. But how can they single out this one incident while there are so many other atrocities and inhuman acts all around? It's inhuman to sink a hospital ship with defenceless people on board, they say; but is it not also inhuman to force objectors to go to war, to put them through brutal training, and eventually send them off to be killed?

26 January 1942

I have organized my affairs so that I can die at any time if required. I'm living in an orderly manner. I take photos. If you borrow someone else's ideology and make it your own, you're not responsible for it, are you? You can only be fully responsible for the things you think and believe in yourself. I have to establish my own thought system, and keep my feet firmly on the ground. My heart is pounding.

Exempt from immediate enlistment as a student, Hachiro Sasaki knew his time would come.

In Soviet Russia, seventeen-year-old schoolgirl Ina Konstantinova had also been taught throughout her childhood at school, and by her parents, both Communist Party members, that there was no higher honour than to sacrifice one's life for one's country, the Motherland. Yet citing her age, Ina's parents talked her out of volunteering for the front and instead sent her to be evacuated. Once the German troops were pushed back from her local area, Ina was allowed to go back to Kashin. She returned home desperate for news of her school friends fighting at the front, especially her first love, Misha Ushakov.

9 February 1942

I only feel able to write about this now that I've lived with my loss for a while. The pain is just as bad, but it has lodged itself deeper inside my heart. I was so happy to be back at last, I had been looking forward to being back with all the people I love. And instead ... I shall never forget the almost physical sensation, the terrible chill inside me when

I heard Father's words: 'Misha Ushakov ... is no more. Died from his wounds ...'

I couldn't take it in at first. Then, later on, I began to cry, but how can tears ever convey the pain of loss? I shall never forget the night I went to see Praskovia Vasilievna [Misha's mother]. I threw my arms around her neck. We cried and talked about him, only him, all night long.

I couldn't stop thinking about him, every little thing, the whole story of our love, from that first evening in April, to our last party. He had so much love inside him, so much to give. I remember the day he told me he loved me and asked if there was anything I wanted, anything at all. He promised he would do it, whether it was possible or not.

And now he will never tell me he loves me again. We used to be so happy together, we could sit for hours in silence, as if we were listening to this glorious music inside us. I remember him saying once: 'Shame I don't know how to cry; I think I could cry with happiness right now, if only I knew how.'

What wonderful, unforgettable moments we shared! He once told me a secret, something he never told anyone else. And I, yes, I loved him too. My love was strange and wild, perhaps, but it was love all the same. I was suffering, and because of that I made him suffer too. I was cruel. I annoyed him, all too often; I upset him very badly, many times. And at that last party, he cried even though he had never cried before in his whole life.

He left me two photos, a key, a bronze flower and a lock of soft black hair. That's all. And now I shall never, ever see him again, never kiss him, never feel his hands, so strong but so loving ... This is the end, the end of everything. I know one thing for sure: no one will ever love me the way he did. No one!

Why did it have to be him? So brave, so strong, so clever and fine. Such an amazing human being. He died at 11.50 p.m. on 31 December. He missed the New Year by 10 minutes. I had some kind of a premonition that moment; I was at a school party, but I suddenly felt very sad inside.

Misha is no more. My *Mishka*. No more and never will be. How can this be?

18 February 1942

Why did I take our relationship for granted? I used to feel ashamed of it. How stupid of me! I mentioned our love so rarely in my diary, and wrote so little about it. And now I'm going over every moment of it, every tiny detail. Now I can see how wonderful it was …

No news from 'there' yet. I am desperate to get a positive reply! How I long to be 'there', where life is so full, where there's danger and hero-ism and a chance to distinguish myself and take revenge on the Germans for ruining my happiness. Is it possible they won't accept me? I am so anxious, so impatient! I can't carry on living like I did before. I really hope they take me. I know I can make myself useful!

A year to the day older than Ina, nineteen-year-old Herbert Veigel was becoming less enthusiastic about the idea of personal sacrifice for the Fatherland by the day. Herbert's older brother Gerhard, a doctor, had been killed during the German advance eastwards in July 1941, and that Febru-ary Herbert discovered that another of his four brothers, Fritz, a thirty-eight-year-old father of two, had been sent to fight on the Eastern Front.

19 February 1942

My dear Parents,

It's a shame the pullover only arrived today, the worst of the cold is over now. But I will make sure I wear it a few times so it didn't travel in vain.

I am really sorry that Fritz is in Russia now. I would have been really happy if none of my brothers had set foot in this awful country.

The Russians are starting to look exhausted. We will overrun them with a massive onslaught in spring. I realize there will be more sacrifices, but I believe and hope our family won't have to make any more. That would be too hard to bear.

I am really pleased Gotthold is in Crete. There might be a few air raids there, but they're nothing compared with what we have to put up with here, night after night. We don't think anything of them any more. It hardly even wakes me up any more.

The situation here has been critical, but what gains have the Russians made compared to what we achieved in just a few weeks last year? And the Russian casualties are unbelievable. They're fighting a peasant's war, with ten men to a gun, or fighting with clubs, that sort of thing. You can imagine how disorganized they are.

We've got to get some new transport as nothing's working any more. We should also get proper tanks instead of these scout ones. At least then we'll feel safer during an attack. It's been pretty hairy up until now. But that's enough about war! Whenever I hear that one of my schoolmates or friends has been on holiday, I feel a pang in my heart. Not that they don't deserve it, but it makes me realize I haven't had any leave in over a year.

My warmest greetings to you all,

Yours, Herbert

Six weeks later, Herbert wrote to his parents, trying to make sense of some
devastating news.

8 April 1942

My dear Parents,

When I got your letter and the news that our dear Fritz has died a
soldier's death, I was nearly destroyed. It was so unexpected. I had hardly
grasped he was on the Eastern Front, when he should have been at home.
And now he's been snatched away from us, so abruptly. I can hardly
believe it, I can't take it in that our Fritz is no more. But it's true and I
have to come to terms with it, just as you will have, my dear parents, even
before you get this letter.

It is harder for you and for dear Elise than it is for me, but at least you
were able to say goodbye to him and prepare yourself for the possibility
that he mightn't come back. It is very hard to know what words to write
to you, when only grief and pain can express how I feel. How can I
comfort you? There is much that could comfort us, but we must first rid
ourselves of all superficial, selfish and trivial ideas. We must see the hand
of God in all this. He wanted our dear Fritz to crown his life with sacrifice; the biggest sacrifice a man can make. His life was not in vain; his
every minute was filled with work and fighting. Though he did not live
to see victory, we know his deeds will live on. We must carry his spirit
with us, to help us make the breakthrough. Fritz will always be with us,
not just through his children but whenever we feel him near. We must
be strong and brave and worthy of his life and death.

Just as he was prepared to sacrifice his life without any weakness or
fear, so we, too, must not have any doubts. If we did, we would be betraying the idea of death for the Fatherland, and in particular the heroic

deaths of our beloved Gerhard and Fritz. We must not argue with our fate, which has asked such great sacrifices of our family, while others haven't had to give up any of their loved ones. It is my belief that everything happens for a reason.

My dearest mother, however hard this loss is for you, I know you'll bear it with a strong and faithful heart. It is much harder for you, and you must feel so lonely now. But I hope I can visit soon.

It will perhaps be some comfort to you that I am coming back to Germany soon. I'll get leave, at the very least. A transfer might take a little longer. I'll write with more details later.

I don't know what to write to dear Elise. It must be terrible for her. The three little ones have no father now. We all want to help her. We must take her right into the bosom of our family, in place of Fritz who can only be with us in spirit.

My dear ones! Let me sign off for today. I hope my words have not hurt your wounded hearts too much. It is so hard for me to express what I'm feeling. I hope I will be able to say it all in person soon.

Your grateful Herbert is sending many heartfelt thoughts and shaking you warmly by the hands, in spirit at least.

The day Herbert mourned his brother Fritz, Ina's dream of fighting for the Motherland finally came true.

8 April 1942

What great luck! I am so happy. I've never felt this good in my life! Today I've been accepted for work behind enemy lines. I am so happy! I'll write about everything later.

At night:

I'll continue now. After school, our teacher told us the Deputy Secretary of the District Communist Party Committee wanted to interview five people from our class: Klara, Sasha, Valya, Galya and Lelya. Why? What was it all about? No one knew. I decided to go along with them. We waited and waited … It turned out they were being called up to work behind the German lines. The very thing I've been dreaming about for so long, so intensely! And I wasn't among those chosen, to begin with.

Sasha's name was called out first, then Klara's. They both came out beaming! Then I went in. They told me what my job would be. I immediately said yes, I'd do it. We were so happy, the three of us!

We are going! Going 'there'! To the front. I know it will all turn out well. I feel fine again, and happy.

A few days later, Ina ran away from home to join the partisans without telling her parents, leaving behind a note to explain and apologize.

Undated

My dear family!

Please forgive me! I know it's cruel of me to tell you like this, but it's better this way. There was no way I could bear Mummy's tears. Please don't be too upset and don't feel sorry for me, because my biggest wish has finally come true. I am so happy! Please remember that. All I can tell you right now is that I am going to join a partisan detachment. Dear Daddy, please forgive me in the name of everything that is sacred, please forgive me for 'deceiving you', as you put it. I went to the Regional Party Committee … and it was too late to back out … My dearest family, please don't cry and please do not feel sorry for me. After all, this is what I want to do with my life, this is happiness, to me … It would be so good to see you, and to kiss you. I will be back in the autumn.

Mummy darling, please don't cry. What's the point? Don't you want me to be happy? I feel really good, please believe me.

That's all for now. I'm going to write to you about everything tomorrow, every last detail. Don't be angry! And please don't feel sorry for me!

Lots of love to you all.

Your disobedient Inka

Two months later, Herbert Veigel found himself transferred to the German rear. Sharing the news with his brother Gerhard's widow, Herbert tested his latest plan on Luise before confronting his parents.

22 June 1942

My dear sister-in-law Luise,

My easy life as a radio operator is over, we're all in the infantry now. We were ordered to move back, 200km behind the front line. That gave us all a break, but then we were ordered to secure an airport targeted by the partisans. We were sent to a place no German soldier had ever set foot in before. It's very hard to catch these guys. They look like friendly peasants by day, but by night they become really dangerous. They're very well organized and get all their arms and supplies by air. We have to be very cautious, because there are only fifty or so of us. I spent the weeks building defences and bunkers from morning till night. I'm on duty for 12 hours at a stretch every other day and I spend the rest of my time at the gun emplacement in the bunker, or digging trenches.

Five days ago we were attacked from three sides simultaneously. It was pouring with rain and so dark that I couldn't see my own hand. I was on duty and only noticed the partisans when they were 20 metres away. Luckily, my machine gun worked beautifully, and I managed to hold off the attack from one side single-handed. When it got light they were forced to retreat, having achieved nothing. We've been on high alert since then and yesterday our dive bombers targeted several nearby villages, so I hope it will all be nice and peaceful here for a while. It's getting better already in fact, these night-time shoot-outs have died down a little.

We are not allowed to leave the immediate area. You can imagine what a dull life we lead! It's dark by nine and our use of lights is restricted. The guard is changed at 8.30 p.m. so there's just enough time to eat something before crawling into bed.

All this has made me completely disgruntled. I feel more useless and superfluous than ever, so every spare minute I think about the future. I haven't come to any decision yet, but life as a mere private gets more and more unbearable every day. I believe I am capable of greater things. My commander advised me to sign up to be an officer. I wanted to tell you what I think about all that, as best I can.

First of all, I have realized that I can never be an army doctor. Through this whole campaign I have never been able to look at wounds and injuries without feeling sick. So I don't think I would be able to help people in those circumstances.

Dear Luise! You will understand that I am torn, especially as I said in front of the whole family that I would follow in Gerhard's footsteps [to become a doctor]. Can I go back on my word?

And the other thing is that we are at war and I am a soldier. Nobody knows how long the war will last. It can't last more than another 2 or 3 years, but for as long as it does I have to delay training for a career. But if I were to become an officer, I'd have a career, with a salary. I could even end up as a captain. Obviously all the professions have their downsides and nothing comes for free. But at least here I have the advantage of knowing what the dangers are. Like all soldiers who have done this job with their eyes open, I disapprove of the behaviour of most of our officers. There's no reason why I can't do a better job, give the men in the company confidence as they go about their duties, and in battle as well. I am very keen to do better than my 'superiors'.

Warmest greetings,

Your Herbert

A day later, Ina Konstantinova, now a member of 2nd Kalinin Partisan Brigade, described her first confrontation with the enemy in the devastated German-occupied countryside near Toropets, over 200 miles west of her home town.

23 June 1942

I haven't written for a long time, but so much has happened! I wasn't wrong when I said that this exercise book will see a great deal of action.

I remember the events of June 19th very well. That night, a large detachment of one of their punitive units came very, very close to our village. Fire was exchanged right throughout the night and at dawn there were villages burning all around us. Soon the first casualty was brought to me. My hands were covered in blood. I took this heavily wounded man to a doctor 6 kilometres away. On my return, we had to execute a certain village elder, for being a collaborator. We picked him up, read out the sentence and led him to the place of execution.

He kept his head up, didn't say a word. Just the tips of his fingers were shaking. He went quietly. Zoika shot him, her hand didn't even tremble. She's so great! But I felt weird for some reason, really awful.

My life is so different now, compared to what it was like just a month ago. School, friends, Kashin have all faded away, far into the past ...

Yesterday I was called in to see my commander, who suggested I become a scout. This would involve working on my own away from our unit, and coping with a lot of hardship. And it would be more dangerous. I said yes, so I am getting ready. I am on cook's duty today, making breakfast and dinner.

If only I could see Mummy, Daddy and Rena, even for just one minute!

His mind fully made up, a few days later Herbert wrote to his parents to tell them about his ambition to become an officer.

28 June 1942

My dears,

What can I tell you about life here? We work really hard, constantly exhausting ourselves, and we get hardly any free time. I must admit, though, all the fresh air is good for me. I look well and I'm very tanned. I drink at least 1, sometimes 2 litres of full-fat milk every day, which I get from local farmers in exchange for cigarettes; I sometimes get a lot of eggs too and use the camping stove Fritz gave me for Christmas to fry them up. But as for being on duty, that's really wearing me down, except for guard duty perhaps.

I hope you can understand why I'm so anxious to find a way to leave this company and get out of Russia. I've given up on my idea of becoming an army doctor and have come to the conclusion that I should sign up to become an officer. I won't do it in a hurry, I'm being sensible about it. After two years in the army I have no illusions.

Sometimes I think I'm going mad. Not from overwork, but from the stupefying boredom. I hope I can be among totally normal people again soon. Almost everyone here has *Russia madness*.

Your Herbert

In early July, Herbert left Russia, having signed up for an officer-training course in Poland. Later that month, Ina Konstantinova described another mission behind enemy lines, this time with the aim of inflicting damage on the Pustoshka-Nevel highway, a major supply route between Moscow and Russia's western borders.

21 July 1942

I haven't written for nearly a month. So much has happened since then!

On July 4th, exactly a month since I left home, I went on my first mission. Our group was ordered to sabotage a highway. The boys carried some TNT and mines, while I was sent to a safe house, to discuss with a certain person plans to blow up some German barracks and get hold of some identification papers. I was to rejoin the group later.

The first night went by very quickly. We covered about 18km and stopped to rest in a clump of hazelnut bushes next to a village. We huddled together and fell asleep. The next day was wonderful, and I got to know the boys a lot better. That night we stopped near another village, sat under a fir tree and had a good time. There were so many violets growing all along the side of the road! It was a wonderful sight! I was in a great mood the whole way.

After spending time with the boys I had to leave them and rush off to a secret address. They really made a fuss over me, giving me food to take and helping me pack my rucksack!

I walked and walked and I got there on time, but the contact didn't show up. The police [*Ordnungsdienst*, local auxiliary police] became interested in me, left me to spend the night in a house and took away my passport. Then I heard the place where the boys were heading was crawling with police. I had to warn them as soon as I could, so I decided to run away.

I asked if I could bathe in the stream; I went in fully dressed, up to my neck in water, but then I got out and ran off. The police still had my papers, but I was desperate to get back to the boys. There was no sign of them. I searched the whole of the woods, but it was no use. I had to go back to another village. I was arrested again, and since I had no passport the village police decided to detain me until the German troops came. That was the first time I got really terrified, because the Germans don't even bother questioning people without an ID, the verdict is simple in such cases – partisan, to the gallows with you. What was I going to do?

I was billeted in a village elder's house, with two policemen. I decided to try and escape, I had nothing to lose. All that night I pretended to have the runs. They went with me to the outhouse to start with; then gradually they began to trust me. I ran like the wind, across the yard, along the street and into a field of rye. And that's how I got away.

I was okay, myself, I wasn't even tired, but I was devastated because I was sure the boys were doomed to die. I felt completely useless. I walked back to base, hardly stopping once. I was the first to get back.

I was worried sick until finally Makasha showed up one morning. I jumped up and down for ages, I was so happy! I almost hugged him to death. He told me the boys did manage to mine the road, but ran across several German units. They exchanged fire with them but had to retreat. They lost sight of each other and came back separately. Lyosha was killed by his own grenade.

Igor and Grisha returned the next day, and Boris and Seryozha a day later. I was so happy! I would follow them anywhere now, through fire and water. I visit my dear friends every day, I'm having the best of times!

Four days later, Ina turned eighteen and stopped keeping her diary for fear of endangering herself and her comrades. Whenever she had a chance, Ina kept in touch with her parents and younger sister Rena.

24 August 1942

Hello, my darling Mum!

I thought I'd write to you separately. If you knew how much I long to see you, to give you a huge hug, smother you with kisses. Well, perhaps not smother you, but you remember how I used to kiss you, so madly? You always pretended to disapprove, but you'd be smiling, and I'd carry on, giggling. My darling, I can see you all so very clearly, you, Daddy and Reginka. Sometimes I wake up with a start in the middle of the night, so convinced that you're sitting at the end of my bed, like you used to back home. And it's so nice, such a lovely feeling! But then I wake up, and there's no one there. If you only knew how much I love you, how much I've always loved all of you.

Please don't be sad, my dearest sweetest one. You know what the hardest thing is to bear? The thought that you might cry when you think about me. Please don't! Don't!

I live so well here, and everybody likes me. The boys from our group, the ones I went with on my first mission, they've become like a family to me.

Here is a kiss for you. Can you feel how much I love you?

Your Inka

29 August 1942

Hello, my darlings!

I don't know where to begin. Right then. First of all, I am alive and well, and I feel wonderful. It s only been three days since I got back from behind German lines. I had a bit of a time of it, again. I was caught, again. This time I fell straight into the Germans' clutches. I didn't expect it all to turn out so well ... I've been through so much ... Honestly, I thought I was going to go grey. I'll tell you everything when we meet. I nearly went mad with joy when I crossed the front line and saw our people!

I'll probably be going back 'there' in a few days. But please don't worry about me. I am convinced nothing will happen to me, and I'll soon be home on leave.

I saw the boys from Kashin yesterday – they told me that Mummy is really worried about me – but she really shouldn't be.

I am feeling incredibly well, a hundred times happier than all the girls back home – dancing and thinking they are having fun – because in these difficult times I am doing my bit for my country ... Even if I go hungry, or get captured by the Nazis, or have to walk barefoot for hundreds of kilometres – I would still be very lucky, and feel very happy with my lot.

Well, my dear ones, lots of love and kisses to you.

Your Ina

29 August 1942

Hello, my dear Renok!

I haven't heard from you for a long time. Why? Are you starting to forget about me? This won't do!

Do you know where I'm writing from? I can't believe my 'luck'! I've been arrested, by our very own border guards. It was funny and sad at the same time. And so stupid. All because I no longer have my passport. I was locked up in a bath-house until my identity could be established. They let me out this morning, so now here I am sitting in the commandant's room, writing to you.

Renochek, I have something to ask you. Please look through my letters for Zoya Poryvaeva's address. And hold onto it. Zoya was one of my best friends in the Brigade, she was amazing! She has died a real hero's death. And I really mean that. Lots of remarkable people have been killed, some of my closest friends among them: Zoya, Genka, Igor and Grisha. Do you realize, only Boris is left now, out of our whole group? I am taking it very hard, Renochek. I have every intention of avenging them, I am now driven on by intense hatred.

I hope you'll write to me more regularly. Please kiss our parents for me, lots and lots.

Love and kisses and hugs to you.

Ina

After two years of fighting, and many successful scouting missions, on 5 March 1944 Ina Konstantinova was killed by enemy fire while staying behind to cover her group's retreat with a submachine-gun as they fled, outnumbered by a German punitive detachment. Ina's comrades told her devastated parents that their daughter had died a hero's death.

CHAPTER SIX

The Holocaust

May 1942–March 1943

'There's no help from anywhere'

*I*n the spring of 1942 Churchill and Roosevelt were not yet ready to launch a direct assault on Western Europe to relieve pressure on the Soviet Union and the Eastern Front. As Churchill explained to Stalin, he preferred to 'go round the end rather than through the centre', and planned a landing in North Africa by the end of the year.

While the Allies discussed military strategy, across occupied Europe Hitler pressed on with his racial war, the aim – to create a Reich 'emptied and freed of Jews as quickly as possible'. During the opening months of the Russian campaign in 1941, SS mobile killing units, or 'Action Groups', shot tens of thousands of Jews; others were killed in gas vans, while the rest were herded into newly created ghettos similar to those in occupied Poland.

But as a means of solving the 'Jewish question' mass killing by shooting was deemed inefficient; the gas vans were too limited in their capacity and the ghettos only a temporary solution. To annihilate Europe's Jews on an industrial scale four specially built death camps were created in occupied Poland.

The first of these SS-run camps opened in December 1941 at Chelmno, near Łódź, its purpose to 'cleanse' the area of Jews and Gypsies. Those considered incapable of working – mainly women, the very young and the elderly – were to be sent to their deaths in the gas chambers, while a smaller number of Jews were kept in the ghetto as slave labourers. To prevent panic and deflect suspicion, those selected for deportation were told that they were to be 'resettled' in villages further east, where food was plentiful. By mid-May over 55,000 people had been deported from Łódź to the death camp at Chelmno.

In Germany, details about the systematic killing of the Jews were withheld from the public. On 7 January 1942, an order had gone out to the press not to print anything about 'the Jewish question in the occupied eastern territories'. Yet in Poland local witnesses and a few who escaped from the killing sites began to spread the word; from Warsaw reports eventually reached London and Washington. A few articles appeared in the press over the summer, though it would be months before the Allies publicly acknowledged what they had been told. An American diplomat shelved the first report to reach Washington, advising it should not be passed on until verified by further eyewitnesses. At the time, what was happening seemed barely imaginable.

In the summer of 1942, New York schoolboy David Kogan turned thirteen. He tried hard to remind himself to write about the war in his diary but it still had little impact on his daily experiences.

That summer Herbert Veigel arrived in Poland for his officer's training course. He stayed in Poznań and visited Łódź, both now in the German annexed region of 'Warthegau'. Poznań, the region's new capital, had already been 'cleansed' of its Jews and was, like 'Litzmannstadt' (Łódź), undergoing rapid transformation. Both cities were being renovated so that they would one day rank alongside Berlin, Hamburg and Munich as great urban centres of the Nazi Reich.

On the other side of the perimeter fence, inside the Łódź ghetto, conditions continued to deteriorate. Seventeen-year-old Dawid Sierakowiak had graduated top of his school but with no further education available worked hard stitching German military belts in order to avoid the regular deportations. Hunger in the ghetto was becoming more acute; food supplies would be deliberately reduced before transports arrived in order to encourage more

people to leave for 'resettlement'. In late May, Dawid was told that the next
round of transports would take people from Łódź to a work camp near the
city of Poznań.

27 May 1942

This afternoon they announced the voluntary registration of men from
18 to 50 years old for work in Poznań. Father has been threatening to sign
up for some time (though he often shouts that we're just waiting for him
to go) and registered this afternoon. He's to appear before the medical
examination board tomorrow at one. I thought about leaving myself,
but I don't feel strong enough to go, I have no energy because of the
hunger. Besides, I would miss my books and writings, notes and notebooks. Especially this diary.

The Jews recently sent here from Pabianice and elsewhere are escaping this ghetto hell to go and work in Poznań.

30 May 1942

I don't know why [Father] hoards all the money. He takes all of Mum's
and Nadzia's pay then doesn't want to give them money to buy rations.
He's also managed to borrow 100g of bread from Nadzia (stupid girl!).
I now take my bread with me to work (tomorrow's and Monday's
portions because I'll only get the rest on Monday and it has to last till
Thursday). I'll have to do this every day now. Also, he bought meat, and
a litre of whey (which he got at the dairy, for all of us), cooked it and ate
the lot. There is nothing else, so we are going to bed hungry. He wasn't
at work today, he just wandered round the city the whole day. He must
have spent a lot of money. Mum looks like a skeleton and the worry is

wearing her out. If only he was serious about leaving! But no such luck. He has taken to stealing from us and hassling everyone – as if that's going to help him. It's dreadful. Mum suffers the most, physically and mentally.

9 June 1942

They are sending more and more men to forced labour in Poznań. They took them from their beds last night, or snatched them up from the streets or from work even. A few workers from certain workshops are exempt. Transports are leaving more and more frequently.

14 June 1942

I'm working the afternoon shift again. Today I've been writing 'The Hallucinations of those Dying from Starvation' – a few pages of confessions and hallucinations, influenced by my depressed mood. The constant battle of hope against despair is killing me. What's more, my bad tooth flared up again and I'm in constant, excruciating pain. Tomorrow I'll go to the dentist which I've been putting off as long as I can. No political news.

21 June 1942

We received three 'workers' rations today, with added shredded cabbage and cottage cheese for three. The portions and sharing business are getting really tough at home. Father causes the most problems, obviously, cheating us all whenever he can, while claiming it's *us* who are cheating *him*. There's another reason why I so badly want the war to end: so I can be independent and start a new life, without all the fighting and shouting at home. But it doesn't look like we're going to be parted any time soon. More likely we'll all croak together in the ghetto.

22 June 1942

It's been a year since the German–Soviet war broke out and there's not the slightest chance of it ending soon. For the last few weeks the Jews have been promising that the Allied offensive will begin today, but, sadly, I was right to think that the beginning of the end is still quite far off.

The dentist filled my tooth today. If I'm to be buried here in the ghetto at least I won't have any cavities. And if I get out of here I'll need good teeth to bite and tear with!

3 July 1942

Father has been exempted and doesn't have to go to Poznań. It's still cold and cloudy. But it hasn't rained much.

By chance I read today's *Litzmannstädter Zeitung* [Litzmannstadt newspaper]. They report the capture of Sevastopol, the victorious march into Egypt, victories at sea, etc., etc. Reading the paper made me lose what little good humour and hope I still had. Concrete, irrefutable facts, as opposed to our empty, silly talk.

All of those who fled or were sent to the 'work camp at Poznań' were killed at the death camp of Chelmno.

In July, Herbert Veigel travelled to the real city of Poznań. On arrival, he wrote to his parents, relieved to be away from his life on the Russian front.

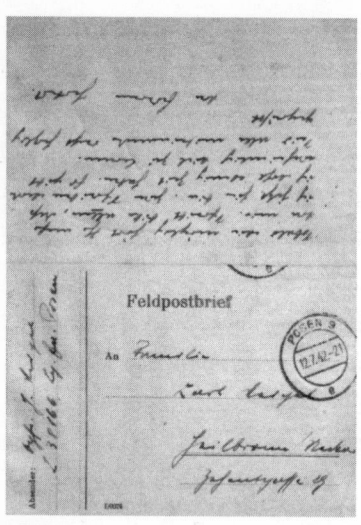

Herbert's letter, 12 July 1942.

12 July 1942

My dear Parents,

I arrived in Poznań an hour ago. You won't believe it but I've been sent on an officer's training course, it starts tomorrow and finishes on 8th August. I doubt I'll get any holiday but I'm hoping I'll be sent to Halle [in Germany] on 1st September for three months, provided I pass this course. It will be tough, but I am feeling positive and brave.

The journey here was fine. We travelled from Smolensk in a group transport, it took five days from when we left the company.

Please tell everyone I'm here, so they can write to me.

Fondest wishes, your Herbert

14 July 1942

My dear family,

A brief hello during my lunch break. The training here is very hard work, I get hardly any time off. It takes a lot out of you, both physically and mentally, there's focus especially on the kinds of knowledge that you completely forget after two years in the field. And we are supervised the whole time. I don't think I'm going to find it easy to pass, particularly as I never did the junior officers' training and I'm the youngest one here.

Over half of the trainees are from more senior ranks. So I have to try really hard. We get harsher treatment here than when we were new recruits, but at least we have a definite goal, and we know it will all be over in four weeks. If you want to send me a small parcel, please include things to spread on bread, and other little things to eat. There's not much of anything here. You can't eat your fill in the canteen because we all have to finish eating when the commander does.

Warmest greetings, your Herbert

20 July 1942

My dears,

We are now in the second week of our training! Everything has gone fine so far. I am struggling a bit to keep up but I think I'll manage. We're working all the time: writing and learning. We're busy every evening till midnight. Poznań is very nice, it's just a shame that I don't have time to enjoy it after all those months in the Russian desert. One more request: send me some cake coupons, as many as possible. And if you have any spare cards for meat, I would be very grateful.

Your Herbert

27 July 1942

My dears,

Thank you for your letters of the 17th and 18th, and the four parcels. I've been looking forward to my first letters from home since the day I arrived!

We are not allowed to go out in the streets. We are living in an old school building in an area of Poznań where most of the people are

Polish. You really don't need to send me so much, dear Mother. I am quite happy with little parcels, and in any case I hope to be home in two weeks.

On Saturday we will have completed half of the course. I will be so incredibly happy when it's over. If I manage to pass, and get leave back home, it will all have been worth it.

On Wednesday we are having a social evening in one of Poznań's best hotels. Actually it's not so much a social event as a way for them to watch us and see how we behave towards each other. I'm sure it will be fun anyway.

If I have collected enough coupons by my birthday, I'll have a cake or a tart made for me. I might even be able to get hold of some pudding. Then at least we might be able to have one little celebration this year.

Warmest greetings from your son. Herbert

On completing the course two weeks later, Herbert was suddenly summoned to return to the Russian front with no leave and had to spend his cake ration in a hurry. Inside Łódź ghetto, Dawid Sierakowiak was writing about bread, not cake. Over the first three weeks of July the ghetto food supply had been reduced once again.

27 July 1942

I've only received half my daily ration of bread – we didn't get any today. People are saying that corruption in the bakeries has come to light and that many commissioners, bakers and policemen have been arrested. Meanwhile, they're not issuing any bread (it'll come tomorrow instead). Mum cooked something this morning but I'm really feeling the lack of bread. Maybe my feeling so weak gave me inspiration, I wrote quite a good Yiddish poem ('*Lebn wil ich*') [I Want to Live].

Still no political news. People are saying large numbers of Jews (10,000 people a day) are being deported from the Warsaw ghetto, and that there are pogroms and that the people leaving are being shot at. The chairman of the ghetto there has committed suicide. In any case, the Warsaw Jews can't have suffered as much hell as we have. And it's still not over.

28 July 1942

The daily ration of bread has been reduced to 250 grams! The atmosphere in the streets is grim. No political news. The same hopeless, choking silence.

17 August 1942

A tiny glimmer of hope, at last. The Germans report that Goebbels said in a speech that the next few weeks will be decisive for victory in the East (the army slogan: 'We're defeating the English in the East!'). A Soviet offensive has begun along the entire Russian front. The Americans are on the offensive in the Mediterranean. The Germans are preparing to repel the attacks everywhere but they admit that they'd be ready to make sacrifices elsewhere for victory on a chosen front. So now there is the hope of a general offensive. Incredible excitement in the ghetto! The Jews are lifting their heads again but they are scared because of the rumours that the Germans plan to finish off the Jews in Europe before the end of war and possible defeat. Even so, everyone is full of rosy optimism. They think the war will end this year. If only! If only our strength could last that long. A few potatoes, some sugar, oil, vegetables, a normal portion of bread, soup at work – then we might pull through, if the food situation doesn't get any worse, if it doesn't last much longer.

19 August 1942

We've nothing to cook at home. We're all living with the growing hope that the war might end before 1942 is out. This evening the news spread – allegedly broadcast by the English – that there's now a general offensive in the West (air strikes) as well as the East, and that English, American and Canadian troops have landed in France. The mood in the ghetto now is like it was in Poland in August 1939. Except that now there's joy, mixed with expectation and hope, where then there was fear. I can feel myself being slowly overcome with joyful excitement, with an anxious and at the same time pleasant yearning.

The Allies had not, however, landed in France. The military activity was merely a practice run for a raid on Dieppe, which was executed on 19 August chiefly by Canadian and British troops to test out techniques to be used in the eventual invasion of France. It would take another two years before the Allies would be ready to invade north-west Europe and open up the Second Front.

Herbert Veigel wrote home that same day, as soon as he arrived back at his post on the Russian front.

19 August 1942

My dear family,

What a huge difference there is between life in Poznań and life here! I am used to it now though, it wasn't so hard. I left the civilized world in stages. We spent two days in Litzmannstadt, which I already told you about. We stopped in Warsaw for almost a day and then in Brest-Litovsk all the trains were so full that we had to wait there for two days as well. We even got the chance to go to the theatre and watch an operetta, *The Geisha*. The last stop was Minsk, where we had a fantastic meal in the beautiful barracks there, and watched a very good film. In Smolensk we joined up with an empty hospital train and travelled first class to our military airfield.

The village here is exactly the same as before, except for the fact that the personnel in our company have changed a lot, not many familiar faces. All our old pals have been sent elsewhere. My papers might come through from Poznań in the next few days, and then, if I'm lucky and I've passed, I should be an officer soon. And hopefully if all the timing works out I should be on study leave in Germany this winter. I wish I'd got here two days earlier, I would have met up with my old tank regiment, but then again it was good to take our time on the journey here. It's midnight now and I'm about to be relieved. Then at 4 a.m. I have to go outside again for 8 hours.

I have to go to the dentist the day after tomorrow, I've had terrible toothache in the last few days.

Warmest wishes,

Your Herbert

The letter Herbert refers to, in which he wrote about his visit to Łódź, no longer exists. In later life Herbert told his son that he visited the ghetto and saw the wretchedness but was so influenced by Nazi propaganda that he believed the Jews had brought it on themselves. Herbert remained on the Russian front for another year before returning to Germany for the rest of the war.

On the other side of the world, in July 1942, David Kogan prepared to celebrate his coming-of-age ceremony, his Bar Mitzvah, when he would become a full member of the New York Jewish community.

4 July 1942

Today I am a man. Bar Mitzvah. It was a great day. At first I was nervous when it began to get late. They say I looked serious on the pulpit, but I enjoyed it. I was only 70 per cent as good as practice, but the crowd liked it, and it was good. Just all of Dad's and almost all of Ma's family were there.

Downstairs we had the reception. Everyone had enough to eat, and I went around taking care of people's wants. I got a lot of gifts, mostly little envelopes containing $207.00 in cash and War Bonds and stamps. A great day. I'll remember it.

It was not like other Fourths, no fire-crackers …

5 July 1942

I couldn't sleep, so I went into the big bed and we talked about the Bar Mitzvah for two hours. It was the first time I did it in the morning since my childhood days on Randolph Street. After supper I went for a walk. I talked with the boys and learnt a little about people. Well, I got the congrats from the whole gang on my Bar. I have found out that when Steve read this diary last year, he spilled and this must have given some people a wrong impression about me.

17 July 1942

There is a French orphan refugee living with some people we know. Mom thought he should belong to the Jewish Community Center, so I spoke to the Director, and the boy will get a scholarship. This is the third straight day I have been hot in ping-pong. I was terrific, beating Ken Stone once 21–3. Then I went swimming. In the afternoon I wanted to go again, but Mom wouldn't let me. There was a long argument with Ma, which was quite humorous. Daddy has decided to go on a vacation to Camp Boiberik [a Jewish summer camp] and wants me to come with him. I will go for a week, and he may stay longer. Discovered a treasure. Old Yonkers postcards at Pinsky's.

29 July 1942

My birthday. A year ago I started these books. What a year for me! I started as Seymour Cohen. I am now 'Biff' Kogan. From an unknown I became known to every Jewish kid in my grade. The baby and mascot of the Athletic and Social Club. It was a momentous year, but not very profitable. My schoolwork was the same as last year. I started with girls. I, at thirteen, am in a world of fourteen. I have allowed my wit to develop. I've got and lost more friends than ever, and will have to gain them back again. Well, good luck!

31 July 1942

This is one part of my life, which I never until now touched – my thinking at night with my I [eyes] closed. Thinking I am President of Palestine … a great baseball player, manager, chess champ, greatest American in history, founder of modern housing projects. It has been going night after night for a few years.

For the fifth straight day it was rainy. In the afternoon I started to really teach Dad to play chess. We played a 'loose ' for two and a half hours, and he became fascinated by the game's possibilities. I kept on explaining, showing and comparing it with war.

1 August 1942

Mother came here today. Boy I am glad to see her, and am getting my dose of her character, her whole life, and my constant source of enjoyment and humour.

In the afternoon we saw the mid-season celebration of Camp Boiberik. It was a play, a pageant on the Nazis and the Yellow Badge. The people of a little East European town are invaded. An old Jew comes to the city and shows the people the Nazis' latest law, the wearing of the yellow badge. The badges were handed out to the audience, and we all wear them with pride.

10 August 1942

Given up the victory garden. The rain, worms, bugs, winds and soil have wrecked just about all stuff, except a pepper plant and a shrivelled tomato plant.

An important part of this diary should be devoted to the war and how it affects me. At present everyone is confident of victory. We have more of everything – on paper – and *are* losing. I, like others, believe in a second front, but do not want so much publicity on it. Nick came over. We played cards. He would bring up Eleanor's name, and I would blush. He is Mr Intrigue himself.

25 August 1942

My teeth hurt, so I stayed at home. My mind was on nothing but my teeth, so they hurt more. I was at my worst, and thus gave everyone a rotten time, but Mom deserved it. She put the braces on me. For four long years they will be on.

Across the Atlantic in Poland, rumours were circulating in the Łódź ghetto about the fate of the deportees, with fears aroused when Jews employed to sift bundles of clothing and bedding found the documents and ID cards of former ghetto inhabitants amongst returned belongings.

Dawid seemed no longer to have any illusions when in early September a new and unprecedented demand came from the German ghetto author-ities. The following week was like no other in the ghetto and Dawid wrote more in his diary than at any other time.

4 September 1942

Yesterday's tragic reports turned out to be true. The Germans have ordered the handing over of all children up to the age of ten, the elderly over sixty-five and all those who are sick, swollen, crippled, unable to work or unemployed. There is incredible panic in the town. Nobody is doing any work, everyone is running around trying to get work allocations for people without a job, and the parents of the unfortunate children are trying everything to save them. There will be a general '*szpera*' [curfew] – during which medical commissions will examine everyone and decide on their ability to work. As I'm a clerk, I managed to get Mum assigned to a furniture division where she can be employed at some suitable work, but it was incredibly difficult. I'm frightened for my Mum, though, because she is emaciated, small and weak. Saying that, she works all the time at the vegetable garden, she is not sick and she still cooks, cleans and washes clothes whenever needed at home.

At two, our office shut and we were told to go home until further notice. All other offices and services were also shut, with the exception of the 'faeces carts', the police, fire brigade, various guards, etc. The panic is intensifying by the minute. All the rumours make us expect the worse. At four o'clock, Rumkowski and Dawid Warszawski, the head of several departments, addressed the people. They said that 'sacrificing the children and the elderly is necessary, that nothing can be done about it, and they ask people not to interfere with the deportation'. It's easy for them to say because they managed to get an exemption from the Germans for the children of departments' heads, fire fighters, policemen, doctors, instructors, the Beirat and devil knows who else. So the Germans, who ordered the handing over of 25,000 people, will send others in their place – people who're capable of work – these people will in effect be the victims of the 'well-connected' children and elderly.

Father's cousin, who has a three-year-old girl, came to see us this evening. Since there is as yet no danger, we agreed to let her and the daughter stay here with us. Then later, we agreed to let her whole family stay, after they descended on us too. They were afraid to stay on at their place in case they were taken hostage instead of the child. Later still there was an air raid and some bombs fell on Łódź. The sound was music to the ears of all the Jews in the ghetto. It was really hot and stuffy outside, and with so many people in the flat I couldn't sleep. If things could only turn out well!

5 September 1942

My saintly, beloved, worn-out, blessed, my own MOTHER has fallen victim to the bloodthirsty German Hitlerite beast!!! She was completely innocent, she went just because of the evil hearts of two Czech Jews, doctors who came to our place to examine us.

There's been unrest in town since the morning because the news has spread like lightning that they were going to take children and the elderly to empty hospitals in the night, and from there they are to be deported on Monday (3,000 people a day!). After two o'clock, when we had a quick soup for lunch, cars and wagons pulled into our street and medical examiners, policemen, firemen and nurses began rounding people up. The building opposite was sealed off and after an hour and a half three children were brought out. The screams and struggling and crying of the mothers and of the whole street were indescribable. The parents whose children were taken went berserk.

While all this was happening two doctors, two nurses, some firemen and policemen entered our building. They had a list of all the residents. Despite protests from the policemen and the nurses, the doctors – old, mean, sour deportees from Prague – began a thorough examination of all the residents, finding many 'sick and disabled', as well as what they called '*frägliche Reserve*' ['uncertain reserve']. My dear unfortunate Mother belonged to the latter, but it's no consolation to me since they were all taken away to the hospital. Our cousin hid with her child behind a bed, her family all ran away and got out safely. They didn't lay a finger on our neighbour Mr Miller, a 70-year-old man who happens to be uncle of the chief doctor in the ghetto, but my exhausted but otherwise healthy mother went in his place! The old doctor who examined her was searching hard, surprised that he couldn't find any illness. He only shook his head and said to his colleague in Czech: 'Very weak, very weak.' And in spite of the protests of the nurses and policemen present, he wrote those two fateful words on our family card. They obviously didn't know what they were doing because they also took our neighbours' son, Dawid Hammer, a 24-year-old youth who has never in his life had anything to do with illness or doctors. But his cousin is a police inspector, so he was examined again, and released. What use is it to me that the two doctors were reported to the chairman of the ghetto and as a result were no longer allowed to examine people? So what if all the hospital staff were outraged? My mother is trapped and I doubt if anything can save her.

And Father? After Mother was examined, while she was running around the place like a poor mad thing, begging the doctors to save her life, Father was eating the soup that the people staying in our house had left on the stove, and he was helping himself to sugar out of their bag! Yes, he was a little bit shocked, he pleaded with the policemen and doctors, but he didn't run to town to ask his friends for protection. On balance I think he was pleased to have got rid of his wife. Their relations were getting worse recently and it was killing my mother. I swear on human life, which is sacred to me, that if I knew for sure my mother would survive the war, that would be enough to make me happy with things the way they are. Despite her great anxiety, my poor mother, who was always ready for anything, and always, unerringly, believed in God, showed full presence of mind. She talked to us about her fate with a fatalism and a logic which breaks my heart. She kind of agreed with me when I told her she had given her life away by giving her food to others, but she said it with such a bitter smile that I could see she didn't regret her behaviour – though she loved her life she valued some things higher, such as God and family. She kissed all of us goodbye, took with her a bag of bread and a few potatoes, which I had to force on her, and went out to her terrible fate quickly. I couldn't watch her out of the window, I couldn't cry. I walked around and sat down and couldn't speak, it was like I'd turned to stone. Every so often a nervous spasm would seize my heart, hands, mouth and throat. I thought my heart would break. But it didn't, and eventually allowed me to eat, think, speak and go to sleep.

I was submitted to a very thorough examination too, like everyone else, told to show my legs, in case they were swollen, but in the end they let me go. Up to now I have always thought of myself as a selfish person, in so far as my life was concerned, but I don't think it would make any difference to me now if I'd have gone with Mum and died. It's more than human strength can bear: the things she said before leaving, and knowing that she was an innocent victim of circumstances. And there was no way to help her! Although she is supposedly on the reserve list, our dignitaries will sacrifice the healthy reservists for their crippled protégées. Damned, capitalist world!

Hala Wolman came round in the evening, the sister of a friend of mine from our block. She works in the hospital where Mum is being kept. She tried to console us that Mum is to be re-examined, and that she'll be released because she was a victim of the crazy doctors. Promises, promises. These promises and consolations don't exactly fill me with joy. If Mum had been out of the house, or if they'd have come to examine her again, nothing would have happened. Someone's else's child is safe at our house, so far, but they took my mum. Nadzia howled, wept, had fits, but it doesn't move anyone any more. And I remain silent and feel almost insane.

6 September 1942

Yesterday afternoon they posted up notices saying that from five p.m. no one can leave the house without a police permit. Of course, with the exception of such and such and such. It looks as if they plan to start rounding people up. It was relatively quiet in our area in the night, but in other parts of the ghetto they took a lot of people. Of course, the Germans and the pogroms have not come yet, and that is what everyone is afraid of. It'd be all the same to me, if only they would bring Mum back.

At half past six today I took Hala Wolman a towel, soap and a clean nightshirt for Mum, who asked for them yesterday. Hala promised she will do everything in her power to get Mum examined again and released. Father's conscience must have been awakened during the night and he went to see a couple of acquaintances to ask for help, but of course that didn't work. Mum is still inside and no one knows if she's going to be examined again or if there's any hope of her being released.

There were no air-raid sirens last night but no one is expecting any miracles from outside now. The heat wave is ongoing. Even though it's forbidden, people are still running around the streets, everyone looking to be saved from their fate. But the curfew continues, and everything is shut. Until noon everything was totally quiet. After lunch, word spread that the commissions are now accompanied by Germans and that it is they who decide who is to be taken and who isn't. They've ordered that all the children that had been released should be gathered together in one of the hospitals. Although Rumkowski assures us that 'safe conduct' is guaranteed for these children, nobody believes him; even the policemen, instructors and managers are in despair. Laments, wild screaming and howling have become so commonplace that nobody pays them any attention. What do I care about another mother crying when my own mum has been taken away from me? There can be no adequate revenge for this! People are hiding children in attics, privies and other holes, losing their heads from despair. Our street is next to the hospital, and we hear the laments of passing hearses and funeral processions all day long.

Father got through to Mum at the hospital this evening. They didn't even want the commission to see her as she looks so bad now, and it's only because of Hala Wolman's intercession that she is to be examined again. Father says it's like hell in there. Everything is messed up and in a terrible state. Mum looks unrecognizable, which makes her already slim chances even slimmer.

Sometimes I get such shivers and palpitations that I think I'm going mad. Even so, I can't stop thinking about Mum and, suddenly, as if split, I find myself in her mind and body. The hour of deportation is approaching and there is no help from anywhere. There was thunder and lightning this evening, and it even rained, but it's no relief for our suffering. A month of rain wouldn't refresh a heart that has been completely torn apart and nothing will fill the eternal emptiness of the mind and soul after the loss of the person it loves the most.

Dawid's mother was deported to the death camp at Chelmno. In nine
months the population of Łódź was reduced from 163,000 people to under
90,000 – those considered fit for work. More than ever, life depended on
work, as Łódź was turned into one great factory producing sets of uniform
for 5,000 German soldiers every week. Over the autumn Dawid worked as
a clerk in an employment office, while his father returned to his old habits,
rarely working and often cooking only for himself, though by January his
health was deteriorating.

4 January 1943

It turns out Father's ankle is broken. The doctor wrote that he 'qualifies'
for a plaster cast at the hospital surgery. So far he hasn't even bandaged
the leg. It's tense again at home. Father says nobody cares about him,
we don't want to save him. He's forgotten how he behaved when Mother
was taken away to her fate. I keep quiet but whenever I have the strength
I drag myself out somewhere.

6 January 1943

Father started a row this morning. He doesn't care if the whole of the
ghetto crumbles – he just wants to go to hospital. I went to see Hala
Wolman this morning, and she promised to intervene at the hospital
where she works, to find a place for him.

14 January 1943

It was minus 8°C today but felt as cold as minus 20. It's terribly cold at home. I didn't get any soup at work because, unluckily for me, the boss was sick. Nadzia went to hospital to see how things were. Father has had his leg put in a plaster cast and he'll be in hospital a few more days. He asks for food the whole time. Nadzia sent him the 250g of bread which she always takes him and that's all. We couldn't give him any of our watery vegetable soup. He's not the kind of father for whom it's worth giving up your own health, like our unhappy mother did. My blessed mother, I remember her every minute, day and night!

24 February 1943

No political news. At home the hunger is growing. We have no groceries left and the soups are not nourishing. Father is worse and there is no help for us.

25 February 1943

More terrifying news for the ghetto Jews. The papers printed the Führer's speech in which he vowed to exterminate all Jews in Europe.

6 March 1943

At four in the afternoon, my unhappy, once powerful father died. He became so weak during the night that in the morning he was lying down unable to move. It got harder for him to breathe, he couldn't pass urine and he said very little, though he was conscious all the time and aware

Page from Dawid's diary, March 1943.

of everything. For lunch Father had a few cooked potatoes with beet-root soup but he was no longer able to eat by himself – Nadzia had to feed him. At three Nadzia went down to get shredded cabbage and cheese and I stayed with Father at home. Suddenly at five to four he asked me to arrange pillows for him. When I did, he turned his head and lay without moving, breathing almost imperceptibly. I watched him all the time from my bed, and, suddenly, it looked like he'd stopped breathing. For a few minutes I couldn't believe it, I was numb with fear. About five past four I called for someone to fetch a neighbour. A neighbour came and tried to move Father's head onto the pillow but she was terrified to when she saw that he was dead. When Nadzia came back with the shredded cabbage and cheese she threw herself at Father, screaming, but it was too late. We sent for Uncle, who came before nightfall. No one else from the family has come.

7 March 1943

I lay sleepless, like Nadzia, all night. Nadzia didn't undress, she just lay on my bed in her coat. In the morning Uncle did the paperwork with the doctor and the burial department and at around 1 p.m. Father was washed – at home, according to tradition – while I lay facing the wall. At three, the hearse arrived. Only Uncle and Chaim Esler went to the cemetery. Nobody came to see us in the evening and we were left on our own at night.

8 March 1943

I stayed in bed today because my fever is not going down. I am really annoyed that almost everyone keeps telling me to get up and go to work, without checking my temperature. I'll definitely go to work tomorrow. We've got 1kg bread, a little white cheese, three spoonfuls of sugar and about 20g cooking oil, left over from Father's rations. We're not selling any of this. The Hammers got us our rations of butter, cheese and milk powder. Added to the soup in the office it's a lot of food compared with the last few weeks. But the fever, having to stay in bed, and my sadness are all bothering me and causing palpitations. I wake up at night with my heart pounding or beating only weakly, and I can't get back to sleep. I'm looking forward to tomorrow when I can go to the office. Oh, to be back on my feet again! I wish I could get out of bed, which is a symbol of the grave in the ghetto. If only I were not in this accursed flat, where there's no help. Maybe I'll manage to get out of doors with the fever. I hope so!

Dawid stopped writing soon afterwards, having kept his diary for nearly four years. He died five months later, on 8 August, two weeks after his nineteenth birthday, of 'ghetto sickness' – a combination of TB and starvation. By the time of Dawid's death the extermination camps at Chelmno, Sobibór, Treblinka and Belzec had been closed down and the SS guards sent to work elsewhere, their work considered done. Over 1.5 million people perished in these four camps alone.

Part Two

Part Two

CHAPTER SEVEN

After Stalingrad

May–September 1943

'Shooting, shooting, shooting …
that's my weakest point'

Klaus Granzow in
1944.

Trudie Lach in 1943.

Brian on duty in the
desert in 1943.

*O*n 31 January 1943, after nearly five months of fighting in and around Stalingrad, the German Sixth Army surrendered to the Soviets. Four days later Berlin radio stations announced two days of national mourning, playing sombre music to honour the half a million lost in 'the Stalingrad disaster'.

It was a turning point in the war. After nearly three and a half years of conquests, Nazi Germany no longer seemed invincible. The surrender of 91,000 troops, including twenty-two German generals, was kept from the German public, who were told the men had given their lives for the Fatherland. Within weeks of the defeat the urgent need for replacements led Hitler to order 'total mobilization'. He cancelled previous exemptions and would come to extend the age of conscription to include all males aged sixteen to sixty.

The German surrender boosted morale in the Red Army and brought hope to those fighting Axis forces elsewhere. By May, Allied troops had driven the Germans and Italians from North Africa and were preparing to attack mainland Italy. Allied success in both campaigns and the prospect of an Allied victory changed the outlook of many of those living under German occupation. In France, more people became willing to engage in acts of resistance, though an increase in such activities, ranging from the spreading of rumours to sabotage and subversion, led to a clampdown by the German occupying forces and increasingly tough reprisals.

In Paris, seventeen-year-old Micheline Singer continued to get away with minor rebellions. Since the beginning of the occupation, she had lived a *successful 'double life': outwardly she was friendly, even attentive, to the indi-vidual Germans she came into contact with, while all the time she longed for an end to the occupation, breaking its laws as and when she saw fit.*

In May 1943, after nearly two years of training at RAF bases in England, Leading Aircraftman Brian Poole was sent to newly liberated French North Africa. Having been called up on his eighteenth birthday, he joined the RAF as he had hoped, but trained as an instrument repairer rather than a pilot with a 'Blenheim bomber of his own'.

Until 1943, fifteen-year-old Klaus Granzow had enjoyed a remarkably sheltered adolescence, his life at home and at school in Germany's rural north-east barely touched by the war. The youngest son in a large and pros-perous family, Klaus lived on a farm in the small village of Mützenow in the rolling hills of Pomerania. Neither his parents nor his teachers at the grammar school in nearby Stolp, where he boarded during the week, were committed Nazis, but nor were they outspoken critics of the regime. In May, with the war disrupting his familiar routine for the first time, Klaus began to keep a regular diary. Earlier in the year he had stopped going to the compulsory Hitler Youth meetings.

15 May 1943

They're saying I deliberately set out to skive but it's not true: I went to a Hitler Youth meeting in Stolp once but all we did was exercises and gun training, I didn't know anyone and none of the leaders wanted me in their platoon, so I just didn't go back. But back in the village I would always say that I had already done my weekly training in Stolp. Every-one in my class knew, but no one gave me away, even though they were all very jealous of the extra free time I had while they were at their Hitler Youth meetings.

Anyway that's all over now. I had nothing to say in my defence. If I'm reported to the Youth Leader I could be expelled from school and I don't want that to happen because I want to carry on studying. Now that they've found out I haven't attended one single Hitler Youth camp, they've signed me up for the big summer camp at Lonske-Düne. From now on I will have to go to the Hitler Youth meetings twice a week! Attendance is compulsory.

21 May 1943

I am scared of going to camp, to be honest. Scared of the drills and the square-bashing. The worst thing is that no one else from our class is going, no one from our village even, and the thought of being there on my own frightens me. So this is why I am going to take this diary with me, the one Auntie Link gave me last year. She laughed when she saw

I was using a cheap notebook as a diary and gave me this one for my birthday. I haven't used it yet because I didn't like the lock and the flowery cover – all right for a girl but not really the thing for a boy. But I think I will take it with me to camp, it will be a friend for me – a girlfriend in a flowery dress.

Klaus's diary.

*Before Klaus had even left for camp, Hitler's recruitment drive caught up
with him at school.*

13 June 1943

On Tuesday, lessons took a back seat. Three smartly dressed officers from
the air force, the navy and the army came to visit. They each talked about
their different branches of the military and then signed us up for officer training.

Our whole class volunteered. A question of honour! We chose the
army, the tests for the air force and the navy looked really tough. We could
then choose which arm of the service to join. Gerd and Muck chose
artillery, Georg Tegge the cavalry, some of the others couldn't decide.

I signed up for the multiple rocket-launcher. My classmates were
surprised, they'd never even heard of it. I told them everything our
neighbour Kurt had told me. He is two years older and tipped me off
about it. It's a completely new weapon, still being developed and
improved. It could decide the war. It will only be used at the hotspots
on the front and it's part of the motorized division, so you don't have to
go tramping through Russia on foot.

The officers said that as volunteers we wouldn't be called up any
earlier than other boys of our age, so we should be able to finish school
first – which would be brilliant!

On Wednesday we were told that our fantastic German teacher won't
be coming back. We have a new one called 'Doris' and she's an old witch!
She wears her party badge on everything – blouse, cardigan, whatever.
I can see we're going to have a lot of fun!!!

I showed Doris my plan for the homework essay 'My Parents' House',
but she didn't like it and she wasn't all that keen on what the others came

up with either so she set us a new one, 'When the Spring Comes'. I will get on her good side by writing about the old Germanic custom, where they used to roll burning cartwheels down into the valley. That will touch her party heart and get me top marks, easy.

She wouldn't have liked 'My Parents' House' anyway. I wasn't about to lie and say that there was a portrait of Adolf Hitler hanging on the front door. What would Dad say? But of course in my diary I can describe our house just exactly as it is:

This has been our family's home for hundreds of years. The big black gate might look imposing but it's easy to open. Once you are through the gate you see the house with its big white door and ten windows, five on the ground floor and five above. My five siblings and I were born and grew up in this smoky old house. Our bedrooms are in the loft, where the walls and ceiling are painted white and are decorated with our drawings and our sports certificates. In the boys' room the beds are along the wall, then there are wooden chests, two chairs, a lamp, a little bench and that's it. I keep my books on the floor. We usually have lots of apples up in the loft too, and also hams and sausages fresh from the farm. The upper loft where the corn dries out is a fantastic place to play when it rains. But as soon as the sun comes out we go straight down to the garden and run about among the many fruit trees and beautiful flowers, the roses and clematis.

That's my parents' house, my home, the place I like to be most of all. I love it, and am often homesick during the week when I have to stay in town to go to school.

Unlike Klaus, Micheline Singer often seemed happy to get away from home, if only on food-finding trips from Paris to the Normandy town of Verneuil where the family had lived during the first year of the war. Micheline travelled alone, staying with family friends in Verneuil. Her previous trip, three months before, had ended in a massive row with her mother when all Micheline brought home to Paris was a live rabbit.

8 June 1943

It's been ages since I wrote anything here but lots has been happening: the Germans have surrendered in Tunisia. They're realizing now that they have lost the war. God is punishing them for their prior arrogance: 'Germany is winning on all fronts!'

When I left for Verneuil this time I took a notebook with me but once there didn't get a chance to write in it, so I have to resort to my old method of catching up once I am back in Paris.

1 June 1943

Mummy told me to come back no later than Friday and she also said that if I don't bring any food back with me and just have fun like last time then she would not pay for my ticket. This time I will apply myself seriously to finding food.

2 June 1943

The cobbler from Verneuil tried to help me with my search. But after travelling about 25 kilometres by bicycle, all we came back with were six eggs. It was exhausting. I fell off my bike, catching my shoes as I hit the ground and all the nails came out of the cork soles. Luckily the cobbler was there and promised to repair them with leather. I cycled back in bare feet.

3 June 1943

I have been given another six eggs, but this time I have to bring a landscape painting in return or I won't ever get any more.

4 June 1943

The cobbler has mended my shoes and they look wonderful, but it's a shame to use so much leather for a pair of shoes when the future is so uncertain. He's been a bit wary of me, ever since I told him I was German.

The baker gave me a pound of butter in exchange for two packets of cigarettes. On one farm I swapped two pairs of blue overalls – I found them at home – for a kilo of butter and two dozen eggs. It's very hard getting food. The farmers prefer to give it to the Germans.

6 June 1943

Today Madame Bissell gave me a dozen eggs, four really good cutlets and half a pound of butter. So I'm sure I won't get into trouble for being a couple of days late getting back to Paris!

Micheline returned to Paris to take the first part of her Baccalaureate exam. For Klaus the school term was already over and, after one final attempt at getting out of going to the Hitler Youth summer camp, this time by claiming that his father needed help with the harvest, he had no choice but to leave for the camp, at Lonske-Düne on the Baltic coast.

Late June 1943

Sand, sand, everywhere sand ... that's the first thing to say about this place. We had to walk from Leba, so it was hardly surprising that we were soon yapping and whining like dogs dying of thirst. My shoes were full of sand, the heavy rucksack pressed down on my back and the straps rubbed my right shoulder raw.

We weren't exactly able to appreciate the beautiful landscape. Not till the next morning when we ran through the massive dunes to the beach to wash ourselves in the sea and brush our teeth. It's fantastic, wading through the sand at six in the morning. Sadly we weren't allowed to go swimming as some people don't know how yet, we could only go in up to our shoulders to wash. When you brush your teeth in salt water the taste stays in your mouth all day, reminding you of the sea. When we run back, the sun is rising in the east.

Next thing in our routine is room duty in the barrack. It's not too bad, as the whole floor is covered in mattresses. We sleep on these sea grass things, two on each, and use our rucksacks as pillows; there aren't any cupboards. It's all very basic but pleasingly romantic at the same time.

I was worried about the drills, but they aren't half as bad as they might be. There's only one square-bashing idiot amongst the company leaders; the others are all fine.

The food is just about okay. Several of the boys in our room have had stomach ache from the hard army bread. The medical orderly gives everyone castor oil to prevent constipation. After we've taken it we all run like the wind to the latrines. You have to run really fast because they are a long way out in the dunes.

The mosquitoes are really terrible here. I've been bitten all over. But I'm also getting a really good tan.

4 July 1943

This morning we had a fantastic singing session. We all lay down on a slope in the dunes and three boys played accordion. We learnt lots of new songs and a really funny canon. One of the boys from my room wouldn't sing two of the lines because it made fun of pastors. That's what he thought anyway, and his father is a pastor. We all laughed at him and the company leader sent him off into the dunes. He made much too big a fuss about it, as the lines could just as well have been about a teacher or a doctor.

I will remember this morning for a very long time: it was so beautiful, singing and daydreaming as we lay there in the white sand looking out over the dunes and the blue sea.

9 July 1943

It's the last night in Lonske-Düne. None of us can sleep. Some boys from the other barracks brought the Holy Ghost to visit our pastor's son. They came into our room dressed in sheets, grabbed him and stripped him naked and then smeared his backside with boot wax. He screamed as they set about polishing it. It was really good fun, I laughed a lot. But I also felt very sorry for the boy. When they let him go he ran straight to the beach with a scrubbing brush. But I don't think he'll get it off. I should go out and help him, really.

We had our final inspection this afternoon. The regional leader was there and lots of high-ranking Hitler Youth leaders. Everything went smoothly, we had been very well drilled for it over the last few days. As we were marching off, we started singing 'Oh you spirit of the mountains', when the regional leader shouted 'Song over!' and shooed us through the dunes. We had no idea why. But he called us to attention and asked why we had sung that song. No one piped up, 'It's just a song we know.' He explained that it's now banned because a group fighting against the Hitler Youth use it as their rallying song. I can't believe there are boys fighting against the Hitler Youth, they'd be fighting themselves really because we're all in the Hitler Youth in the end. But I wonder what used to happen in the past? My brothers used to have grey shirts and they belonged to a 'youth movement' or whatever it was called then. Maybe the Edelweiss Pirates are a group like that? We were not told anything else about them, and anyway we were soon busy getting ready for the farewell party.

Thinking back, I've really enjoyed my two weeks here, though I had actually been quite afraid of coming to camp. But I'm very happy to be going back home again, I'm getting quite homesick.

Unknown to Klaus, the Edelweiss Pirates were one of several youth groups who refused to join the ubiquitous brown-shirted Hitler Youth. Dissidence was rare in Germany and by 1943 most such groups, including the Edelweiss Pirates, had been rounded up and sent to special 'work camps'.

That July, while Klaus was at the Hitler Youth camp, Micheline sat the first of her end-of-school exams. For the past year, she had travelled free on the metro, passing herself off as a German, thanks to a pass that she had forged, secretly, at home.

9 July 1943

I think I can now tell the story of my pass. On the way home on the first day of the exams, a Friday evening, I took the metro. The ticket inspector checked my pass and then nodded to the horrible-looking officer next to her. The officer came over and took my pass away. I could have tried to run but it would have been tricky in my wooden-soled shoes and they would have caught me very easily. Until then I hadn't said a word in French. From the expression on the officer's face it was obvious he knew it was a fake. He told one of the others he was taking me to headquarters.

When we came out at street level I burst into tears. I told him I had faked it for a laugh and that my parents had no idea, it wasn't their fault, I was young and would never do it again … People coming out of the metro stared at us. He asked if I was German, and could he see my papers. I told him I wasn't and handed him my papers. I expected to be taken straight to headquarters, so I was relieved when we passed the stop; we got off eventually at Notre Dame de Lorette. As we left the metro, a woman dressed in widow's black saw me with a German and shouted 'Slut!' The officer took me to a little café and made me drink port to cheer me up. He said he couldn't bear to think of me in prison or the idea that my beautiful rosy cheeks would fade. I started crying again. No need to write down every detail of an episode I will never forget. After taking my name and address he let me go. He wanted to bring me home but I persuaded him to come only as far as my street. After all I'd been through, the last thing I needed was to be seen coming back with a German!

I promised not to tell anyone, knowing full well of course that I would have to tell Monique, so the same thing didn't happen to her. I saw him again the following Monday. He asked me to meet him in front of his hotel and made me go up to his room. I felt so ashamed. The first thing he did was force me to read the German military code which warns that the death penalty will be carried out on anyone who forges official documents. Then he took all my papers and burned them.

He said he hadn't wanted to arrest me because I was very young and he thought my life would be wasted. I would have spent a long time in Fresnes prison, and then who knows what.

When I was at home I felt very grateful to him, since if it weren't for him I wouldn't be able to be there any more. But I was less than happy, annoyed even (though I didn't dare tell him so) about having to keep seeing him and letting him kiss me (luckily just on the cheek, because I would rather have died than be kissed properly by an old man like him).

I don't understand how men can be so disgusting. What pleasure do they get from kissing you? He told me it was over, thank goodness, but I'm not so sure. The worst part is being in his room. I wish I could be rid of him. If only he would just go away!

I forgot to mention that when I arrived very late that first evening, Mummy asked where I'd been. She could see I'd been crying. I told her the Latin homework was very difficult and I had a headache. The next day I told my sister Nicole, told her everything!

12 July 1943

I have been to see my saviour again. He is called Willi. We talked about politics like we always do. He doesn't believe in anything, not even God. But he wanted to kiss me again. I told him if he did I'd scream. We went over and over it for at least three quarters of an hour. In the end he didn't. Why these kisses matter so much, I'll never understand. Anyway I'll soon be rid of him as I'm going away on holiday.

While Micheline could not wait to get away from Paris that summer, all Klaus wanted to do was stay at home. But barely a week after coming back from Lonske-Düne he was summoned to another camp, this time an 'Armed Readiness' paramilitary training camp. Established the previous year, almost a quarter of these camps, including Bublitz, the one Klaus attended, were run by the SS.

20 July 1943

I am in yet another camp, this time it's an 'Armed Readiness' one, in Bublitz. The call-up came quite suddenly. I was soooooo looking forward to the summer holidays, then came the notice that I was to attend pre-military training on 18th July. The letter only arrived on the 17th, so of course I got here very late.

We sleep five to a room. Only one of the others is nice; he's called Klaus Odefey. He's a farmer's son like me, a bit older, with straw-blond hair and light blue eyes. He goes to a grammar school like me, and he wants to be a vet.

Yesterday I had to go on watch first thing. The camp is surrounded by a tall barbed-wire fence with a real sentry box in front of the gate. One person guards the gate while the other patrols. My watch companion ended up in detention for hiding a girl under his raincoat in the sentry box. That is absolutely forbidden. His school and his parents will be informed.

25 July 1943

The first week of 'Armed Readiness Camp' is over. Today they let us get our breath back a bit after all the demanding exercises. We are training for the Hitler Youth Silver achievement award and the National Swimming Certificate. This includes munitions training, drills, map reading, camouflage, sport … it's never ending. And then there's the shooting, shooting, and more shooting. And it's my weakest subject. I always make mistakes when I'm taking aim; I'm particularly bad at starting the recoil. Lying up I can sometimes manage a ten but freehand I always get a 'miss'. I get very annoyed with myself because the others make fun of me. Gerd shoots well, so does Peter. There's a competition between all the boys' units; of course everyone wants to get the most points.

Today, the group leader with the least hits had to supervise the tables in the dining hall, and that was me, of course. The entire hall was laughing at me.

1 August 1943

I am so happy to be outside the fence and on my own. We have been doing a lot of square-bashing since our group came last in the sports tournament and, worst of all, last in the shooting. And from our group the least have signed up for the SS. Every day the deputy company leader comes to our rooms looking for recruits.

Klaus Odefey and I head outside when he shows up; we are both officer trainees for the army so they are not allowed to recruit us into the SS. The others in our group have till tomorrow morning to think about it. Then they will probably all be made to sign up.

Of the other companies, almost everyone has signed up for twelve years of duty in the Waffen-SS. They could choose the infantry but most of them have signed up for the tank division. They've been given light duties now. It's just us officers in training who have to be polished up even more. It's so unfair. Why should we be treated worse than the boys who are going into the SS? We are all fighting for Germany, for the same Fatherland. Or is there really a big difference between us?

I have, however, learnt something very important here. Firstly I stand more upright and don't go around hunched up, and in the lessons about fighting without weapons I learnt lots of holds, so I can defend myself now, which is always useful. It's good to know how to outwit a stronger enemy through skill, speed and cleverness. Before I was always afraid of a fight, but not any more. I know how to get out of a headlock or stranglehold, and lay the opponent out on his back, it's really terrific! I must carry on practising the moves when I get home, so I don't forget them.

Ah – Home! I am getting very homesick. It will be so great to be back in Mützenow again.

That summer, Brian Poole was on active duty for the first time, far from home in Tunisia, which was now under Allied control. Trudie's letters were as vital a diversion to Brian at his base camp in the desert as they had been back home in England.

12 July 1943

Dear Trudie,

I don't know the female equivalent of Casanova but I'm calling you that now. You and your Mr Room 16! I'm burning with jealousy now and I've spent the last few days polishing my rifle in preparation to do battle with this 'thief'. I laughed for days about your little 'frustrated romance'. Anyhow, if you hear of an unidentified aircraft bombing Room 16 you will know it's me after your boyfriend.

Since last I wrote we have moved to a more desolate area still. We flew here and I've never had such a bumpy trip in all my life. We passed over bare mountains and stretches of desert, all of which looked uninviting for a forced landing.

Here there is an abundance of those horrible tarantula spiders with legs about 3 inches long and very hairy. To give you an example of the way you get out here, two days ago we captured two of these terrible creatures in an empty tin and let them fight. All the boys gathered around and cheered their respective spider on until one lashed out with his two front legs, grabbed the other, dragged it towards him and began to eat. Then we tipped them out and killed 'em both. There is a moral in that. The biggest thing we have to fight against out here is boredom. Unlike the Americans out here, who get every consideration and plenty of amusement, we are left to find our own fun. There is one thing I can say about your government: they do treat a soldier with respect while we are of no consequence to our government/we are only the people who fight the war!

One thing that has worried me out here is the lack of things to buy as presents. I've hunted high and low for something you would like and I haven't seen anything worth getting. I've only been in one city since I came out so that is explainable.

By the way! My little trouble, Trudie, has straightened itself out. The little damsel I told you about no longer troubles me.

I suppose this is about all I have to say.

Fondest Love,

Brian x

P.S. Just a little one!

26 July 1943

Dear Trudie,

How are you today? I think you possess an amount of cunning to trap all these men. Now a seventeen year old, poor child! You'll be a financier of worldwide renown if he teaches you to 'shoot crap'. Anyhow if that aged so and so could get some poetry out of you what about ME?

There is no need to go out on a balcony here to get sunburn. I'm nearly black on my back and well browned on the rest. We only wear our shorts and topees (sun helmets).

I haven't received your photo yet so I presume it has been lost. I'm sorry because I was looking forward to it. Is it too much to ask you for another, just to cheer a lonely airman in the barren wastes of North Africa? The old one of you standing in the snow is very cooling but you must remember it has been around in my wallet for nearly four years, two of which have been in the service. Now it gets smothered in dust and swings precariously in that burning breeze which blows across this wide expanse of sweet nothing.

Italy seems to be causing particular speculation at the moment. I don't know whether she will surrender or not. The bombing of Rome seems to have upset them too. Anyhow, the first Dictator [Mussolini] has fallen – quite an omen of foreboding for the rest. Don't you think so?

Well Trudie, I know these letters are uninteresting but it's a deadly monotonous life we lead.

Fondest Love,

Brian

The day before, Mussolini had been ousted from power in a bloodless coup, as Allied forces advanced further into Sicily. Brian would remain in North Africa doing very little for several more months before returning to England later that year.

Micheline's chance to get away from home that summer came at the end of July when, leaving her sister behind with their mother in Paris, she was allowed to travel south to join their father. After the collapse of the French army, their father had been determined to continue fighting. For over a year he had been living with his cousin in Belley, a small town outside Lyon, where they were both active members of the resistance – though at the time Micheline knew nothing of their activities.

31 July 1943

I left Paris on the eight o'clock train for Lyon. The journey was really awful; hot and dusty and the toilets stank so bad, I feel like the smell has stuck to me. Luckily there was a nice boy on the train who gave me a drink, I completely forgot to bring any water.

In the evening we ate in a little restaurant and Daddy had a row over the cost of the charcuterie. He's such delightful company! He's always arguing. At least there's fruit and vegetables here, the food is just fine, in spite of Daddy's complaints.

6 August 1943

There's a really adorable little Italian officer staying at the hotel. I thought about him all night long. I haven't spoken to him yet and I found myself suddenly wondering, why not? I always thought my first love would be an English pilot so this one would have the extra pleasure of being a surprise and blowing all my theories to bits. He looks so sad, with his beautiful blue eyes ... and he's extremely chic. I always pay a lot of attention to dress sense.

My imagination has, of course, run wild and I've dreamed up the most extraordinary schemes for getting to know him.

8 August 1943

In the cold light of day, all of last night's ideas evaporated. He wasn't there at lunch. At dinner I changed places with Daddy so I could see him. Luckily Daddy didn't notice but he did ask who the Italian was, looking at me like a fried fish!

I managed to speak to *him*. But I couldn't think and ended up saying something really stupid. He asked how I liked Belley and I told him I was bored. Then I heard him asking one of the hotel staff to wake him up at 6 a.m. so now I'm scared he's leaving.

9 August 1943

I will have to recount today's events just as they happened:

6.30 A.M. – I get up to see *him* and meet him coming out of the WC – not very poetic. Disillusioned and cross.

6 P.M. – I come back from the lake where I've had a great day walking, sunbathing and forgetting all about this morning. Then I talk to Daddy outside the hotel, in the hope of meeting *him* – and then there he is! I pretend I need to return the bike I borrowed and follow him inside. We say 'hello' to each other and talk. I'm afraid Daddy will see us, so we go up one floor, but the whole hotel has seen us by the time we part.

DURING DINNER – I think I am an idiot for not being able to flirt with him. I find it a bit repugnant that I want to give my first kiss, my first love even, to a man I will only see for a few hours. But I shouldn't be so afraid of a kiss.

AFTER DINNER – I go upstairs and bump into him – we exchange a few words and then Daddy appears. I run off. Once Daddy is back safely in his room, I go and find *him* again. But Daddy returns. This time he is absolutely furious, shouting and screaming like someone on a market stall: 'I come out and find you talking like a whore on the stairs. Just you wait …' I go to my room and Daddy appears again. He tells me I shouldn't go around talking to people I don't know and 'a man only has to put on an enemy uniform for you to like him'. Those were his exact words.

10.30 P.M. – I am going to stop now. I'm so cross that Daddy caught me and so cross that I can't talk to anyone without Daddy the guard dog barking. But I must admit, I can be a bit of an idiot during the holidays; I let my imagination run away with me more than usual.

15 August 1943

I will remember today forever, the best day of my life so far. I am passionately in love with him.

At 10 o'clock this morning we left the hotel together and went for a marvellous walk. On the way back, we sat by the road and talked. He is called Giuseppe, what a wonderful name! We promised to write to each other and I now have his address in Italy, where he's a ski instructor. When I'm with him I don't feel at all uncomfortable, not like I do with Germans. We agreed to meet later on by the cemetery.

After dinner, we left the hotel separately. We smoked a cigarette together, then lay down on the

Page from Micheline's diary, August 1943.

grass. We both said we wanted to stay there all night. It was like a dream. Giuseppe is the most handsome person I know and he has the sweetest nature. He's a real mountaineer, too. Two weeks ago, I could never have imagined that I would meet such an exquisite man, an Italian, and be in love with him. Everything was pure and honourable between us, he didn't kiss me. Although to be honest with you, diary, if he had tried I wouldn't have stopped him. I'd like to know why he didn't try to kiss me, in fact. If only he didn't have to leave on the 6 o'clock train tomorrow morning.

The next day, Giuseppe left for Annency and Micheline for Lyon. But after ten days apart, Micheline slipped away from Lyon to find Giuseppe, back at his barracks in Belley.

26 August 1943

I got up at 5 a.m. and set off for the station on foot. I had been worrying about the possible consequences of my little escapade, but I felt better once I started walking.

Once in Belley I had to summon up the courage to go to the barracks. I told a French-speaking Italian soldier who it was I was looking for, and someone ran off to find him. I had forgotten how good-looking he was.

We went for a walk and talked about the war. Giuseppe has this one fault: he likes the Germans too much and said that if Italy stopped fighting, he would join their army.

I said everything I wanted to say to him. I won't try and describe to you, diary, what our talk was like, nothing could recreate the wonderful atmosphere and the loving silences. Now I have a reason for living, for hoping and for waiting, because my Prince Charming has finally arrived. It was strange and amazing when he took my arm and we walked along in the mist, our fingers so tightly squeezed together that it hurt. I could have walked on like that forever. And I'm happy he believed me when I told him he was the first; I don't mind that he didn't kiss me, I can wait till we see each other again. I never realized how beautiful first love could be.

27 August 1943

I want the Germans to leave France, of course, but now I really want just one thing: I want the war to end, so we can see each other again as soon as possible. We went to the station at 7 in the morning. I bought my ticket and we had breakfast in a café. Everyone stared at us, which is only natural.

I like him being Italian, but from the point of view of everyone else, Mummy in particular, it would be better if he wasn't. Then they wouldn't be able to call him 'Macaroni'! Of course, he will come to Paris, if he can, but we can hold out to see each other. Maybe the war won't go on too long. Everything is going so fast (the Russians are already 150km west of Kharkov). Giuseppe is twenty-six, just the age I hoped he would be – isn't that funny!

When it was time for him to go, he suddenly bent down towards me, smiled, and then straightened up. He has beautiful bright blue eyes. I don't like eyes that are too dark.

Two weeks later Italy capitulated. Giuseppe never replied to the passion-
ate letters Micheline wrote to him on her return to Paris.

For Klaus the end of the summer brought brief respite from military
training and a temporary return to normality.

August 1943

BEGINNING OF SCHOOL: We are such a great class! We felt this so strongly
when we met up again today. However good the holidays have been, our
friendship is just as good. We started lessons right away after a great deal
of commotion. Doris is indeed our new teacher. She was quick to
demonstrate the tough new methods she is going to use on us. 'Heil
Hitler!' she said when she came in. 'Heil Hitler!' we replied in unison,
then we went to sit down again, but she shouted: 'Gentlemen, we'll begin
our lesson with a word from the Führer!' So we had to get up from our
benches again and stand up straight while she read us a paragraph from
Mein Kampf. She then wrote our names in the register, including our
Hitler Youth rankings. She was furious to note that not one of us has any
decorations against his name.

We all gossiped about her during our lunch break. We were very
depressed. Muck and Kaspar had found out from their older sister what
Doris had been like at the girls' school. Of course no one had liked her
there either and they were delighted when she left. She once measured
the girls' heads to find out who had the most Nordic skull, but never
announced the results because it turned out the Jewish Meyer twins had
the most Germanic features. We had seen a cat running across the
school yard and it gave us the idea for a devilish plot: we locked a cat in
Doris's desk, so that it would fly out in her face when she opened it to
look for her copy of *Mein Kampf.* The lesson began. Yet again it was

'Heil Hitler!' this, and 'Heil Hitler!' that. And yet again she went to bring out her 'bible'.

'*Miaow! Miaow! Miaow!*' came from the desk. Slowly, a head emerged from the hole where the inkpot goes. Doris stopped mid-sentence and shrieked out in horror. We all burst out laughing and tried to hide under our desks while Doris moaned, 'Poor creature! Help the poor creature!' We were all scratched and bitten by the time the headmaster came in from a neighbouring classroom, alarmed by the noise. 'You will all be punished!' he shouted.

When he left, Doris gave us detention: we had to write out the life of Frederick the Great ten times! I've only done three and it's torture!

1 September 1943

The war started four years ago today. I can still remember the day perfectly, though I was only eleven. I was woken up early by an air-raid siren and saw wave upon wave of our air force flying east in strict formation towards Poland. None of us had any idea what war would be like. Now we can barely remember life without it! So many people we know, friends and family and neighbours, have fallen at the front, there's hardly a family left who hasn't lost a soldier. At home we have been largely protected from the war so far. People in West Germany, in the Ruhr, Hamburg and Berlin have already been through terrible things. We hear about it from the women and children who've been evacuated. There, boys of my age are already in the emergency services or the anti-aircraft units, or trained as dispatch riders or for the fire brigade, trying to deal with the effects of fire-bombing.

We've already done some anti-aircraft defence drills at school. There, and at home too, sandbags, buckets and brooms stand ready in every room. There are bomb shelters in every house but we haven't had to use them for real yet. Pomerania is too far away for the English planes. I hope it stays that way.

CHAPTER EIGHT

Inside Germany

September 1943

'*The Land of Sculpture*'

Vasily Baranov, clarinet pupil at Orlov
Music School in 1941.

Lieselotte G, c. 1942.

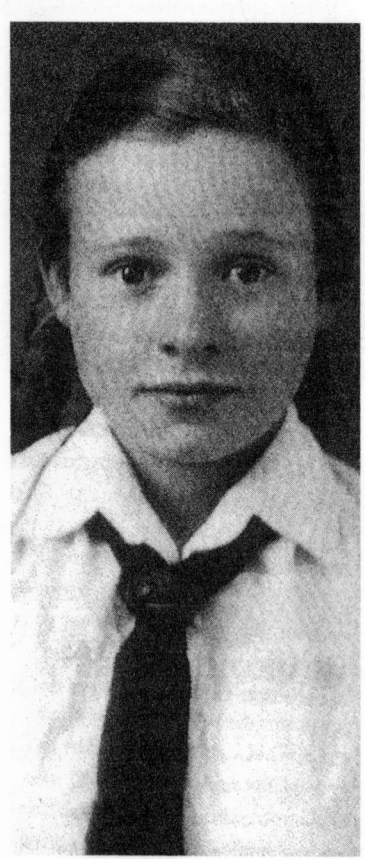

*O*n 24 January 1943, Roosevelt and Churchill emerged to face the world press gathered outside the Anfa Hotel on the outskirts of Casablanca in Morocco. Declaring the Allied war aim as the 'unconditional surrender of Germany and Japan', they rejected any notions of a separate peace with either side. In private the two leaders signed a secret directive to launch a joint strategic bombing campaign, aimed not only at destroying the German military, industrial and economic capability, but also at 'undermining the morale of the German people to a point where their capacity for armed resistance is fatally weakened'.

After a series of highly destructive raids on Germany's Ruhr valley, Allied Bomber Command targeted Hamburg, Germany's main seaport and second largest city. By the end of July 1943, over half of Hamburg lay in ruins; 45,000 people had been killed and close to a million made homeless. On the night of 23 August 1943, 700 bombers headed for Berlin to launch a new and relentless series of raids on the German capital.

That autumn, 200,000 German teenage boys, some as young as fifteen, were sent to man anti-aircraft guns in defence of German cities. Previously exempt male workers were dispatched to replenish troops on the Eastern Front, but women were not expected to replace them in Germany's factories. To preserve morale on the home front, mothers and widows were provided with substantial allowances and told to look after the future generations of the 'Aryan master race'. Instead, forced labourers from occupied Europe were brought in to alleviate severe labour shortages. By the autumn of 1943 one in three workers in German factories was foreign. While in

Western Europe, German recruitment methods were more restrained, in the East, men, women and children as young as ten were often seized off the streets; SS detachments burned down entire villages if volunteers failed to come forward.

Among the nearly 2 million forced labourers conscripted from German-occupied Soviet territories by the summer of 1943 was eighteen-year-old music student, Vasily Baranov, from Merinovka village in southern Russia, who arrived in the east of Germany in September after a gruelling ten-day journey in an overcrowded cattle car.

The same month, German teenager Klaus Granzow turned sixteen, reaching the newly lowered age of conscription. Having voluntarily signed up for the army that summer, Klaus was assured he would not be called up until January 1944, and so resolved to enjoy his last school term to the full.

As a schoolgirl, fifteen-year-old Berliner 'Lieselotte G.' (the 'G' for anonymity) was not required for military service. A patriotic and active member of the BDM – Bund Deutscher Mädel – the girls' branch of the Hitler Youth, that autumn Lieselotte went back to school in Friedrichshagen, an outer eastern suburb of the capital.

While Lieselotte confided her most intimate thoughts to a diary she had begun in 1942, and Klaus carried on writing in the flowery notebook he had started that spring, diary-writing was strictly forbidden for young Russian forced labourer, Vasily Baranov. Defying the ban, Vasily recorded his experiences on anything he could write on – German newspapers, railway timetables – beginning the day after he arrived in Germany.

1–2 September 1943

In the morning, at about nine, all sides of our cattle car were opened up and I was woken by the bright sunshine. The weather outside was just beautiful. News soon spread that we had reached our destination, a town called Dresden. After a bit of to-ing and fro-ing, we all lined up with our gear and three guards led us along the streets. Dresden is a big city, with huge, ancient houses, like nothing I'd ever seen before. They were built with square blocks of a special kind of stone, so their walls shine in the sun like a chessboard. There wasn't a single house without a sculpture or a relief, and it was then I remembered a book I once read about ancient Germany. It said that Germany was the land of sculpture. There was greenery all around us too: lime trees, chestnuts, even fruit trees. We walked along an interminably long road, paved with asphalt the whole way. Germans of all ages pointed at us in the street, and from windows, muttering about us, singling out those of us who looked particularly strange to them. And so we had to walk on under the disapproving gaze of those mugs, revolting to us though they were. There were, perhaps, two hundred of us, four men to a row, our faces looking down in shame. From time to time one of us dared lift his heavy head to look up, as if to send our hatred of these pathetic creatures all the way up to the seventh floor, where the windows were stuffed full of them. They laughed and pointed at a straggler who walked slowly, dragging his injured leg along the pavement, dressed in rags that were actually his Russian clothes once, now in tatters. Frightening, stormy feelings brew inside me. I have never felt anything like this before.

An hour after lunch, we were lined up and divided into three groups. Skilled workers were taken out, though there were very few of them. My group was told we were going on to Leipzig. We got there late at night, by electric train. The station had a dome not unlike the one on our village church in Merinovka. The place was jam-packed, endless crowds of people (Germans) moving up and down. You could really gorge your-self on new sights and sounds there and then, no need to visit a circus, or a museum! Sculptures, paintings, drawings, chandeliers, the Germans themselves, their clothes, etc., etc. At the same time, I felt this revulsion towards them, such hatred that I couldn't bear to examine their ugly faces too closely. Because I already understood what they were like inside. Suddenly a very big tractor on huge rubber tracks arrived, tugging a large trailer behind it. All our possessions and half of the men were loaded onto it and taken to a two-storey house. Each of us was allocated a bed, a mattress and a blanket, I just wanted to go to sleep, really badly.

Before bed, we got checked to make sure everyone had a wash. Stripped to our underwear we looked dirty and miserable, like a herd of sheep that just escaped from the wolf's jaws. Two of us got a slap on the face and I went to sleep gritting my teeth in pain.

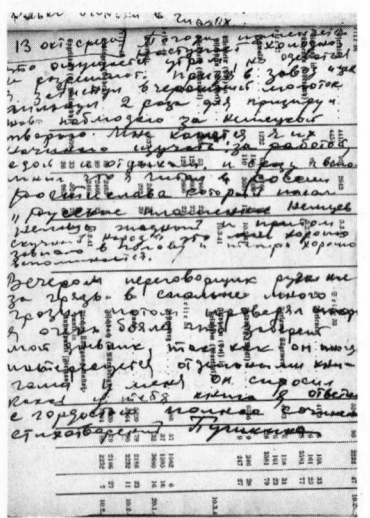

After dinner we were taken to a bathhouse for delousing.

3–5 September 1943

The weather brightened up before dusk, but I felt uneasy, as if my soul was full of buzzing flies.

I remembered what clever Nina told me back home: 'You'll

Page from Vasily's diary.

work like a docile bull.' They treat us like slaves here. We're forced to work without breaks, even though what we do is pretty useless, we've only just learnt how to use a filing tool. They're always laughing at us, they think we're dirty and uncultured. The master beat up one guy because he blew his nose onto the floor, and another one because his neck and hands were dirty. His laughing and sneering are killing me. I'm starting to hate myself and wonder if I really am a swine like they say I am. I just wish I were back at my dear old home, by the two pussy willows and the beautiful fluffy poplar tree. I'll never see my house again, even a crow won't carry my bones back there.

8–10 September 1943

Same old thing again. The masters who beat up my friend Strelsky because he couldn't work are now beating up anyone who shows any reluctance. Which is all of us. We walk around grim-faced, we frown and we swear at them, we use every Russian swear word we know. As I stand at my work table with my filing tool for hours on end, I think about all sorts of things. How long can I survive in this captivity? My legs are weak from the endless standing up. They don't let us sit down and you get hit in the face if you try ...

I have made my mind up, I've got to run away. Commissar and I have been plotting together, because he's a brave guy and he speaks German. We are leaving on Sunday. We'll jump on a train heading for Poland and keep going as long as our courage lasts.

17–19 September 1943

We've been really hungry. Things get stolen every day, but no one can find the thieves. We've been issued with fifteen cigarettes and 60 Pfennigs to last us a week. Sunday goes by fast. It brings two different feelings with it. Great to have a day off, as I might get to talk to one of my friends, or even better, one of the girls. The other feeling is anguish, such pain in my soul, especially when I talk to someone from back home, even someone who used to live 300–500km away from my village. I feel as if I'm going to die of heartache. It's best talking to a girl about it, because more women have died or killed themselves from heartache than men. No matter who you talk to, though, if they've been here for a year or two they say you get used to it, and that dying is the easy option, life is precious …

Today was our day off, so we went to town. I sold ten cigarettes for 1 Deutschmark and a few baked potatoes, found Commissar and we set off to a goods train station. I wore two pairs of trousers, two shirts and a pair of boots. A destination card on a carriage said one train was heading for Lvov, so we hid amongst boxes and waited. We were glad when we began to move at last, but then by looking at the setting sun we suddenly realized we were travelling West, not East. Desperate, we jumped off at a small station, but a railway worker spotted us. Soon there were Germans all over us. One of them took us to a railway hut and ordered an elderly guard to keep an eye. But then the poor old guy went to answer the phone and we flew off like a pair of sparrows.

A Ukrainian guy with a cart and horse told us Leipzig was 17 kilometres away. We decided we had to get back, come what may. We got in through the window at about 2 a.m. Our pals guessed where we'd been and told us everyone who'd been out late got beaten up with a rubber hose. I talked to them about life back home, my music college, and told them I never realized how happy I was. Back then I had all the time in the world to sleep or to go for a walk, and, most importantly, I could always fill my belly. My friend Strelsky said I was a good lad, bright for my age and with a good understanding of life. But as for trying to escape, I should grit my teeth and bear it.

24 September 1943

Everyone wants to run away. My heart is breaking into little pieces. We found some newspapers, which said our area back home has been retaken by the Russians, the Germans are on the run, all the way back from Stalingrad. I was so happy. If only we could get home, we'd grind those barbarians with our teeth. We fantasized about this a while. I've got to get out of here, or I'll die in this place.

In Pomerania, Klaus Granzow's school term was interrupted that autumn by the annual potato- and swede-picking duties. But this year the harvesting was helped by the arrival of forced labourers from France, Poland and Russia. By mid-October Klaus was back at school.

22 October 1943

No lessons this afternoon. We were sent to collect scrap paper. We filled an entire barrel with old drawings and photos of naked women from magazines! When we got back, some older boys stole quite a lot of our stuff, so we lost points! Never mind, I got a prize for the most scrap last year, there was even an article in the *East Pomeranian* about my record.

Anyway, there was little time to fret about it, because the headmaster came in to tell us we'll be leaving to join the Naval Auxiliary Helpers unit on Monday, much earlier than planned. What a happy roar went up! I must have pulled a stupid face, because [our teacher] Doris said I didn't look at all happy, but I was, except maybe for a brief moment wondering what it's going to be like, not to be at school any more. But the thought of going off with all my friends soon cheered me up.

Someone said that now Doris would have to make do with getting the little girls to march up and down, and even the old girl herself smiled and laughed a bit. And I thought, at least I won't have to put up with you any more, you stupid Brown Hen!

And then we left school!

In the afternoon we went to the cinema for the last time. *The Wife* was playing, with Jenny Jugo. We had no trouble getting in, luckily. A couple of my friends showed me a new trick to get into the adult films. Sticking your collar up and pulling your hat down no longer works, so now we wait till the film starts and rush in, preferably behind an adult, saying loudly in a deep booming voice: 'Oh, I must catch the latest bulletin from the front!' And then we're in! It's crazy though – we're not allowed to watch adult films, but we're old enough to be soldiers, even if we're just 15 or 16.

25 October 1943

On Sunday the headmaster gave us a big send-off. He handed out our call-up orders and told us we're leaving first thing on Monday.

As I cycled home over the Wedding Bridge, I finally began to let go of school. How often I've cycled this way over the past few years! I thought. Riding above Mühlenberg was my favourite part of the journey, because I could look right down on my little village, Mützenow, far below.

As I said my farewells, I cycled along as if in a dream. I tried to take it all in and bury it in my memory, so I wouldn't forget it. But my heart was heavy with sadness, and I couldn't say goodbye.

My parents were shocked when I told them. I am the first boy of my age from our village to be called up. My mother said: 'I hoped the war would be over by the time you were big and grown up!' And Dad said: 'He might be big, but he's not grown up! What the hell can be going on, if they're calling up kids like him?'

My sister and I took ourselves off to the village, I wanted to go one last time. We met some of our friends and a few other girls. They were all tickled to see me in a sailor's uniform. Agata was there, too. For some reason, everyone thinks she's my girlfriend, but it's not true. Not as far as she and I are concerned, anyway. The village gossips have paired us off, which has made us allergic to each other, nothing could ever happen between us now. It's that stupid. I got cross about it all, and went off to bed early.

We had a big farewell meal at lunchtime. My father killed two chickens for the occasion! We even had lemon cream for desert, my favourite. (We only ever get it at weddings and other special occasions.)

All in all, leaving wasn't too bad, partly because we've been promised a few days' leave every five weeks. So it really isn't that different from going away to school. My mother took it hard, though, because so many of our relatives have been killed, or gone missing.

As I set out this morning, some kids saw me off to the edge of our village. I pressed down on my pedals – and off I went!

On the day Klaus and his classmates were sent off to be trained to use anti-aircraft guns on Germany's Baltic coast, fifteen-year-old Berliner Lieselotte G. could think of little but her German teacher 'Frau L.'. While Lieselotte's Social Democrat parents openly criticized the Nazi regime, Lieselotte drew ideological and spiritual support from her school teacher, the devout wife of a Nazi officer. That autumn, Frau L. became not only Lieselotte's role model as an 'Ideal German Woman', but the focus of her growing infatuation.

25 October 1943

I am waiting on the most important decision of my life. I wrote Frau L. a letter, telling her everything, how I feel for her. I dared myself to do it! My friends say she will either be really understanding, or she'll want to bring me down to earth with a bump for writing such outrageous things. They say they would never have taken such a risk. If she's unsympathetic, it will be over, I'll never see her again. But what's the point in seeing her, if she doesn't know how I feel? I want Frau L. like this, or not at all. I really believe she will understand me, that she'll write a lovely reply. I'm sure she'll blush when she reads my letter. She'll probably read it out to her husband. What's she going to say?

1 November 1943

I have my answer! I rifled through the post as soon as I got home from school. I recognized her handwriting on one of the letters. I picked it up with trembling hands. From L., it said. I was so nervous! My knees were shaking, my stomach was churning, I felt really sick. I staggered to the sofa, flung myself down and lay there for a long time, holding the envelope, and talking to myself.

Then I sat up, begged God not to disappoint me and opened it, heart thumping. With quivering hands I unfolded it and read: 'Dear little Lilo …' She wrote about all sorts of unimportant things first, about the parcels I'd sent her. I buried myself in the cushions thinking she was not going to respond to what I told her in my letter. But then there they were, her words of understanding, as she gently urged me not to flatter her so, she was only human, a woman like any other. That I should keep both of my feet on the ground. That I shouldn't forget my mother's love for me.

When I finished reading, I felt crushed. I lay my head on the cushions and wept. Why? It was a nice letter, but I was bitterly disappointed. I was shivering and I felt sick. Eventually, I calmed down. I walked to the lake and read the letter over and over. Only then did I thank God, and feel a warm glow, as I began to see how loving the letter was. She was so right about everything, apart from saying she was a human being like any other – she is so much more. She took my letter to be a teenage passion. She said she was once a teenager like me. She wanted me not to get overexcited, to keep both feet on the ground, not to confuse myself. There is so much love and understanding in her words. I am worried about this talk she wants to have with me, to help me find the right path. I'm supposed to treat her as a human being, but I can't. I am so ashamed now of how gushing my letter was. If only she were blessed with children. She has boundless love for children. She is such a good person. I will see if I can think of her as more normal, find something more of the human being in her. I am already standing with both feet on the ground, but sometimes it's hard not to fall over. Her letter makes me feel stronger. I will keep it safe in my heart. Thank you, dear Frau L.

8 November 1943

I am listening to Hitler's speech. He just said: I too am religious, deeply religious. If only he were! Then he might be able to pray, and I would not be so afraid for Germany. If Hitler had been praying all throughout the war, maybe then I could look forward to a future that would bring the German nation nearer to God because of this war and his leadership. Hitler made me believe in victory once again, he talked about invading England and taking revenge for the bombing.

I'm torn. My faith forbids me from supporting the war, any war, but my love for my country cannot bear the thought of surrender. Thousands have died, thousands have been living in mud and dirt for years, thousands more are in pain in the hospitals, thousands of women, mothers and sisters are at home worrying about the men at the front, they're crying for their fallen sons and brothers. Must all that be in vain? Is it not our sacred duty to carry on fighting? But if Germany were wiped out, wouldn't we all carry on being brave? Sacrifices have to be made to achieve a victory. But if victory is impossible, would it not be better to ... before thousands more die, before more pain is inflicted on Germany ... but no, that must never happen, then all those who have died would rise up to shame me. And if we are destroyed, at least it won't be 1918 all over again. Adolf Hitler, I believe in you, and in a German victory.

Three weeks into his training with the naval auxiliaries on the Baltic coast, Klaus Granzow was practising to intercept Allied bombers en route to Berlin.

15 November 1943

We're square-bashing again. Infantry duty is enough to make you sick. Our instructor is young, but he's also ugly and bad-tempered. He drags us all out on a so-called gentle tour of the sand dunes and makes us go up and down with our full kit on.

Weapons training is far more interesting and enjoyable. We knew all the basics already. I am assigned to the second gun. There are air raids almost every night, Berlin is being bombed non-stop.

The bunker for the light anti-aircraft unit is about 50 metres away from our guns, and it's a daily trek to the canteen. The food isn't nearly as good as it was in the last place. We found a mouse in our soup not long ago: it caused quite a stir, and put us right off our food. Some people wanted to complain, but what's the point?

We haven't had any leave, as we haven't been sworn in yet. We were allowed to visit a nearby town, in strict military formation. We felt like idiots, marching through the streets two abreast. Only the boys from Schneidemühl enjoyed it because they got their first glimpse of the sea. For the rest of us it was no fun at all.

18 November 1943

We have fired the guns for the first time! It was fantastic. We only shot two rounds, but it was a great experience, hearing them for the first time. Berlin was under attack again, not for the last time I'm sure, so hopefully we'll be shooting a lot more often soon.

We've had three films in the canteen; one mass said; one talk on the fighting morale of the Japanese and another one on England and India.

Though Klaus and his group failed to hit any aircraft, 9 of the 440 British
bombers heading for Berlin that night were shot down. After another Allied
raid on Berlin four days later, Lieselotte described the destruction caused
to her city.

23 November 1943

There was a terrible bombing raid last night, the worst one on Berlin so
far. Mummy is distraught, everything is at a standstill. The underground
is shut; the trams are not running. We tried to phone people, but we
could barely get a connection. All our relatives are still alive, but half of
Berlin city centre is in ruins. I'm so worried about Frau L. I don't know
if she is still here, but I am so frightened for her.

I am so weak. I just want to cry, but I should be thankful that we are
all alive. Daddy talks about revolution all the time, Mummy cries.
Everyone has a terrible story to tell. I am so worried about my dear, dear
Frau L.

24 November 1943

Another air raid. The centre of town is just a pile of rubble.
Friedrichstrasse, Linden, Leipzigerstrasse, Alex, all in ruins. Aunt K. was
bombed out. My school has burned down, so I won't be going there any
more. The underground is out of action. Daddy says Hitler can't keep
the war going much longer. But I don't think he will give up. Daddy
thinks there will be peace by Christmas, but I don't want peace, or
surrender. Oh, it's all so ridiculous! There's no news of her, why can we
not get news of each other in these terrible times? If I heard her house
had been bombed, I'd run to Frohnau to dig her out.

Though Lieselotte's own suburban home remained undamaged, the Allied raids carried out on central Berlin in the four days to 26 November 1943 killed nearly 5,000 people and left half a million inhabitants homeless.

By the end of November, Vasily Baranov had given up his plans to escape. Stricter measures made escape even harder and the wooden shoes issued to forced labourers made walking difficult. With their loud clanking noise at every step they were quickly nicknamed the 'shackles'. As the Allied bombers extended their attacks further east, Vasily tried to adapt and survive, and wait to be liberated.

28 November 1943

Stealing has become my main preoccupation. I have to steal, no matter what, because death is snapping at my heels. Volodya's mate died yesterday. Ten or so of us here live well, but they are just ten out of the 3,000 here. They go out robbing at night like real bandits. It's dangerous, yes, but very profitable too.

Today I got a haircut and stole a turnip. Most of the lads escape into town through the Belgian barracks. I haven't tried it yet because I'm sure that if I steal anything in town I'll get caught. People have become good thieves, because they're angry and it makes them reckless.

4 December 1943

An alarm woke me at 4 a.m. There was shooting, the electricity was down, and fires were crackling and sparkling up everywhere like huge lightning bolts. I tried to find my 'shackles' under the bed, but then there was this terrible cracking noise and the ceiling fell in. I thought my heart was going to burst from the fear. I ran outside without my shackles and saw the whole town was on fire. The bombers droned overhead and a cold wind was blowing, but I was afraid to run out of my barrack without the shackles! Two emotions were fighting inside me – one was fear, today's my baptism of fire, I said to myself, and it would be terrible to die like this from a bomb, even if it's a bomb dropped by friends. My second emotion was that of revenge, a powerful, persistent feeling. I wanted these American planes to flatten the factory where we Russians have been tortured so. And then, for the sake of all our people, I wanted to overcome the fear, because patriotism is a finer feeling. We went back to work at 8 a.m. Our supervisors were late and some didn't turn up at all. Judging by their faces, the Germans must have had some depressing conversations. The French [workers] turned up to work in their blankets, forgetting about their hairdos and their manners. Some escaped in just their underwear when two huge French camps were destroyed by fire.

While Vasily's camp remained unaffected, that night the Allied bombers destroyed most of Leipzig city centre, the main target of their offensive. In Berlin, Lieselotte now spent nearly every night in an air-raid shelter.

8 December 1943

People are so mean and small-minded. They want to take absolutely everything away from me, all my ideals, everything that makes life beautiful. But I won't let them succeed! It's so sad there won't be any Christmas trees this year, but it's even sadder to hear people saying: 'There's no point in having a Christmas tree at a time like this.' I took an electric oven and a woolly blanket to Aunt Else's today because her building was damaged. I always thought she was quite religious, but she said: 'I don't think we should be celebrating Christmas. If there was a God in heaven, he wouldn't allow all this to happen.' How flimsy people's beliefs are. I think we should be celebrating Christmas now more than ever. Of course there is an incredible amount of pain and suffering in the world. But how does it help the homeless and the cripples if we let our own heads drop? Why shouldn't we light a candle, sing a Christmas song? This Christmas will be a prayer for everyone in need! I am going to celebrate it even if others think I am wrong to do so, if they say it's heartless to be cheerful while others are in distress. I'd celebrate even if I was bombed out and living rough, even if all my loved ones were dead and I was a cripple myself.

Like Lieselotte, Klaus was also looking forward to Christmas, and his first leave home. Although he was manning an anti-aircraft gun, Klaus still hadn't been officially sworn in as a soldier.

17 December 1943

The sirens went off this afternoon. We thought it might be a test, but then we got the order to fire. We were only meant to shoot three rounds, but in the heat of the moment we shot four. We got a lot of stick for it later from our commander. As luck would have it, our fourth gun only let off one round, because someone's glove was stuck in the breech-block.

We didn't hit anything, but we could have. We could have fired more too, but it all happened so quickly, and the air-raid warning was so sudden. We had a fire drill straight after, but I couldn't hear a word, my ears were still ringing. I should have blocked them with cotton wool like we're supposed to.

In the other bunker, Grote is back from his Berlin leave. He was there during the last air raid, he said whole areas have been reduced to rubble, but the Berliners haven't lost their sense of humour.

21 December 1943

We were marched off to a review inspection yesterday. I am 185 cm tall, I weigh 58 kilos. Incredibly, my eyesight has improved.

The main check-up was carried out by Dr Liebe. He told me I couldn't go with the others, because my body isn't fully developed yet. He said I wasn't ill, exactly, but he still had to hold me back for three months. The other doctors couldn't find a clause for my case, except under the section for those 'still growing' and 'late developers'.

I don't really care. I'll have another check-up in six months and join the army a bit later. I might even manage to pass my end-of-school exams, which would be great.

I am getting ready for my Christmas leave. We were given some of our rations to take home, even a bottle of red wine. I don't need the food, as we still have plenty at home, lucky us.

I had a letter from Mummy today. She was upset by my description of our first shooting episode. Why did I have to go into such detail about our baptism of fire? It was stupid to send a letter like that back home, I realize that now. And it's against the rules to write to civilians about anything military or technical.

As Klaus headed home, Lieselotte also prepared to celebrate Christmas. Her determination was reinforced by Minister of Propaganda Joseph Goebbels, who called upon the nation to celebrate the traditional German Christmas that year as one of 'austerity and ideological determination'.

24 December 1943

Christmas Eve! There was an air-raid warning at 3.45. We thought it wouldn't be too bad because it came very late, but it was awful. We were all in the cellar when there was a terrible crash and the lights went out. We jumped up, grabbed our bags and went to rush outside, worried the walls were about to collapse. The ceiling shook, the windows rattled, we saw red clouds of ash outside. The men wouldn't let anyone leave, because bombs were still falling. We sat in the dark for half an hour, listening to the awful banging and crashing, cowering together, waiting for the end to come. I can still feel it, the fear of death, but in spite of everything I didn't lose my faith in God, and Her. She was always in my heart. I would have died happy with God and Her in my heart.

Then came the all-clear. We left the cellar, full of thanks that we were alive. The flat was full of dust. We walked over splinters of glass. Most of the windows were smashed, the blackout curtains were in tatters, the floor was covered in broken glass, china and mortar, our beds were black, the cooking pots were smashed, gherkins and pumpkins spilled all over the place. The baubles on the Advent wreath were smashed, the clocks still said five past four. I thought I was in a dream. We started clearing up. We rolled up all the carpets, took down the curtains, swept up the glass and threw all the rubble into the street (like everyone else had). Though it was still dark and the blackout was in place, all the windows in our neighbourhood were lit up (we still had gas, light and water) –

everyone's blackout curtains had been shredded when their windows were smashed. So it looked like peacetime! And it was Christmas Eve!! I was so happy.

It was dawn soon after. Most of the wreckage was already cleared and our windows covered up with blankets and bits of cardboard, but we didn't have enough, so the living room was cold. I spent hours sewing the blackout curtains back together. When everything was more or less in order, we decided to celebrate Christmas, even though it was freezing. I put up the tree – and as I was decorating it, my brother Bertel came home on leave!

Then Daddy came home, and we gave each other presents. The Christmas tree was done, the manger was out – everything was just as it's always meant to be! So beautiful! Our lovely old German Christmas. The best thing was that Bertel was there. I was only sad we couldn't go to church. Then we ate the duck we'd been cooking the whole time, with candles on the table, and there were candles on the Christmas tree too (four of them homemade). I kept thinking of Her, she must have been happy too, because her husband would be home for Christmas.

The air raids on Berlin on Christmas Eve killed 178.

On the outskirts of Leipzig, Vasily Baranov hoped the festive spirit might allow the forced labourers some respite.

24 December 1943

There's no night shift, so I decided to boil the swede I've been hiding for ages, and read a magazine. My friends went off to look for vegetable peelings in the kitchen waste after lunch. They were arguing whose turn it was to use the stove first, but I am used to that kind of thing now and no longer pay any attention. They say it's Christmas tomorrow and that Germans celebrate it heartily and they might give us something as a present.

In the evening a couple of lads brought in cabbages. I bought one for 70 Pfennigs but I couldn't boil it because there was no wood left, so I ate it raw.

Someone was playing an accordion next door, and some cripple was dancing along to the music. The whole atmosphere was depressing and revolting. As soon as I got back to my room, I started writing a song called 'A Harmonica is Playing Next Door'.

25 December 1943

I got up late and looked over the song I wrote last night. I am loath to spend much energy writing about anything now. There's not much to write about anyway, and apathy is winning. We lit up a stove this morning and cooked vegetable peel in a pot. At lunchtime, we were given our Christmas present: 100 grams of cake. I wish they'd given us 200 grams of bread instead, or half a kilo of potatoes.

27 December 1943

Terrible weather, endless rain. It's cold and damp in the barracks. When I got to the factory this morning my grumpy supervisor said nothing to my 'Gut Morgen'. He said I had to work faster because I spent my night shift sleeping in the lavatory. He kept rushing me, and wouldn't let me go to the toilet. He told me I could have five minutes before lunch and five after. I sold a pack of tobacco today and bought a large swede with the money. I managed to cook some and ate the rest raw. I was using a cauldron the Germans use to warm up their pots of homemade soup, but my swede stank so much they swore at me and chucked my pot away.

But as I was walking home from work, a young German woman nodded to me, and I had pudding for the first time in my life.

29 December 1943

My master's brutality is not easing off. He is constantly tormenting and mocking me, and muttering under his breath. I don't even try to learn their idiotic language, I don't want to understand it, I'd only get more upset by the taunting. Dog, swine, these are the kind of words that never go out of fashion here. What has happened to me! I am no longer Bara-

nov, Vasily Maksimovich. I am now a 'Russian swine' number 25795. There's 'OST' on my chest, my work number on my cap, and my own number in my pocket. I'm covered in numbers, all over.

Placed on close watch as a trouble-maker, Vasily was required to wear a larger 'OST' sign – short for Ostarbeiter, *'worker from the East' – on his chest, rather than on the left*

Vasily Baranov, Ostarbeiter #25795, Germany, 1943.

arm as was usual. Writing less and less in the days that followed, Vasily gave up altogether in January.

In Berlin, as Lieselotte G. emerged from her shelter after weeks of disrupted sleep, she too was feeling a different person.

29 December 1943

We've just left the cellar after another terrible air raid. We have one up on previous generations, because we truly know what it is to be afraid of death. The fear strips you bare, all the veneer rubs off, even the things I thought most dear to me have vanished – apart from God. Even my love for Frau L. (I would never have believed it.) Fear has driven it away. The only thing that remains, my only comfort, is my eternal love of God.

It was a great comfort to repeat my confirmation prayer over and over in my head. When I came out of the cellar, I was so grateful just to be able to live for another day. Mummy says that this is the triumph of life over death, one minute you're in the cellar, waiting for death, then an hour later you are safe and comfortable again back in the flat. Oh Lord, please bring this to an end, in accordance with your will.

31 December 1943

Dear Frau L.! I swear to you that despite our distress, death and sorrow I will keep the flame of my life lofty and pure. I will be cheerful and brave, as you told me I should be. Whatever happens, I will become a good German woman. Dear God, please make me strong.

2 January 1944

I spoke to Daddy today about the war. I can see it clearly now: we cannot win. It would be stupid to want to deceive myself. The Soviets are at the Polish border. In Italy, the enemy is approaching Rome, the Anglo-American planes have landed in France. German towns are being destroyed, turned into ashes night after night. Everyone says we can no longer win, and I think that way too. Daddy thinks defeat won't be that bad, that the Western powers would make us a Republic under American control. Daddy and Mummy want peace at any price, but lots of people are afraid of Bolshevism, and the Soviets are coming nearer and nearer. And chaos is coming with them. I don't think the Western Powers would let European culture be destroyed, but what will become of Germany, my Holy, Prussian Germany? We will be an American colony, our economy propped up with American gold.

But that would be the end of everything that makes my heart glow with pride: Prussian traditions, Frederick the Great, our German, Prussian officers, all that will be over. Every national honour would be taken away from our Holy German Reich. What do I care about a healthy economy? We will become a satellite state of America. Wouldn't it be better to die?

3 January 1944

There was another terrible bombing raid last night; they come every day now. As the bombs start falling, there is an indescribable roar and death grips your heart with its cold hand. All you can think is: if only it would stop! But it doesn't, and you think your nerves will snap, you want to scream but you can't, you have to keep your dignity, you mustn't weaken, that's what Frau L. begged me to do, and her strength and her example keep me going in the face of death. Where her love is too weak, her example is still there before me.

As I am writing this, I feel as if I'm dreaming, and all this is unreal; but it is all too terribly real. The world could be so beautiful and peaceful! It's impossible to think about all this without going mad. Poor Germany, poor mankind!

I should feel so good inside, lit up by Her look, my heart should be so happy because She lives inside it, but I can't bring myself to be cheerful and happy. I am shaking with fright, the ghost of death is haunting and threatening me.

Goebbels goes on and on about our strength, our strong hearts. If he sat for an hour in an air-raid shelter he'd see how weak the human heart is. Though I am a believer, my heart is too weak, my fear of death is so unimaginably great that nothing is left of that strength, or the idea of sacrifice in the name of God's Will, only a quivering human heart. Father K., aren't you afraid? Martin Luther, don't you know fear? I'm constantly asking God to keep my heart strong. Dear God, hear my cry!

17 January 1944

I don't know what to do. Everyone says I should save my life, leave Berlin. That if I stayed in the city I might be made to work as there is no school. It is tempting to run away from death, and it would be good to go to school once again. But could I really leave my dear mother in danger and all alone, sitting in the cellar all by herself? Am I not bound by a child's duty to my mother? I do also have a duty to save my young life for the Fatherland, but which one is stronger?

CHAPTER NINE

Waiting for Liberation

April–August 1944

*'Please God don't shatter
our hopes and dreams'*

Wanda Przybylska in 1943.

Micheline Singer in 1944.

Signature du Titulaire :

LIVRET UNIVERSITAIRE
INDIVIDUEL

N° du Dossier : _____

Nom et prénoms de l'Étudiant. { M Icheline George Singer

Date et lieu de naissance. {
Date 17 Avril 1926
Lieu Paris
Pays France
Département ou province Seine

Adresses de l'Étudiant. { 23 Rue du Cirque Paris 8e

(Signature de l'Étudiant.)

Sceau de la Faculté ou École

(Signature du Secrétaire de la Faculté ou École, ou de son Délégué, attestant que les pièces authentiques d'état civil et les diplômes ou certificats ont été présentés.

(Signature ou griffe du Doyen ou du Directeur.)

(Légalisation des signatures.

*I*n November 1943, Stalin, Churchill and Roosevelt met together for the first time, in Tehran, to discuss the final phase of the fighting. Churchill outlined to Stalin the plan to launch a cross-Channel invasion of France in the spring or summer of 1944, in order to open up the long-promised Second Front in northern Europe. Stalin in turn agreed to increase simultaneously the fighting in the east to prevent the Germans from redeploying more troops to France. Over the course of their four days of talks, the Big Three also discussed the division of influence in Europe once the war was won. Stalin met separately with each of his allies to discuss his plan to move Poland's border westwards. Both gave their tacit consent, though the future of Poland would be a source of contention between them. The Red Army would be responsible for liberating eastern and central Europe, while the Anglo-American forces would concentrate on the north-west.

In the spring of 1944, after four years of occupation, France and Poland were about to become war zones again. The Red Army was already within striking distance of the pre-war Polish border, as Anglo-American troops prepared for the biggest amphibious landing of the war. The Germans, aware a major attack was imminent in the west but unsure from where it was coming, doubled the number of troops stationed in France. With their regime under threat in the west and east, they increased their efforts to root out resistance and wipe out Europe's Jews. Harsh reprisals were meted out to all resistance and Jews taken from all over occupied Europe continued to die at the combined killing centre and concentration camp of Auschwitz-Birkenau in Poland.

Amongst the Polish Jews hoping to survive the war was a boy in the Łódź ghetto whose name and details are unknown. By 1944, Łódź was the only ghetto still standing in occupied Poland, the rest long since liquidated, their inhabitants sent to their deaths or held in concentration camps. Both the anonymous boy's parents had died and he and his twelve-year-old sister were among the less than 70,000 Jews surviving from an original Łódź ghetto population of over 160,000. In the summer of 1944 the boy began to keep a diary, as an outlet for his hopes that the war and his suffering might soon be over.

That summer in Warsaw, fourteen-year-old Polish schoolgirl Wanda Przybylska also hoped that the German occupation would soon come to an end. Ever since her father had escaped from prison, where he had been held for being an intellectual and an enemy of the Reich, the family had kept a low profile, living in a succession of tiny flats in Warsaw, trying to shield young Wanda from the worst effects of the war. Wanda's older sister, Jadwiga, was involved in the Polish underground, but kept the details from her family for their safety.

In Paris, Micheline Singer was already dreaming of liberation. On 1 April, she was back in Verneuil, where, four years ago to the day, on the eve of the German invasion, she had begun writing her diary. Then, she had hoped she would look grown up when the victory parades came. She was now almost eighteen.

1 April 1944

A letter arrived from [our friends] the Le Nédélecs asking me to come and stay [in Verneuil] for Easter. I am taking Darak [the dog] with me as the Germans are requisitioning all large dogs and training them to run in front of tanks by throwing meat ahead of them. The dogs are sent to the Eastern Front, deprived of food then sent towards the Russian tanks with sticks of dynamite attached to their stomachs. The poor things are crushed and then blown up, along with the tanks. I don't actually believe this story, but Darak will be happy to go back to Verneuil and the Le Nédélecs don't have a dog.

8 April 1944

I fetched my roller skates, I'd left them behind last month, but one of the boys had used them and I couldn't get them on. As I was sitting by the side of the road fiddling with them, the Commandant spotted me and some Germans rushed out offering to help. They were very kind and fixed them for me, they even greased them. Their headquarters was even dirtier than last year and the poor things weren't a very attractive bunch. As I was leaving I ran across someone from the tank division who had given me dirty looks before but then when he saw Darak he bent down and started stroking him. He asked if he could come and visit me. I said no, of course, telling him I lived with some farmers who might not like it. His division was in Normandy for some rest after two years on the Russian front. They've really wrecked the roads with their tanks.

9 April 1944

When I was out with Thérèse Le Nédélec this afternoon we bumped into Karl, the SS guy from yesterday. He said he had come especially to see me. This annoyed me but Thérèse insisted he come in and even offered him Calvados. I must admit he did look rather smart in his black tank division uniform with its silver death's head insignia. And he has very beautiful eyes. He asked me how come I speak such good German. I said

I learnt it at school. He then told me he had volunteered for the SS because he was fanatical about Hitler. We talked about fanaticism, dictatorship, the English, the Lycée. He was quite interesting but I was glad to be rid of him in the end, which took ages because Thérèse invited him to stay for dinner.

11 April 1944

What a day, I'll never forget it. I don't know if I will be able to describe what happened yesterday evening. Before bed I was going out to walk Darak, same as usual, but just as I was closing the gate behind me, Karl showed up, not drunk exactly but you could tell he'd been drinking. He greeted us both, then took my hand. I didn't like it at all, but didn't say anything. Then suddenly he tried to take me in his arms, but I held him off, he said he wanted just one kiss, said I didn't understand, he'd spent two years in Russia without talking to a woman. We kept repeating ourselves, he kept saying 'just one kiss' and I kept saying I couldn't because I didn't love him. When I tried to shut the gate on him, he kissed my hands through the slats, which felt weird. He hadn't slept a wink since he met me, he said, and could think of nothing but me. 'You're drunk,' I said. 'Not drunk enough,' he said, he wanted to be but he wasn't. Then suddenly he changed his mind and said he was leaving, because he didn't want me going round saying that Germans behave like pigs. I should have bitten my tongue and let him go, instead I shrugged and said I wouldn't be so stupid as to judge all Germans by the behaviour of just one. I don't know why but this sent him into a rage. He shoved open the gate, took a pistol out of his pocket and said, 'It's very simple. Kiss me or I'll kill the dog.' So I had to let him kiss me. Then I ran inside the house, wiping my mouth with my arm. He just stood there. When I got to my room I was still terrified because it's on the ground floor and the shutters don't close properly. I managed to get my night things on somehow, tried to read *Les Fleurs du Mal*, but couldn't concentrate. I was worried he was going to come back and attack me. I heard the clock strike every hour right through the night. I was just so unbelievably scared.

13 April 1944

I was really depressed yesterday. Instead of going into Verneuil I spent the whole day running around the fields with Darak who was being chased by cows. I kept thinking, I am eighteen years old and I used to be proud of the fact that at eighteen I still hadn't kissed a boy. It also made me miserable to think that I always believed my first kiss would be something really wonderful, that it would carry me away like in a dream, but now all that's ruined.

The weather is beautiful and I am sitting under an apple tree with my paint box but I'd rather just think about things. I have always been honest with my diary. So he's German and he loves dogs. Deep down I knew he wouldn't really have killed Darak, even if I'd still said no. So why did I kiss him? I think I wanted to know what a kiss felt like but I was an idiot to think it would be like it is in books where people are in love. I think that's why I was so disgusted. I don't love him. I forgot to say I didn't sleep all night. An English plane circled over Verneuil for hours, too high up for the anti-aircraft guns to shoot at it.

I should be doing my science revision but the weather's too lovely.

Six weeks later, Micheline was back in Paris to prepare for the second and final part of her end-of-school Baccalaureate exam.

6 June 1944

I got up early with Darak to go and queue for milk. And in the queue what should I hear but the English and the Americans have landed in Normandy. I ran home as fast as I could to tell Mummy the news. All excited, we rushed in to wake Nicole who was still asleep. I have been waiting so long for this, I've dreamt of it so often, it almost seemed like it was nothing special. Please let them hold on this time! Please God, don't shatter our hopes and dreams!

8 June 1944

They have taken the area around Carentan, Bayeux and Caen. They have established a beachhead. Don't let them be driven back into the sea!

I listened to the English radio with [my German friend] Alice. She says that this time Hitler is well and truly beaten and she is happy her home is in Western Germany because the English will get there before the Russians.

12 June 1944

Carentan has been taken. Alice is leaving at the end of the week. She asked if we could hide her until the English arrive; lots of the Germans are doing that, apparently, putting on civilian clothes and hiding. She doesn't want to return to Germany, but what else can she do? She didn't press us; she knows very well we can't feed her.

Marigny, the Champs-Élysées and Avenue Gabriel are full of camou-flaged German lorries, waiting to be dispatched to Normandy. Lucky devils, I'd love to go with them.

I dreamt about the landing again.

The Allied landings in Normandy met with strong opposition. German reinforcements engaged the newly arrived troops in heavy fighting for the next month in an area the Allies had hoped to overrun in a day. Just over 100 miles away in Paris, Micheline waited impatiently.

10 July 1944

Now Caen's been taken. We spent the weekend sunbathing. I'm hoping to have a really nice tan by the time the English arrive. Victory is so near and yet so far. But this time, I really am convinced it is only a matter of days.

RESOLUTIONS FOR THE FUTURE:
I will be hard, so no one can make me suffer.
I will be morally depraved, so men will love me.
I will be strong and cruel.

Micheline's hopes had been raised prematurely; it would be another ten days before the Allies took Caen, enabling them to finally break out from the beachhead and move inland.

By 24 July, the Red Army's summer offensive, timed to coincide with the landing of Allied troops in Normandy, was into its fourth week and Soviet troops were rapidly advancing into German-occupied Poland. That July, Wanda Przybyska had been left for her own safety with relatives in the town of Otwock, just east of Warsaw, while her family remained in the capital. As the Soviet troops approached, Wanda resumed her diary, interrupted the year before for fear of betraying two Jewish women hiding in their Warsaw flat. Wanda determined to write only about her own experiences and to keep her diary a secret.

24 July 1944

It's really hotting up, the war is rushing towards us. The Bolsheviks are flying, the Germans too but only to get away! I don't think we will have to cry for much longer, there won't be a single German left here soon. Lots of people have left Otwock already, mostly on foot because the horses have all been requisitioned and the trains reserved for Poles are very slow and unreliable. I don't know what's going to become of me. Mummy still hasn't come and I must get back to Warsaw! There are rumours about 'surprises' in store for us! Here in Otwock everyone says the Bolsheviks will get here within three days. The main road, which is not far away, is full of military transports from the east. They are digging trenches. I wish I was in Warsaw with my family.

25 July 1944

Last night was awful! I had pains in my chest in the evening. Then at 11, I was just about to go to bed when a terrible explosion tore through the air and the silence of the night was destroyed. Bombs! Bombs! You could hear them from anywhere in the house, they must have been falling very close by. Everyone jumped up. The sound was deafening. 'Hurry, into the garden!' I grabbed my dressing gown and ran out. My heart was pounding and my whole body was shaking so much I thought I was going to fall over. I lay down in the grass and that calmed me down a bit. It was a beautiful, warm, starry night.

All of a sudden, a rocket lit up the sky. It was very beautiful to watch. It fell slowly and then hung over the forest, lighting up the whole. If it wasn't such a danger sign you could sit and marvel at it. But it lights up the place where they're going to drop the next lot of bombs. After the

Page from Wanda's diary, July 1944.

first rocket, there were more. The light was bright as day. But then the bomb … The windows rattled and almost smashed. We were in shock. [My friend] Anna was feverish, really terrified! We clung to each other, I held her tightly in my arms, and she said after that that gave her the strength to hold on. The rockets continued to fall, followed by the explosions. Each time we thought we were done for. I was petrified to begin with but then I calmed down. I was only worried about everyone who was still in Warsaw. Then the artillery began to fire at the planes circling over us and we had to go down into the air-raid shelter, or rather the big hole in the ground, because of all the shells flying around. I didn't get to bed until 3 in the morning.

28 July 1944

No, it's really bad now – a whole week of bombing! And everyone says it's going to get worse, that they'll start bombing during the day as well. Karczew has been taken already and it's only 4km from Otwock. The bloody hour is near. The war is very close now. A friend of my sister's came to say goodbye today. She's been called up. One of our cousins too. God! All these young lives, is it worth it? It's all for our country and you're not supposed to hesitate for a second. 'Everything we have, we give to our country!' You may not question the price. The hour of battle approaches – but will it be the hour of victory? Yes, it will be victory, we just have to believe it, defend our country and drive the enemy out. They invaded us. As soon as we join the fighting we cannot think about the cost! We must have faith and hope, for the sake of our country.

It is 9.30 in the evening. I am not going to bed. It's not worth it. According to our sources there will be an attack in the next half hour. I am dressed and ready to go down to the cellar. I will go but I don't know whether I will ever come up again. Anything could happen tonight. It's possible that within a few hours the house I'm sitting in will be gone, and this notebook I am writing in, and yes it is even possible that I will be gone too … Oh! Such pessimistic thoughts!

News of the fighting on the outskirts of Warsaw reached the Łódź ghetto, bringing renewed hope to the anonymous boy diarist. With the Soviet troops now just over 80 miles away, the boy poured his thoughts out onto the only paper available to him, the end pages and margins of a French novel called Les Vrais Riches, *where he wrote alternately in Hebrew, Yiddish, Polish and English.*

25 July 1944

[*In Hebrew.*] I can't sleep. I was patient for five years and now my patience is gone. We can feel the coming liberation in the air. The Russians have captured Lublin. In Germany war is being waged, there was an attempt on Hitler's life. They definitely oppose the war and want to end it. The end is knocking on our doors. Another moment and we will be free. Just thinking about it makes me cry. Really this whole awful war is so senseless and crazy, for every person killed on the front, when the Germans are already convinced of total defeat. It is hard to believe that they will harm us but we are fearful because who can foresee the depth of the intentions of the crazy Hitler! He is irresponsible with regard to his own nation's future. We are full of hope, and impatience.

26 July 1944

[*In Polish.*] Rumours are spreading, one more sensational than the other! We cannot foresee what the next few days will bring us but one can feel that they will be loaded with significant events. We expect, more than ever before, that we will be allowed to live. But every one of us knows that we cannot be certain. Can you expect logic from beasts of prey?! Negotiate with a tiger? I am very tense and excited the whole time. Everyone is trying to guess what the future will bring.

27 July 1944

[*In English.*] During the past five years, which have felt like five ages I have been tolerably patient and calm. I supported all the interminable, innumerable, unnameable sufferings which bottomless, fertile German inventiveness heaped on us so lavishly – with an incomparable stoicism. But now, when the solution is near, I am quite at my wits' end, and got to be very impatient and nervous, full of anxiety. I meditate over the future – if we have any at all! Then if we should walk the same path our heroic brethren have gone – can we speak about any future – eternity has no future whatever! The dead and murdered don't have any calendar! But sure of either life or death we can't be – maybe that they would be thwarted in their 'noble' plan, our infernal, devilish, satanic German fiends – and we shall have the narrowest of escapes? – to tell decent unGerman humanity about their deeds! And curse their abominable name for evermore!

28 July 1944

[*In Polish.*] My excitement and terrible impatience grow with every moment – I would like to find myself on the other side of the barrier. I want this so badly I can hardly breathe. Can anyone imagine a condemned man in his awful dungeon when he can clearly hear the hammering on the other side of the walls of his prison? We can also hear the hammering – every night we have several alarms. No wonder, they themselves are admitting that there is fighting in eastern Warsaw. What magic words – what times we live in. Perhaps our relentless fate has become more kind to us and we will survive nevertheless!

29 July 1944

[*In English.*] I am in a state of terrible excitement mixed with disbelief and fear. Who of us who are subject to such sufferings could believe it that we should get out, that we should be among those who survive! Oh! If I should be a poet, I should say that my heart is like the stormy ocean, my brains a

bursting volcano, my soul like ... forgiveness, I am no poet. And the greatest of poets is too poor a fellow in word even to hint, only to allude at what
we passed, and are presently passing by. Never has any human being been
put into such a state of 'the *profundis*' as we have been. Imagine a Jew of
Litzm[annstadt] ghetto not wholly deprived of imagination when he is
being told the few magic words: 'Bitter fighting has reached the outskirts
of Warsaw.' At last it is not in Asia, it is not in Africa ... but in Europe, in
Poland, in Warsaw ... If we lived up to this time perhaps shall we live up
to the moment of our dreams, to the moment of our deliverance, which
seems so discouragingly *incroyable* [incredible] perhaps.

I have been saddened by the fact that a ghetto inhabitant has been
wantonly murdered by being shot at by the Nazi 'Kripo' (what fiends).
I, with my easily impressed mind, have begun to reason: if they could,

Page from anonymous boy's diary, 27 July 1944.

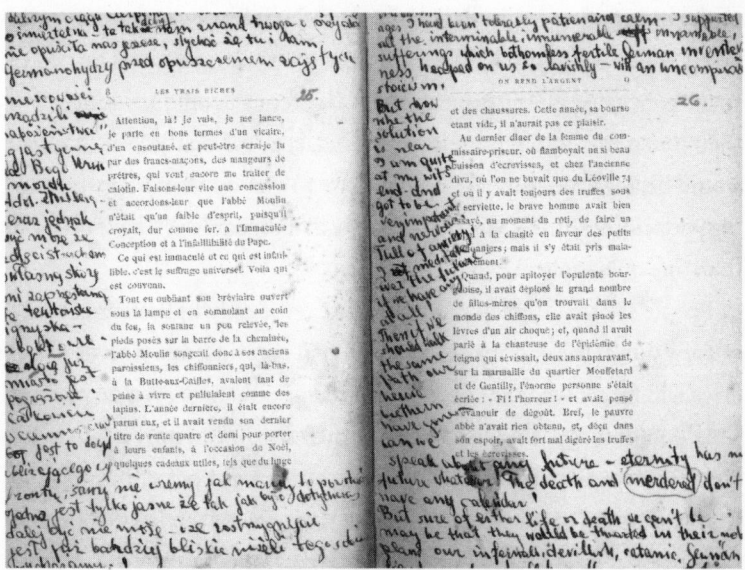

what will they do with us at the last moment? But away with such thoughts. If we live up to the time when our capital is taken, it is nearly sure that we shall see also Litzmannstadt delivered. Meanwhile, I am walking along as a lunatic, fevered with impatient expectation, full of hope and fear. I should like to become a few weeks older and still be alive!!

29 July 1944

[*In Hebrew.*] We can hardly believe, and will not believe till the last moment, that we will survive. If only the thugs won't do us harm! They have so many worries of their own now, that they may not do to us what they intended. When I look at myself and at my little sister, who has suffered so much in the last few years, it is hard to believe tomorrow will bring us life. We will see, and we will tell, we will remember and mourn our relatives, the murdered ones, victims of starvation, martyrs of the holy nation, annihilated in such a terrible way. Is that not so?! I joked with Mr Bohon that I don't know what transgressions helped us survive. Because all the honest, quiet, righteous people are gone, all of them (also my father, honest, warm, wise, a real man). How happy I would be, my little sister, if I did not have to see you so unhappy, mending your clothes, full of worries. I can say that certainly you have no more than one of Napoleon's soldiers.

People say that if we survive we must settle only in Palestine. Without any doubt the nations of the world that commiserate with us to our faces will forget what has been done to us. Some may even be pleased. This 'do not forget' understanding of our sorrow can only happen in a Hebrew state. Because every utterance, every word out of our mouths will be devoted to our sorrows, to the suffering of the Jews of Europe under Hitler's rule. Others, outsiders, will not be interested in those matters, they will turn to their own business, grieve for their own losses. There are no more Jews in the Diaspora! Who will acknowledge our distress, who will console us in our grief – the Poles, Hungarians, Romanians? Only a Jewish heart is able to feel the sadness of our troubles, the depth of our pain. We have no more strength, no more patience. If God will let us live, we will console ourselves!

31 July 1944

[*In Hebrew.*] Tension and anxiety have increased to an indescribable level. There are rumours that heavy fighting is taking place in eastern parts of Warsaw, and that the Russians have crossed the Vistula. Will we be liberated, will we be human again? Those who are not here will never believe that it was possible for us to live as long as we have. Maybe they will be forced to flee the city in panic and confusion without being able to harm us?

3 August 1944

[*In English.*] I write these lines in a terrible state of mind – we have, all of us, to leave Litz[mannstadt] ghetto during a few days. When I first heard of it I was sure that this meant the end of our unheard of martyrdom equatanously [together] with our lives, for we were sure that we should be '*vernichtet*' [annihilated] in the well known way of theirs. People were regretting that they didn't die on the first day of the war. What for to have suffered five years of '*Ausrottungskampf*' [war of extermination]. Couldn't they give us the 'coup de grace' in the very beginning?

But evidently some pressure on the part of the victorious Allies must have had some effect on the brigands and they become more lenient – and

[Hans] Biebow, the German Ghetto Chief, held a speech for the Jews – the essence of which was that this time they are not to be afraid of being dealt with in the same way all the other outsettled have been – because of a change in war conditions 'in order that the German Reich should win, our Führer has ordered to use every worker'. Evidently! The only right which entitles us to live under the same sky with Germans – though to live as the lowest slaves, is the privilege of working for their victory, working much! and eating nothing. Really, they are even more abominable in their diabolic cruelty than any human mind could follow. He further said: 'If force has to be used, no one will survive!' He asked the crowd (Jewish) if they are ready to work faithfully for the Reich and every one answered '*Jahwohl*' [Yes, indeed] – I thought about the abjectness of such a situation! What sort of people are the Germans that they managed to transform us into such low, crawling creatures, as to say '*Jahwohl*'. Is life really so worthy? Is it not better not to live in a world where there are 80 million Germans? Oh, is it not a shame to be a man on the same earth as the Ger-man? Oh! shabby, miser-able human, your meanness will always surpass your importance!

When I look on my little sister, my heart is melting. Hasn't the child suffered her part? She, who fought so heroically the last five years? When I look on our cosy little room, tidied up by the young, intelligent, poor being, I am getting saddened by the thought that soon she and I will have to leave our last particle of home! When I come across trifling objects which had a narrow escape all the time – I am sad on the thought on parting with them – for they, the companions of our misery, became endeared to me. Now we have to leave our home. What will they do with our sick? With our old? With our young? Oh, God in heaven, why didst thou create Germans to destroy humanity? I don't even know if I shall be allowed to be together with my sister! I cannot write more, I am terri-bly resigned and black spirited!

Undated

[*In Hebrew.*] My God, why do you allow them to say that you are neutral? Why will you not punish, with all your wrath, these who are destroying us? Are we the sinners and they the righteous? Is that the truth? Surely you are intelligent enough to understand that it is not so, that we are not the sinners and they are not the Messiah!

These were the anonymous boy's last words. On 6 August 1944, the German authorities began deporting all but 700 of the Łódź Jews who were kept back to clear up the ghetto; another 200 managed to go into hiding. The rest, over 67,000 men, women and children, were sent to Auschwitz-Birkenau where more than half of them were taken straight to the gas chambers. The anonymous boy's diary was found in the ghetto, after the war, by a survivor. It is presumed that he died in Auschwitz, along with his sister.

Wanda Przybylska was now back in Warsaw, reunited with her family. Outside the city, on the eastern banks of the Vistula river, the Red Army waited, having halted its advance. Inside, the Polish resistance, amongst them Wanda's sister, were about to launch an uprising in an attempt to liberate the capital, though relying on the Allies to drive the Germans out. This time, Wanda's sister, Jadwiga, confided in her the 'Home Army's' plans for Warsaw.

1 August 1944

Finally, the hour has come. I am on the balcony. It is half past three and the uprising is meant to start in half an hour. The Bolsheviks reached Warsaw today, on the Prague side, but the Germans pushed them back. Only fifteen minutes to go. Blood is going to flow. It's crazy what's going

on now! A great racket ... shooting everywhere, grenades, bullets,
machine guns. At every shot, my heart leaps and I wonder, who just fell?
Is it someone I know? My hands are shaking. I am now lying on the floor
by the balcony doors. Our soldiers are in the street already. They are
wearing red and white armbands and a car taken from the Germans just
went by flying a red and white flag. Is it really going to work? Will we
manage to beat them? I've just heard the caretaker shouting that the
water supply is about to be cut off and that soon we won't have any lights
either. This time, it really is war. It is 9.30, I'm going to lie down and pray
for the dead, the living and those who are in grave danger.

4 August 1944

I don't much feel like writing today. There is no good news. Our young
fighters are holding out, they've even taken up new positions, but they
can't keep going much longer, they're running out of ammunition. There
is no help from the Bolsheviks, or from the English. And the Germans
are very busy.

The beautiful weather returned today, and with it came more bombing and shooting. What can we do? We are powerless. We have no anti-
aircraft guns so those swines take advantage of the fact and fly so low
that they can fire at us with a machine gun. We keep hoping to see
English or Soviet planes but there's nothing but black German crows
circling over our heads. We had to go down into the cellar several times
today. Luckily the bombs have been fairly small, dropped from light
aircraft, not bombers. But in spite of everything, we are in good spirits
and, more importantly, so are our soldiers. They are fighting well and
have announced that it will all be over by next Sunday and then all the
divisions of the Polish Home Army will have a big parade. Oh, how we

long for those celebrations, for peace and tranquillity, for no war! There are two more incendiary bombs burning.

9 August 1944

Really, I have no desire to write today. There is no news.

I have almost nothing to do now. I wish I were two years older, then I could work as a nurse in the hospital like my sister, or do something else useful. All I can do is stand guard for a couple of hours a day at the entrance to our building and that's it. Otherwise, I sit and read, if I can concentrate, or tidy up (and then make it all untidy again), I cook a little, but really I don't do much of anything. I sit all day waiting like everyone else, waiting for the end result of all this. Waiting for the future.

After ten days of the uprising, only a few British supply planes had arrived and Stalin was refusing to allow operations beyond the Red Army's front line, across the Vistula river. The despair felt by Wanda mirrored the desperate situation in the city, as SS reinforcements slaughtered civilians and the Wehrmacht fought the determined but poorly equipped rebels.

In France, Allied troops had secured Normandy and were now just over 30 miles from Paris, where Micheline waited impatiently as German forces began to pull out.

16 August 1944

So much has been happening. I walked to the dentist, as the metro isn't working. The receptionist, who's from the suburbs, said the Germans are on the run everywhere, using horse-drawn carts, stolen bicycles, taking with them everything they can carry. I hope someone takes it all back from them later. Outside the hotels, all you see is luggage, cars and lorries. I watch them, the defeated enemy, with contempt. We have been waiting for this for four years! I wonder, had we known it would take this long, would we have had the courage to wait it out. We are all exhausted. The Germans have left the hotel opposite. There's a rumour going round that the Germans are meant to be leaving Paris in the morning.

19 August 1944

11 o'clock. I don't know what's happening right now because we are not allowed to go out, but revolvers and submachine guns are going off constantly on the Champs-Élysées. The window panes rattle when the guns go off, and a man has just shouted, 'Stay close to the walls.' No one knows what to do in the streets, which direction to take. German lorries pass by with submachine guns aimed at the crowds. I wonder if the Americans are 'here' already. Nicole heard someone say they are at the gates of Paris. It's all very exciting! I don't think Mummy will let me go to the dentist this afternoon.

Evening: There were more people killed in Paris today than in all of the English bombing raids; 400 dead on Place de la Concorde alone. It's amazing that we can hear everything but see nothing because of the angle of the house opposite. Nicole and I were desperate to get out, so we said we had to walk the dog. We got as far as the Champs-Élysées where we saw lorries full of soldiers with so many gun barrels sticking out they looked like pincushions.

No one knows anything; there are too many rumours.

20 August 1944

At 4 o'clock, a car drove past announcing through a loudspeaker that the Germans have negotiated with the resistance and an armistice has been signed; they will let the Germans leave and the people of Paris are to remain calm until the English and American troops arrive. Waiting is only hard when nothing is going on; but now we know they are coming … My God, we're going to be so bored when all this is over! …

23 August 1944

Everything was very calm yesterday. We now have newspapers and therefore news, which has reassured everyone; and we have been promised food within five days. They're saying it has been agreed the French will march in first, with General de Gaulle at the front (but for the past two weeks they have been saying the Allies are at the gates of Paris). Everyone is madly excited.

We went to bed. Then two huge explosions went off to the east of us. The house started wobbling like jelly. Then more explosions, like a storm coming towards us. It seemed as if the skeleton of dead Paris was moving in the wind. A huge red light spread on the horizon … it was like a *danse macabre*.

We went back to bed and I went straight to sleep. I hate them, I hate them. To think that I believed they were human, once. I hope we know how to avenge ourselves. They burnt down the Grand Palais, which was full of the wounded. After all of yesterday's explosions, set off by the Germans to vent their anger, Paris smells of tar, smoke, rubber, more smoke, gunpowder and even more rubber. There are still a few Germans opposite, but they're lying low.

24 August 1944

11 p.m. Paris is literally in revolt. The Allies are entering the city right now, the radio is reporting mutiny at the Hôtel de Ville. Nothing but noise and colour. But people are still dying, which prevents us from rejoicing completely. All the stars are out for the arrival of the Allies in Paris, all the windows are lit up, flags are flying and everyone's singing *La Marseillaise*, as out of tune as possible. Radios play military music. Young women sing the departure song or *Tipperary*. The whole of Paris is out on the streets or at the windows, in spite of the Bosches' bullets.

I feel very weak from not having eaten anything, but I'm so happy. I don't dare get undressed. There's been no gas since yesterday. Luckily there's a little bit of alcohol but everyone's pretty fed up. We have been given some butter and 150 grams of meat, some sweets and some biscuits! Everything will end well, it's almost over. We can't say where the Allies are now but in the time it takes me to write this sentence they will have moved a little closer.

25 August 1944

I just went to see the first three American tanks arrive with French soldiers sitting on them, they are the victors of the 'battle for the Champs-Élysées', covered in red and white gladioli. The Allies let the French, the Leclerc division, be the first to enter liberated Paris! I had to scream at Mummy to be allowed out, because the fighting isn't completely over, they are still shooting from the rooftops. It's a complete free-for-all, young boys and girls climbing all over the tanks, even dogs are wearing the tricolour. The French soldiers are covered in lipstick; they look fantastic, brown from the sun. I didn't kiss them though because I thought they'd had quite enough.

Paris Liberated, Micheline's drawing, 1944.

I hurried over to the American press car and shook hands with a fantastic guy with a little black moustache. A little further on I found one of Nicole's friends in tears, her father had slapped her because she was kissing a soldier. It seems as if all of Paris is comforting her, a soldier gives her some chocolate. A little American goes by, chewing gum. I have to go home, sadly, so Mummy doesn't get worried.

Evening: I felt most alive today when they burnt the German flags. They managed to take all their champagne with them but left their flags behind. It looked fantastic from the balcony. The flames went up and all the young girls danced around it, singing *La Marseillaise*. I will never forget it all, not even if I live to be a hundred. It was like Hitler was going up in flames.

As Micheline and her fellow Parisians celebrated, in Warsaw, three and a half weeks into the uprising, there was still little help from the Allies. Wanda resumed her diary after an enforced break, when her area was targeted by German 'Nebelwerfer', multiple rocket launchers, which were used against the rebels with devastating physical and psychological effect. The Poles called them 'bellowing' or 'roaring cows' because of the loud howling noise made by the incoming rockets.

28 August 1944

I haven't written for three days, and even now it is hard for me to write after all I have been through. It started on Saturday when we were targeted by a 'bellowing cow'. And from that moment on, it was horrendous. It is hard to describe what a terrible thing it is to go through something like that. Our house was hit first, it was very early, we had no warning. The 'cows' bellowed a few more times but quite far away and they didn't explode. They were just a nuisance, compared to the real thing, like the buzzing of a fly. I was in the dining room when we were hit. Everything was over within seconds but I will try to describe it.

It went very dark, like it was the middle of the night, at the same time a flash of fire swept through the air. Then, a terrible cloud of dust and smoke rises up and suffocates you, filling your throat and your lungs. And it is all accompanied by a terrifying noise. The furniture smashes and falls over, tiles and bits of the ceiling fly around, the whole house shakes. That's what it was like. You have no idea where to go, which way to turn or how to get out.

After five minutes it began to get lighter, the dust settled and I realized the flat was ruined. Everything was dirty and damaged. The people looked worse. When I looked at their faces, they looked so comical that instead of crying I just laughed. They all looked like Negroes or chimney sweeps. After the explosion, we spent the whole time in the bomb shelter. But it is just as hard in the cellar as it is in the flat. Everything shook and there was so much dust that we had to make ourselves masks out of wet gauze to put over our mouths and noses so we could breathe. We spent the whole day like that down in the shelter while everything above and around us was being destroyed.

When I emerged from the shelter in the evening, I was greeted by a horrible sight. Everything was in ruins, not a single house was standing, including our own. The courtyard was completely covered in ash and rubble. It was just terrible. The night was calmer, spent in the cellar, of course, but it was a real nightmare for me. We had to sleep on the ground. I felt really dirty and exhausted after such a horrendous day. My hand was wounded and hurting badly. I was almost killed out in the yard when I was caught by surprise by a 'bellowing cow'. My coat caught fire. Luckily I had enough presence of mind to throw it off me before I fainted. It's amazing I survived.

The next day, the 'cows' left us in peace. We all emerged from the cellar and set to work like ants whose anthill has been destroyed but gather together in the same spot to build a new one. We moved the rubble to the side to make a path through to the road and cleared out the air-raid shelter and then began to live again, after a day when we barely managed to stay alive.

That's what we are like; we fight for our lives right to the end.

29 August 1944

Today, I lay in bed, or rather, on a kind of straw sack in the cellar. My temperature has gone down a bit and I feel a bit better. I was very ill yesterday and I still feel very weak. I can hardly move. All is quiet, and I feel very lethargic. My spirits are low. That's what happens when you don't even have a place of your own. Life is awful now. All we do is just sleep or sit around in this damp and dirty cellar. We can't wash because water comes at a price – the pipes are broken so if you want water you have to go out and fetch it from a well three streets away, under constant gunfire. And even then it doesn't taste any good, it's not even good for washing in. When you go out all you see is rubble and ruins.

Six days later, Wanda Przybylska was killed in crossfire as her sister Jadwiga led the family to safer shelter in the ruins of the city. Wanda's distraught family discovered her diary amongst her belongings.

The battle for Warsaw continued until the beginning of October when the Poles capitulated and Hitler ordered his troops to raze the city to the ground. The Red Army would not enter Warsaw until January 1945.

By the end of August 1944, Americans had replaced Germans on the streets of Paris, which had been spared from destruction by the armies on both sides. Several days after liberation, Micheline noted the first signs of change.

31 August 1944

I just got news from Verneuil. Everyone there is well and they weren't bombed too heavily, thanks to the old pastor who went by bicycle to tell the Americans that the Germans had already left.

I took Darak for a walk before dinner and bumped into Monique Léger, she was out with her mother. Meeting her had a weird effect on me. She looked so glum, her lips shut tight, and she was wearing a dress that would have looked better on her mother. It's funny how quickly she lost her Germanic air.

I forgot to say that there are Americans in the hotel opposite now, instead of Germans. There was a whole row of them, sitting along the wall, like birds. I am only just now starting to feel happy and take in the fact that THEY ARE HERE …

CHAPTER TEN

Inside Japan
October 1943–December 1944

'I feel nearer to death than life'

Mikiko Kato in 1944,
aged 15.

Kukimoto Nobuhide
(second from right),
Haramachi Air Base,
1944.

*B*y the autumn of 1943, Allied forces in the Pacific were on the offensive. After a decisive naval victory at the Battle of Midway in the summer of 1942, which prevented the Japanese from taking control of the central Pacific, the Allies embarked on an 'island-hopping' campaign. Despite encountering ferocious resistance all the way, they were able to successfully overrun Japanese garrisons one by one. Along with the liberation of the Philippines and other Japanese-occupied territories, the ultimate Allied aim was to advance close enough to the Japanese mainland to launch a major campaign of strategic bombing, to force Japan's unconditional surrender with minimum losses to their own troops.

Strict censorship ensured few ordinary Japanese citizens were aware of the real situation. As war approached Japan's own shores, the entire population was asked to redouble its efforts on the home front, being told that 'to die for the nation is to live'. Despite doubts among the Japanese high command about whether the war against America could be won, surrender was regarded as unthinkable. In the autumn of 1943, the idea of 'body-crashing' into American aircraft carriers and destroyers was mooted for the first time as a means of 'rendering the impossible possible' and taking the upper hand by eliminating the superior American navy as it approached. While Japan's most experienced pilots were saved for air battles, the idea of the suicidal kamikaze, as they would become known in the West, was promoted to university students as a means of achieving 'a splendid death' in the name of the Emperor and the nation. While extreme, the sacrifice demanded from the 'Special Attack Squads' was not *unthinkable for a generation brought up on patriotic education and regular military drills. Even young Japanese girls, sent to replace adults in the munitions factories and fields, were required to prepare to die rather than surrender.*

Unable to work at a munitions factory with her school friends because of a chronic kidney complaint, fourteen-year-old Japanese schoolgirl Mikiko Kato stayed behind in Haramachi, a small town on Japan's eastern coast. In the autumn of 1943, as she recovered, Mikiko began to help out at her family's 'milk and ice-cream shop'. As the only café in town, it became a popular meeting place for young trainee pilots and junior officers stationed at the nearby air base. Mikiko would devote much space in her diary not only to thoughts on the war and self-sacrifice, but to the young pilots she befriended.

Thousands of miles away in New York, David Kogan, now also fourteen, was enjoying the company of girls and taking pride in America's effort overseas. War remained a distant concept, though to do his bit for the war effort David bought war bonds with his pocket money and signed up with the Red Cross Mobile Corps to deliver 'What I Can Do' booklets.

Unlike David, Tokyo teenager Hachiro Sasaki had privately opposed his nation's war since the start. Refusing to join in the national celebrations at the time of Japan's attack on Pearl Harbor, Hachiro had buried himself in his studies, graduating with top marks from Tokyo High School and going on to read economics at the University of Tokyo. Yet by the autumn of 1943, Hachiro had begun to feel that abstract study was futile at a time of national emergency, when patriotism and self-sacrifice were hailed as the ultimate virtues. Keen to distinguish himself from the crowd, Hachiro decided to apply to become a trainee pilot, despite opposition from his father. Since the death of his eldest son, Hachiro's father had pinned all his hopes on his surviving children: Hachiro and his younger brother Taizo. But to Hachiro, *his father's expectations were those of a 'selfish capitalist' bent above all on family wealth accumulation.*

Writing at the end of a day in which he had dared to confront his parents about his decision, Hachiro reflected on his decision to become a pilot.

10 October 1943

I told [my teacher] Mr Ideta that I have chosen the Naval Pilot Preparatory school. 'If I don't go, who will?' He was very pleased with my decision: 'I am grateful to all students who are making such great efforts. They couldn't wish for a better young man than you. Do try your very best.' I felt so relieved. My mind was suddenly clear. I've been throwing hints to my Father every day and he has been looking very annoyed with me. But in the end, there they were, my mother and father, to hear what I had to say.

I have to set down here two things I am worried about, however.

First, my parents.

I think my mother has come to terms with my decision, more or less. She is an optimistic person who doesn't look too far ahead. I feel so sorry to have been nothing but a burden to her all these years, and for leaving her now, and like this, but it can't be helped. I will beg her forgiveness, but I'm going to defend our country so I will be defending my parents too.

I upset Father again today. He is an intelligent and ambitious man, but he just can't let go of his conventional ways. He will praise someone else's son for getting on a plane, but his own children are there to look after his investments, first and foremost. They are there to take care of him. They are forbidden to go on a dangerous flying mission – not all of their own will! Not voluntarily!!

According to him, sons who wish to go and fly a plane are the ungrateful ones. I am supposed to think about all his hard work, his struggles for his own family, and be thankful. Thank you, Father. But why can't I feel this in my heart for real, not just acknowledge it in my head? It must be the generation gap.

I'd like to say to him, 'Well done. Thank you for everything.' But when he tries to hold me back from my own journey into a new future, I want to push him away. It makes me even more eager to leave. I want to explain to him, 'Father, Father, this is not the world you grew up in.' But my father is not one for listening, no matter what I have to say. He just gets angry and says: 'What do you know?'

Maybe I was a bit tactless tonight, but he got really furious with me. I feel sorry for fathers. If you have two sons, doesn't it make sense to dedicate one of them to your country, especially the way the country is right now?

What would happen to our country if all fathers kept their sons at home to look after them? Why not just say, 'Go and do your best for our country'? What's so bad about that? It's hard to go and fight with a clear conscience with my old-fashioned family dragging me down.

My second worry is that I keep hearing about these new students hanging around in Shinjuku and going wild. Despicable! So low and uncouth, where is their conscience?

19 October 1943

Living is more difficult than dying, to my mind. I am not going to be afraid of death, right now in fact I would welcome it. I feel closer to death than to life. I don't actually care what's going to happen.

I am still a human being who has to live, and I have to control myself. I believe that I have got what it takes to fly a plane. If you can see the right thing to do, but don't do it yourself, that means you don't have the courage. No matter what happens, I will go straight to where I'm most wanted. My will is invincible. I am bright, I've done very well at school and I've got excellent physical fitness. If the Japanese navy waste the talents of someone like me who has everything they need, they really don't know how to use people at all. If I die, it means I was not needed. I will know I wasn't perfect after all. But if I survive, it means the world needs me. To die is to live, so be prepared, and wait.

Two days later, Hachiro marched with other student recruits around a rainsodden Tokyo stadium in a mass send-off, broadcast on national radio. They were hailed as heroic warriors, yet in an essay composed a few weeks later, Hachiro wrote: 'I pray to see the day when we do not have to kill enemies we cannot hate. For this end, I would not mind my body being ripped apart innumerable times.' In early December 1943, Hachiro was required to report for military training.

8 December 1943

Today is the second anniversary of the Great East Asian War and I am going to enter the barracks tomorrow, finally. I am writing the diary on my last day of civilian life.

I was given a truly splendid farewell party last night, I was deeply grateful. Each person wrote a few characteristic words for me on a Japanese flag. I was so moved to receive such honest and truthful feelings.

I was especially surprised when my friend Hirasawa gave me a haircut! It was such a wonderful thing, and so unexpected.

After everyone left, I talked to my brother about our family and how I felt, as much as I could. I can leave with no regrets because my brother is still here. I can wholeheartedly rely on him. I trust Taizo will carry out my will, he will make up for my shortcomings even, and I am certain he will earn the Sasaki family a noble reputation.

I'll throw myself into the eternal flow of history, and I shall prove my quintessence. Our personal feelings in relationships cannot escape trivial fluctuations of love and hate, fondness and envy. But all will be solved by the mighty power.

I am not writing my will at this time. All I wish is for those who have been blessing me to follow their own true paths without distraction and live their god-given lives to the full. Everything is in the hands of Almighty Heaven. I pray that each of them will face judgement by the course of history, straight and without fear. I wish all my friends happiness and the best of health. I sincerely hope each one of them will continue further on their paths, retaining, however vividly or faintly, their own impression of me, the human being called Hachiro Sasaki. With this, I am closing my diary.

2.40 a.m., 9 December 1943

The next day, Hachiro was sent to the Yatabe naval air base. On the first morning, each new recruit was shown how to kill themselves by pointing a gun directly under their chin and using a toe to pull the trigger, so as not to be captured alive. Months of strenuous physical and mental training followed, including daily corporal punishment, all deemed necessary to create 'god-like soldiers'.

Convalescing at home in provincial Haramachi, fourteen-year-old Mikiko Kato was troubled by feelings of guilt and frustration, and thoughts of her father who had died when she was a baby.

15 January 1944

I think I'm turning into a wicked child. I got too upset this morning. My mother and grandmother were talking about my father, remembering him. I didn't want to get out of bed. I cried under the blankets. I used to feel proud whenever I heard anything about him, my kind-hearted, beautiful father. But I have become such a bad child. How sad. I don't smile any more. Mother has noticed. Sometimes I don't even answer her. I don't want people to say that I am ill and that's why I am twisted like this. But when I am unhappy, I just ignore what other people might be thinking. I am becoming wicked. Father never quarrelled with his brother, I was told, not once. He never dared talk back to his parents. How can such a fine father have a wicked child like me? The more I think about it, the more upset I get.

25 February 1944

I couldn't sleep last night so I started humming a few school and army songs in the dark when my mother called out to me, 'Mikiko?' When I replied, she said: ' I know you are ill, but don't tell anyone you are happy here. Parents who have sent their children to Tokyo to work in the factories might think it is unfair that while their children are working so hard for our country, here you are enjoying yourself doing nothing.' My heart skipped a beat, but I acknowledged what she said, then carried on singing. But it really wrenches my heart that because I am ill I have time on my hands and can play whenever I want. And it really pains me to be ill and useless, a burden to my country while it fights this Great War. People judge me from how I am on the outside, but they have no idea how I feel inside. I might look happy, but when I think about all those soldiers out there, I curse my own body and am plunged into dark thoughts.

People never really care how I am. They just say they do to please Grandma and Mother. They ask, as if they're bothered, 'How is Miki-chan? I hear she is so much better,' but they're obviously thinking about something else. They say it even when I'm feeling lousy and look pale. What's the point in telling anyone how I really feel? I may not be the brightest, but I can tell when people are being sincere and when they're not. If I said I was feeling sad, they'd pretend to console me, but if I said I was lucky, they wouldn't like it. What are they really thinking? I can't understand them.

4 March 1944

I have started to think about death in quite a casual way. How can a Japanese girl living through this Great War be scared of death? Wherever I am, whatever the circumstances, I must be prepared to die with honour. It would be a great shame if I couldn't. I tell myself that I must train my mind to look death in the face.

Since the end of last year, I have begun to understand that death will bring no enjoyment or fun, but no pain either. I am no longer afraid of it, death, of dying itself, but I still don't like the idea of my body being burned or buried in the ground. Some might say it's silly, but I've been thinking about these things very seriously. Then I said to myself, it's no good, I had to train my mind even more, to rid myself of such worries.

Even with something you thought you could never do, just willing yourself to do it makes it possible. Even dying becomes possible. This thought exercise taught me a lot. However hard I try to imagine it, I don't think I could use a sword like people did in the past. I just can't bear the idea of it. But with enough thinking and willing, could I perhaps do it, in fact? Shall I think about it?

5 April 1944

There is a full moon tonight, it's bright and clear. It has tempted me out into the garden. The view is so fresh here, and looking at the moon makes me forget about the war. What war? Where? But when I look carefully, I can see an air-raid shelter out there, with its dark gaping mouth. Even this lovely scenery, deep inside Japanese land, does not and cannot forget the war. As soon as an air raid starts, even the beautiful moon shines a light on all the terrible things on earth. Lovely moon momentarily turns into a frightening moon. Is such a thing possible? Before the war, I would have been lost in romantic thoughts, but now the moon, the stars, everything is somehow connected to the war. There is absolutely nothing that is not connected to it somehow, when I think of it. Sentimental souls of the past could never have imagined, even if they stood upside down, that there would be a time when people would look up at the moon and think about war. But here we are, right now, thinking exactly that. Though our time is full of endless suffering, we still feel a little proud and say: 'Aren't we doing just fine?' Tonight the moon has made me think all manner of things.

That April in New York, David Kogan remembered his resolution to maintain a regular record of his life in such historic times. Deeply affected by films such as The Human Comedy, *which, David thought, 'painted a picture of America at war which tells the message of courage, DON'T GIVE UP ON THE WORLD', he started writing his diary once more.*

20 April 1944

The last few months contain stirring events, and I can kick myself for not writing. Have been a paper boy for over a year and last Saturday I quit. With the money accumulated from my paper route I purchased the Encyclopaedia Britannica.

I realize how tall the members are in the ASC [Athletic and Social Club]. Of twenty-one members, four are six feet. Seven are five foot nine.

22 April 1944

8.30 found me on my way to a party in the home of a Lincoln Park girl. Was acting as usual – dancing awkwardly; then eating, then talking to the stag line, and so forth. Suddenly Sandra takes an interest in me and feeds me the 'only dearest one' line. To my surprise, she continues. I find myself in a corner with her, my arm around her – we're holding hands, laughing, talking, joking. I was having a wonderful time. It was the first real enjoyment I had with the opposite sex, besides talking to BD and looking at Eleanor. But then – just as suddenly – she loses all interest in me. I did not see her the rest of the evening. I was in a daze, and the last period went slowly. By the time I got Hank out and got home, it was 1.30.

10 May 1944

I guess I am one of the boys now. I've learned the facts of life, smoke, gamble, curse. Don't misunderstand me – I am able to do these things, but don't practice them.

I'm a fellow with so many faults. I know my faults too, and that's what gives me the conscience. The thing to do is to strike out and cut the forest around me. Unfortunately I pretend I'm lost and complacently sit on the axe – it'll cut a hole in my undersides yet.

After I did some homework, Gil came to my house. We went hunting for some really sexy book. Later we went over to Gil's house, where we listened to his swing records.

13 May 1944

Tonight was the night of the ASC anniversary dance. Strangely I had a pretty nice time. Hank took a liking to Bernice, and so, after I had him understand that his cutting in was welcome, I had a chance to look around and dance once in a while. The band was excellent, and the sandwich counter, whose monetary situation was so successfully handled by Steve to the latter's advantage, had some good fare. Ken dropped in about eleven o'clock with a delicious piece of feminine pulchritude whom we nicknamed 'Legs'. What a face! And can she dance! There were a lot of other dames who couldn't exactly be called rotten tomatoes.

24 May 1944

Sandra is very warm to me these days. I can't resist her charm, so I took her up by inviting her to the club party. Today she said that Arty had invited her before I did, and that her mother had forgotten to give her the message. In the words of Steve watching a fire, 'Ain't that a burner?' I wonder if Sandra had her finger in the pie?

27 May 1944

Tonight is the official 'House and All Night Stag' of which Mrs Meltin does not know. She is in Atlantic City, and the goings-on are taking [place] in her house. I would have gone, except for you-know-who, and was not in the mood to invite anyone else.

My family spent the evening playing bridge, and when I went to bed at 11.15 I said: 'Why not?' I waited till all was quiet, closed the door, got dressed in finery, wrote a note, and with heart in throat sneaked out the back way. There were two crowds: the respectable – dancing and talking in the living room, and the loose ones in Gil's pitch-black room, necking. The party broke up at 12.15 and the few stags talked, smoked, surveyed the damage, waiting for the fellers to return. Mike and I had an enjoyable time, playing cards until we went home. I sneaked in, put things away, went to bed, and nobody in the family knew I was gone.

6 June 1944

When I got out of bed this morning and groped my way towards the bathroom, Dad told me FRANCE WAS INVADED. I could not believe it. We turned on the radio, and all the stations had the same news. Most of the news were German rumours. Everyone in New York is inwardly excited, but grim.

To coincide with D-Day in Europe, an Allied offensive was scheduled to begin in the Pacific. In Haramachi, Mikiko recorded what she knew about her country's situation in the war.

12 June 1944

It's been a week since the Americans and the British landed in Northern France. We keep hearing about Northern France on the radio, but there is no mention of what's happening here in the Pacific. We've got 70 thousand enemy soldiers against us, they say. Well, congratulations. Meanwhile, the Germans are being pushed back, bit by bit. Everyone is delirious about how well we've done, but can't see that Germany is retreating. Getting overexcited is a bad habit of the Japanese people. Though it can sometimes be a positive thing …

29 June 1944

I heard today that a coastal guard unit is to patrol our shores in Haramachi. It came as a shock to me. I didn't realize things were that serious. Are they worried about the enemy landing here? I really didn't know it was that serious. I never dreamt of it. I thought we'd be fine until the autumn at least, but things must be getting very tense. We've been kept busy just following the news every day. When the war started, we were wondering where we would land next, but now we keep hearing things we used to think were impossible.

*After the death of a young neighbour that summer, Mikiko did not write
in her diary again until November 1944, when the first teenage pilots and
junior officers began to leave the local air base for Special Attack Squad
missions in the Philippines. Mikiko, now fifteen, turned again to her diary
to record her impressions of some of the pilots she had met.*

3 November 1944

Lieutenant Saito was waiting for his car this morning after breakfast.
I brought him a newspaper. After reading a couple of articles about the
Special Squads, he gave a big smile and said: 'I have made it in time for
the decisive battle. We were supposed to graduate in December but it
was moved forward to October. It was a close shave.' He talked a lot. How
gallant he was! You can tell he's a graduate of an officers' college. So
different from the ordinary pilots who fly civilian planes. He told me
once: 'The moment you go in to blow yourself up, your target looks
bigger, so subconsciously you try to lift the plane up to escape. You must
make it impossible for your plane to go over and above your target. If
you do, you'll have to blow off your head with a pistol.'

I kept thinking, is that what a human being is like? I had never thought
that deeply about self-sacrifice before, it had never entered my head. Is
this what each and every one of them does, acting against such strong
human instincts? It got me down, thinking about it. I was thinking about
all sorts of things, and then it really hit me. Will he be just a memory one
day? I thought he'd be staying for another month at least, but he is definitely leaving.

6 November 1944

Lieutenant Saito left on the five o'clock train today. We all went to see him off – my mother, brother, sister and I. The eastern sky was getting a little lighter, it was faintly purple. I couldn't say a proper goodbye. I think the last words I said to him were to ask him for a poem. Lt Koyama went with him, too. Ever since I first met Lt Koyama, and every time I think about him now, I can't help feeling he is destined to die in battle very soon. This feeling always comes over me. Is that a human instinct? My sister says she has the same feeling about him. I don't know why, but his face makes me think of death. As for Lieutenant Saito, I just can't imagine him dying. Is it because we've been looking after him and got to know him? The idea that he may never come back breaks my heart.

Several weeks later, Mikiko read a newspaper report which hailed Lieutenants Saito and Koyama of the Imperial Flower Regiment as heroes for successfully 'body-crashing' (tai-atari in Japanese) into their targets.

   That November in New York, David Kogan had sad news of his own.

9 November 1944

Miss Grant died today. It is not often that somebody I know dies, because I am young, and my acquaintanceship with older people is slight. It makes one pause and reflect on life and death, on death and life. Somehow I feel there will be no Resurrection, and there is no Heaven. I realize it is a crime to waste a day. Everyone feels it when he steps into bed at night. Therefore it is my opinion that it is a crime to die without having lived. A man should not 'gafoodle' a minute, he should not 'gafoodle' a day, so that he should not 'gafoodle' his life.

18 November 1944

It has lately become a pleasant custom of mine to go to the Yonkers Public Library on afternoons. I look at the people, browse, and do schoolwork.

I went to Gladys's 'Sweet Sixteen' party today. I had a fairly nice time – danced, chatted, and ate. Saw 'pretty little, witty little' DB, still as charming and as unscrupulous as ever. I gave Gladys a nice 'Sweet Sixteen' kiss – it tasted good.

It was the first kiss since my first party in December 1941. The girls are beginning to look.

In Japan, Mikiko befriended twenty-one-year-old trainee pilot Kukimoto Nobuhide, a member of the newly arrived 'Progressive Assault Regiment'.

24 November 1944

On the way home today, I was thinking about the lyrics of 'Dreams Are Gone'. I was looking down and not paying attention, when a soldier walked past. I looked up and it was Kukimoto. I was surprised, but he seemed to have seen me before I noticed him. He said he was going to a local bar and left in a hurry. Then at about 8 o'clock he came round, on his own. We played fortune-telling cards in the sitting room, until my sister came in. I don't know why, but Kukimoto said to me: 'Why don't we see what your love line says?' I was a bit embarrassed, but I said to myself, it's only a card game, there's no need to worry. He said, 'Okay, so you are sixteen …', and started cutting the deck, quick as you like. I was watching him, smiling a little. The cards said that our hearts were in love and our friends were supportive, that our mothers and aunties were in agreement, but both our fathers would disapprove. Then Kukimoto said, with a straight face: 'The cards say, drunks like me are no good.'

Undated, a few days later

Kukimoto has been coming round a lot and we've become very close. I talk to him like he is my brother. I want to know what goes through a soldier's mind. I wish I hadn't told him my thoughts. When I talk to Mother, she tells me we are fighting a great war. People are joining special squads and going off to die. But because of those who are dying, I worry about myself. They say we are desperately short of fighter planes. And however much I agonize over it, there is nothing I can do. It is painful having to spend days on end just reading. Friends the same age as me are manufacturing weapons. How can I carry on like this every day?

That's what's been troubling me. It's so painful, it makes me cry. It's impossible to say or write here all that I feel, so I told Kukimoto and he said: 'Everyone has their own worries and concerns. Our comrades have been going off to the front and some have gone flying with the Specials. We didn't know what to think any more, either, so we've started drinking, out of frustration and anger. Our Lieutenant told us we were too impatient. That the wind might change direction tomorrow, but it was no good worrying about it. Best not to think about it too much.'

Kukimoto said the wind might change the next day, but it came a little too early, that very night. He got an order to leave the Haramachi airfield on 2 December at noon, never to return. When he came around the second time, he was sitting down in the guest room with his back against the pillar, smoking a cigarette, and repeating the words: 'As the saying goes, if you wait with patience, good weather will come.' I was messing around playing the cherry blossoms song on the *koto*. I would have practised harder if I'd known I would be playing for him. I can barely finish the first movement of the Six Pieces. Looking back, there are so many things I should have done. But when I was with him, it didn't feel like goodbye. I couldn't help thinking I'd see him again. That was why, whatever he said, I never looked upset. He would never have thought Mother and I would be crying our eyes out when he left. He would never have dreamed that the day after we saw him off, I would cry again, all day.

4 December 1944

It has been two full days since Kukimoto left the airfield. He told me to check the newspaper, I might read something about him. There is a 'pain in my heart'. Last time I saw him, I couldn't look at him properly – now I realize I will never see him again, and we didn't even say goodbye properly …

He rang just after twelve to tell us his departure was confirmed. I took the phone but he didn't say a word. I couldn't bear the silence, so I said: 'Take care of yourself.' I said the word goodbye first, then he didn't say anything, then finally he said goodbye too. I ran out into the garden to cry. It's all over. I hoped he would leave by train, but no. I shall never see him again, or hear his voice. I think about his voice saying hello on the phone, again and again.

He rang us at 12.20, ten minutes to go, he flies at 12.30.

I can hear his voice. I watched the plane fly south, and then it was gone.

That day Kukimoto Nobuhide left for the Philippines to prepare for his mission. Shortly before his final flight, he wrote to Mikiko.

Undated, mid- to late December 1944

Warm breeze. We really have flown south. I can feel it. All the trees I see around me tell us so. Are they pine? No, they don't appear to be, someone says. Leaves on the banana trees sway in the wind, they look quite dashing.

A beautiful coral reef, enclosed by the deep blue shores. Why here of all places, I wonder. But the weather is still miserable. Silent rain still falling.

We slept inside a mosquito net. It was nice.

At our dormitory they turn out the lights at 8.30. Thinking about all the people I met and left behind, I can't help feeling a little lonesome.

Listening to the sound of raindrops in the garden, I wonder how they cry for me now, but who are they really crying for?

Planes take off in fine rain. One after another. We set off on our journey. We thank our beloved planes, we pray for them. Almost touching the sea, we push up into the clouds. I am glad our squadron is strong. My engine

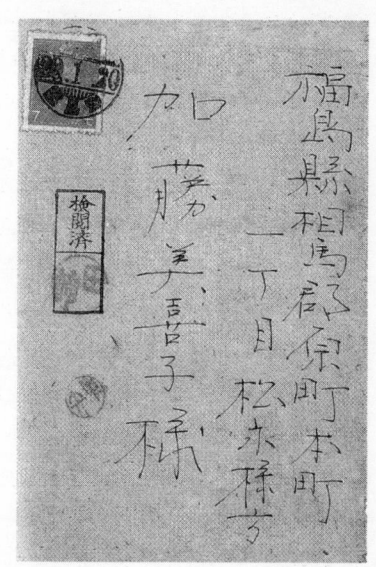

Kukimoto's letter to Mikiko, December 1945.

sounds fine. Just seen a shadow of the island out of the corner of my eye, then suddenly the sky opens up. Taiwan! Capped by the clouds, the Yushan Mountain stands high and proud. There are tears – of joy? – my vision's blurred. I can't see clearly. My silver wings tremble with excitement. Off I go! I slap my arm and squeeze the controls as hard as I can.

I've come far, far away
Thousands of miles
Over the ocean
Wind blows wherever (it doesn't bother me)
Rain falls whenever.

I don't care if arrows and gunshots come flying at me. We have made it, all of us, safe and sound. Next stop, the Philippines. We are ready. That's all for now. Good night.

On my Lord's order
I've come far and away
Awestruck
The southern sky is not clear yet
Wait a little longer, my comrades!

And enclosed here are my poems, answering yours:

A fair maiden prays
Head down with pure heart
I am going
For the Lord

I miss her more than Kunimi
My home town deep in the north country
How is she tonight?
I long for her always.

Yours sincerely,
Kukimoto Nobuhide

Soon after, the Asahi *newspaper reported that Kukimoto and four other pilots had succeeded in their mission, sinking 'a number of American ships and destroyers' near Mindoro Island in the Philippines, though the claim has never been verified. The successful American landing on Mindoro Island would pave the way for the liberation of the Philippines.*

CHAPTER ELEVEN

Germany in Retreat

September 1944–April 1945

'I can't believe this is the end of Germany'

Elvira Filippovich in 1952, aged 18.

Page from Elvira's diary.

Page from Klaus's diary, October 1944.

Дома нечего есть кроме маленького кусочка хлеба. У нас живёт кот Мочек, и питается тараканами. Бабушка жарила на плите тараканов и сказала: Скоро и нам придётся есть тараканов, потому что этот сорт Доменко мамин начальник до сих пор не имеет деньги.

B y mid-September 1944, the Allies were closing in on Germany. To the east the Red Army had already liberated Russia, the Ukraine, White Russia and half of Poland and advanced through Bulgaria and Romania to the Hungarian border. To the south the Allies now controlled much of Italy and in the west the liberation of France and Belgium was almost complete. On 10 September the first American soldiers crossed into Germany. Some hoped the Germans would capitulate by the end of the year, but on all fronts, as Allied forces neared Germany's borders, the rate of advance slowed.

Hitler was determined his country would fight to the end, even though by the middle of 1944 few in Germany believed that the war could still be won. A new German offensive against France was planned for the end of the year, and on Germany's eastern borders men young and old prepared to mount a final stand against the Red Army. As German troops retreated from previously occupied territory in the east, Hitler ordered all traces of the concentration camps to be erased. At Majdanek outside Lublin, the SS ran out of time, leaving unburied corpses and seven gas chambers to be discovered and photographed by the Soviets in July 1944. It was the first camp reached by the Allies and the vivid reports which appeared in the press intensified the hostility felt by the advancing troops. The German Propaganda Ministry exploited the population's fear of reprisals by the Red Army to keep the German people fighting to the end. Over a third of the total number of German troops killed during the war lost their lives in these, the war's final months.

Klaus Granzow turned seventeen in September 1944. In just over a year, he had gone through every form of pre-military training available in Germany. But months of mindless repetitive drills, indoctrination and bullying instructors had failed to turn him into a committed member of the Wehrmacht, ready to sacrifice himself for his country without further thought. Soldiering would never be for him; he still dreamt of becoming a writer, an actor or someone famous one day.

In February 1944, fifteen-year-old Lieselotte G. had agreed to leave her family in Berlin and be evacuated to save herself, as she saw it, 'for the future of the Fatherland'. Sent to board at a private girls' school in Droyssig, west of Dresden, she was often lonely and missed her mother, feeling both out of place amongst her wealthier peers and increasingly isolated as the Allied troops approached Germany.

On the other side of the front line, ten-year-old Elvira Filippovich could hardly remember her life in Moscow before the war. Her parents had separated when she was very young, and just before war broke out between Germany and the Soviet Union in 1941 her mother, a geologist, was sent to work on a project in Southern Russia, near Stalingrad. Elvira – or 'Elichka' – had spent most of the war being looked after by her grandmother, her 'Baba', in a small village never reached by the Germans near the town of Kamyshin on the Volga. After the Red Army liberated the Ukraine, Elvira's mother was sent to work on a rebuilding project in the Donbass region, taking Elvira and her Baba with her. It would be the first time that Elvira had been in an area directly affected by the war. Her mother had always kept a diary and as they set off for their new wartime home Elvira began one of her own.

15 September 1944

Today I am travelling by train from Kamyshin to Donbass with Mama and Baba. At Kamyshin we barely managed to squeeze into a carriage. We had a permit to go to Donbass and tickets as well, but the carriage was full. It was a goods carriage and the whole train was a goods train. The conductor finally managed to push us in even though all the people who were already in the carriage screamed that they didn't want him to let us in. We had to stand up. There wasn't even room to put our suitcase down. But the conductor said she reckoned it was all going to be okay. She was helping us because Mama gave her half a litre of vodka as a present. When the train started moving, everything settled down. Mama sat down on the suitcase and sat me on her knees and Baba sat down on a bundle holding a round yellow cardboard box in her hands. That box isn't for sitting on: my great grandmother brought a fashionable hat back from Paris in that box, and we had put all our things in it. There was a lot of noise in the carriage. They were talking but not quite in Russian. At first people only pushed and shoved us but then they started speaking to us too. Someone even offered us unsalted dry biscuits – called *matza*. They were Jews who were returning home to the Ukraine from the Saratov region. I made friends with one boy called Edik.

16, 17, 18 September 1944

The train stopped often, and they were long stops too. They let us out to 'go'. The whole way there were broken-up tanks, motorbikes, cars, planes even, right next to the railway track, all mixed together, all twisted and torn up. And also helmets that had been shot through, and tins and mugs. Edik and I collected all the utensils. And bits of shells. But these were heavy so we threw them away. People say there are still dead people inside the tanks. But we didn't climb inside them. There were signs everywhere saying: 'Mines!'

We didn't step on any mines and during our entire journey no one from the train stepped on a mine. But we kept stepping in shit. Everyone in the carriage called these yellow piles 'mines'.

We went past the huge Stalingrad field for a very long time. For more than a day and a night. And we stood next to it too. You could see the city of Stalingrad, or its ruins more like, far away beyond the field. In the morning we saw a huge red sun rising through the fog. It came up from behind these black ruins. And during the day you could barely see the city. We saw so much else though. Once we saw a tank, almost half of it dug into the ground, just standing there.

You can get boiling hot water at nearly every stop. Edik and I run to get hot water in his bucket. We crumble bits of dry bread which Baba made especially for the journey into the boiling water. Baba crumbles the bits into her mug of hot water and says: 'I wish we had an onion, or some dill.' And Mama says: ' I wish we had a tiny bit of meat, I am so hungry.' And I don't say anything, I just grit my teeth and tie my stomach up with a towel so I feel less hungry.

19 September 1944

We have arrived at Debaltsevo, at last. We are walking along a very very tall and narrow railway bridge. It is so long! We can see the tracks underneath. Ten, twenty, maybe thirty rails, maybe even more …

We can also see the town from the bridge, or to be more precise, what's left of it. The station is in ruins. We are waiting for another train. And the platform is full. Everyone has bundles and suitcases. Mama says: 'You just watch our suitcase so no one steals it.' So I watch it. Then finally the train comes and we have to get in, quick. But we looked and the suitcase was gone! It all happened in a flash. It was there – and then it was gone! Mama ran along the platform. But there were so many people. Then she came back crying. People asked what was in the suitcase to make her so upset. And Mama said it had all her diaries. From years and years of her life.

Mama was very, very upset. It was then I understood that diaries are more precious than the finest silk dress. And that was why I decided to keep a diary.

20 October 1944

We've been living in Alchevsk for a month now. It is a small town, but beautiful. There's a cinema and a library in the centre, and on the outskirts, where we are staying, a market. And there is a school near us. We live in the Degtiariovs' flat, in their main room. It is a big room. They all live together in their front room. There are four of them – the mother, eldest daughter Lyuba, Tanya and the youngest son Andrei. Their room is smaller than ours, but it's warm. They have a big stove in their room and they cook on it. And for warmth there is a stove in the wall too, but it doesn't give off much heat because it is very hard to get coal, all the mines have been blocked up.

Baba keeps herself wrapped up in her woollen shawl, Mama wears her coat indoors, I wear two jumpers, but Andryusha, our landlady's son, walks around completely naked. He is only three years old but he is tough. He comes to visit when we are eating and says: 'Here I am.' So Baba and Mama always give him something to eat.

19 November 1944

'THE STORY OF A PARTISAN GIRL'

It was a dark and quiet night. Partisans walked along a narrow path. Among them were two girls, who had voluntarily joined the partisans. One was called Anya, the other Lisa. They were trying to reach the nearby German HQ. There was a German colonel inside, and important documents about the actions of the German army. Suddenly they heard shooting. Partisan commander Ivan Vasilievich Volkov ordered Anya to go and find out where the shooting was coming from. Anya saluted and disappeared into the darkness. Enemy bullets whistled over her head.

Anya lay down but soon the shooting stopped so she carried on walking. Nearby, perhaps thirty steps away, she saw the Germans, who had just attacked a group of partisans, running away without looking back. Anya laughed and went back to her group. The commander ordered Anya to go on a scouting mission to the HQ to find out how many Germans there were and where would be best to start a battle. Anya went searching for Lisa, who was nearby, and off they went. It was dark in the forest and Lisa was quite scared, so she held on tight to her friend. But Anya kept on marching bravely and wasn't afraid of anything. She used to live outside Moscow and had spent her whole life in the forest, she was a forester's daughter and knew all about forests, and now it became useful. When they were right near the village where the HQ was they heard loud voices and then saw lots of German helmets. Lisa cried out accidentally and was immediately shot by an enemy bullet. Anya was seized, she resisted but they hit her with a rifle butt.

She woke up at dawn in a dirty damp barn …

Anya was tortured brutally, they pushed needles under her nails, hit her with sticks and cut off her ears, but she remained silent. They threw her back in the barracks, bleeding.

At dawn several soldiers came for her. They called up all the soldiers and made a gallows. Anya was tortured again for the last time. They tore out her nostrils and burnt a star on her forehead. They led her to the gallows and threw a noose around her neck. Anya looked at the forest she loved so much and said in a loud voice: 'I am dying a good death for my Motherland, for my people!' And suddenly she went quiet and only an echo responded in the forest and all around her went quiet.

20 November 1944

This morning I read out my story to Baba. Mama had left for work already and Baba was listening half awake. By the time I finished reading, tears were rolling down my face but Baba was smiling. She calmed me down and said: 'Elichka, why are you crying?' And I couldn't stop crying. 'But she was hung, don't you understand? She was hung!'

At school, I read my story to my girlfriends, and they cried with me.

In the evening Mama came back from work and I read my story to her. She too just like Baba didn't cry but smiled instead. And once again I couldn't hold back my tears. And I got cross: 'Mama, aren't you sorry for Anya the partisan girl? She was hung!' And she just asked in which newspaper I had read about it. And I said to her: 'But I saw it with my own eyes!' And I really did, in my head. But very very clearly. Then she told me it is best to describe what you really saw with your very own eyes, and what impressed you. So, for example, what made an impression on you today?

Today our school toilet made an impression on me. Bits of shit froze and made a pyramid that rose out of the hole. And one of the girls called it 'Stalin's Peak'. But I felt very embarrassed. So I couldn't go and kept it all in, all day.

That autumn Klaus Granzow reflected on why he kept a diary and decided that it was important to set down his own personal thoughts rather than describe external events. He had been placed on yet another training programme, this time with the 'Reichs Labour Service'.

25 September 1944

The training is becoming really tedious because we know everything they're telling us already. In compensation, I've been reading *William Tell*, much to the astonishment of my roommates. They're all only interested in banned jazz music. One of the boys is a keen pianist, another plays the accordion; the rest make jazz with their hands and feet, with wood, tin and their mouths. I can understand why they want to numb their fears with jazz. We all want to be free. The way power is abused here can only have a bad effect on us. We're told it is essential to keep the German people together in bad times. I can't judge that, I can only speak for myself and I so long to have my own career. I'm going to suffocate otherwise! I don't know if I have any thoughts of my own any more. They have all been drummed out of me. Would I even be able to act independently? What would I do? Write, of course! But I haven't had any big experiences yet. Unless this is a big experience and this war will later be seen as the life and death struggle of the German nation. Our group leader is always giving us talks about the military and political situation, telling us youngsters we need to become as tough as steel, just as the Führer says. One word of Hitler's is used to justify all the bullying by those training us.

Tomorrow we have another medical inspection and beforehand our hair is always cut as short as matchsticks. I hate this. Why can't we have long hair? Why do we all have to look exactly the same, all branded as idiots? Everyone should be allowed to look his best.

1 October 1944

We have had schnapps distributed to us but it tasted revolting. We were also given cigarette coupons today. Luckily I haven't picked up the habit yet. I'll save mine and give them away as Christmas presents. When we finish our work duty we won't be eligible for them any more as we're not eighteen yet. For now, as long as we're wearing the uniform, even though we're only sixteen or seventeen, we count as grown ups. What a mad world!

It's the same with the cinema. We're not allowed to watch anything exciting or abnormal yet because we're too 'small' and it could have a bad effect on us. But at seventeen we can go to the front. Do they think it's any easier there?

4 November 1944

The call up to the eastern defences is going quicker than expected. We are going to be dismissed from Labour Service. To be honest, I'm rather frightened of the future and going to the front. But I must conquer this weaker part of myself and let the other, better part of me, the cheerful, fearless part, win. What's going to happen to me? I think my fate has been decided by a higher being. I believe God preordains death. I cannot put off the meeting. I have been thinking a lot about God and death, as I embark on this new part of my life – which is bound to continue until the war ends. I am sure I will come through if I stick to my childhood motto. 'Always cheerful, never lose heart'.

27 November 1944

I am now a soldier, a gunner, so volunteering worked. I am attached to the multiple rocket launcher, just like I wanted to be.

I've been steadily improving myself, I've gone from being a Hitler Youth to a naval auxiliary, then a senior naval auxiliary, now I've reached the heights of gunner!

We were released from officer's training on 13th November. By Monday I was already home. We had Monday and Tuesday to ourselves. Dad killed a couple of chickens and we all sat together around the big dining-room table. Mum and Dad were happy, even if they didn't really show it. It was soon time to say goodbye, it went much too quickly, the break between training and military duty was too brief. Strangely, I found it easier to say goodbye this time, I've left home so many times this year already. But maybe this was the final goodbye. I realized it could be when I saw how hard Mum was taking it. Oh dear Mum, I don't want to die at the front for her sake, the pain would be too great for her, it would be too hard a blow because I know how much I mean to her, as the youngest. For myself, I don't really care. I don't want preferential treatment.

1 December 1944

I was given my uniform today. But it's a horrible First World War uniform, with a stiff collar, green in colour, like grass, endless buttons, knee breeches and puttees. None of us knew how to put it on. It took ten minutes to make it look right. I think it's disgraceful that the German army makes us wear these uniforms. The army has run out of supplies. I hope we get proper uniforms soon, we look really pathetic. If we went on leave looking like this everyone would laugh at us!

10 December 1944

Our swearing-in ceremony! We practised for the big occasion all day Saturday. It went well, in spite of all the nerves.

It was a beautiful December day. In the morning we all lined up in Market Square for the ceremony. There was a huge platform in the middle with a lit-up swastika and us recruits lined up four rows deep in front of it.

The major came and gave a speech about the point of our oath and how we should remember those who had given their lives to stay true to it, and to Germany. We sang *I Had a Comrade* quietly. It was very solemn, that song is really moving. Loads of spectators reached for their hankies.

Then the swearing-in. We all had to repeat the oath, swept along by the occasion, putting our heart and soul into it. I kept reciting it to myself, thinking: I have sworn on the German flag and to Adolf Hitler, and I must keep my oath. But can I? People say so many malicious things about National Socialist Germany now, I'm bound to get into arguments.

Then, to finish it off, we had an amazing meal. We were completely stuffed. It was only then that it sunk in how seriously the oath is taken. And now we have the whole afternoon off. Fabulous. But it will be our last taste of freedom, we leave tomorrow for four weeks of training.

Right now, I have time to write and dream. I would so like to write something great one day but I must wait until I'm free again. And when will that be?

11 December 1944

The first snow fell today, it is nearly Christmas. We were practising some hymns and it turned out that the younger ones knew more of the words than the old soldiers.

The singing reminded me of the feeling I had at the Hitler Youth camp: the enjoyment of belonging to the group. It is wonderful to 'have friends around you, who have the same spirit as you'. At the Christmas celebrations this feeling of togetherness should be even stronger. Unfortunately it never lasts long. It disappeared again after the singing. Our lives don't belong to us any more, they belong to Germany and we have to shut out all personal feelings. Sometimes I wonder whether I did the right thing, volunteering for officers' training. I am not really suited to being an officer, I am too good-natured and soft, I can't hurt anyone and can't order other people around. I sound so ridiculous giving orders that the others just laugh at me. But I've done it now and I must suffer the consequences. The only consolation is that there are a lot of others around me who are going through the same thing.

This was to be Klaus's first Christmas away from home. In Berlin, Lieselotte G. was briefly reunited with her family before returning to her boarding school in Droyssig. As the battle for Germany intensified, she received news of the death in the fighting of the husband of her beloved former teacher, Frau L.

25 December 1944

What will Christmas feel like this year in her house, dear Frau L.? So many more men will have died, as Hitler has just started a new offensive. What will it be like in Germany next Christmas?

4 January 1945

I don't expect I'll get married because all the men are dying and the ones that are left will marry the girls who run after them and I can't do that, I wouldn't want to. I will survive without a man, though I would have loved to be a housewife and have lots of children.

Today I received Frau L.'s reply to my letter of condolence. My heart swelled as she allowed me a glimpse of the sublime love between a man and his wife. I realize that she didn't just love him sexually, in a really good marriage the love between a husband and wife is more than just a physical bond. Because she hopes to meet him again in Heaven and surely there is nothing physical left of us there. Once again Frau L. towers over my life with untarnished purity, the light of my life. Through her suffering, she has risen even further in my estimation. She bears it as I would expect my ideal German woman to, I cannot believe that any woman has felt the loss of her husband more deeply. If only they had had children. I know I can never see her or write to her again. But she will shine on forever inside me.

14 January 1945

We saw a beautiful film today! I cried loads and it did me good. By the end I wasn't crying over the characters in the film but about Frau L. and her pain, about the evil of mankind and about how easily our ideals vanish.

22 January 1945

We are about to fall into their clutches, unless there is a drastic change in the situation. The Russians have broken through into Germany, East Prussia is cut off, they are fighting for Silesia. It really can't be true! Holy Germany, does this have to happen? Oh Lord in Heaven, please help us.

Millions of civilians were fleeing west ahead of the Red Army, creating an estimated 8 million refugees by the middle of February. Travelling in the opposite direction were German troops who had been diverted east via Dresden to form a bulwark around the city of Breslau. Klaus, billeted at Hainichen, less than an hour away from Lieselotte's school, now underwent further training before joining this defence force.

31 January 1945

I have been here for a week. Most evenings I am invited to spend with the Butz family upstairs. Hanni is a very pretty girl and has brought loads of film magazines for me to look at. There are always lots of people upstairs in the evenings, all playing fortune-telling cards. Everyone wants to know what's going to happen to their family members.

I don't know why I don't get letters any more. Mummy would write to me if she had to leave Mützenow. Dieter had a letter from his mother saying she was packing. It's bound to be the same at home. I still can't quite grasp it: to be expelled from you own home! But Daddy wouldn't leave his farm. So Mummy and [my sister] Waltraud would flee alone! And what about all our relatives? It is hard to imagine, hard to understand. Yesterday, we all waited tensely for the Führer's speech, but there wasn't one. Or maybe we missed it? He won't be able to talk for four hours like he used to, you don't really see pictures of him any more or see him in the weekly news reports. On the map it looks as if the Russians are heading for the Oder to cut off the whole of Pomerania. They are caught in a trap. Oh God!

2 February 1945

It is odd, that we are being trained as officers, without having any experience of the front. Next week we should go into action for the first time. Oh well, let's get going! I really don't care any more, I have no home left, I have no idea where my parents and siblings are. If only I had a letter! But nothing more will get through. The Russians are 70km from Berlin, whether you believe it or not. Hopefully, everyone back home will get to safety in time. But where is safe?

There's nothing left but to pray: God protect them.

11 February 1945

They are distributing notes to those of us not suitable to become officers, who'll be sent to their first posting at the front instead of further training. My terror was indescribable when my name was read out today.

I think I have our group leader to thank for that, he enjoyed bullying me. I have now overcome my fear and accepted that it is pre-ordained whether or not I will survive the war. I had to say my goodbyes and was very spoilt on my last evening. Hanni spent the whole time crying uncontrollably. I found it hard to leave, too. My marching orders are to head east, to join the 3rd Battery. Tomorrow we're going to Dresden.

18 February 1945

We have got ourselves into a terrible mess. We haven't reached the 3rd Battery yet. After a thorough inspection at Dresden we were hauled off the train by guard dogs. All soldiers passing through Dresden were stopped and sent to Front Headquarters at Coswig where they're making up new units and regiments from the sick, the wounded and soldiers on leave, and sending them off to the front. I don't volunteer for anything any more, I just let myself be shoved around wherever it suits them. I have learnt this from the older soldiers over the last few days. Everybody here is as tough and unfeeling as a tank. Which is hardly surprising after what we've been through. We just survived the attack on Dresden. I was on the last transport of soldiers out of that hell. We watched the horror from Coswig: the pine trees were lit up as bright as day, the flares rained down in unimaginable quantities and then came the bombs! It was terrible watching without being able to do anything, while heaven and earth went up in flames. We knew that thousands of people were burning to death and we could only look on, our anger growing. It looked like a firework display over the Baltic but it was hell, purgatory.

There must have been many, many waves of carpet bombers. They began at 10 p.m. and the bombs were still dropping at midnight. The air-raid sirens didn't stop. There was no more 'all clear'.

In the morning we were all loaded onto lorries. First the medical orderlies, then the old soldiers from the front and finally us young ones. What we saw was so terrible my pen refuses to describe it. We didn't even get to clear up or help. It wasn't possible to reach the city centre. They say there are 200,000 dead. But this is only an estimate as there were thousands of refugees from Silesia at the station; they all burned. No one knows how many there were, no one even knows their names. Dresden is one mass grave! I saw it in all its glory just a few weeks ago. Now it has been destroyed forever. But even more shocking are the deaths of so many people. Perhaps Mummy and Daddy and Waltraud are also fleeing right now. The same thing could be happening to the Pomeranian refugees in Stettin as happened here to the Silesians. But I must force myself not to think about it. I must stay tough, always tough, or I won't be able to cope.

I am completely exhausted. Is this war? It's murder! Where is the 'Front'! Isn't what these civilians are going through much worse than what soldiers endure at the front? And the worst thing is, we can't help them!

For the next month Klaus and his unit were moved around behind the front lines until finally being sent into action east of Dresden at the end of March.

Ten-year-old Elvira Filippovich was still in the Ukrainian town of Alchevsk, in the Donbass area, which had been under German occupation for two years of the war. Her mother had just returned from a six-week trip to Moscow, with an assignment to a new project in nearby Mariupol.

28 February 1945

Mama is back finally. She said we are moving to Mariupol. We'll have our own rooms there! Baba can't believe this is true. She is pleased we are going to Mariupol even though it isn't the same as being in Moscow. When will we go back home?

Baba and I often talk about our little wooden house in Moscow and our dear neighbours.

Baba keeps asking Mama to take us back home to Moscow but in reply Mama just whispers something to her. All I can understand by that is, if we do go back to our flat we won't be allowed to stay there anyway and could even be put in prison. Why? Because an NKVD [Soviet Secret Police] man lives in our flat now, he's a bad man. I suggested we take a big stick and kick the NKVD man out but Baba started crying and Mama put her hand across my mouth and started looking around to see if anyone had heard what I said. Then she and Baba started speaking French, and I don't know a single word of French.

8 March 1945

Today is International Women's Day. Mama got back late from work because they had to do extra work today to commemorate it. Mama came back grey with tiredness. Baba asked: 'What's up with you, Manyusia, you look awful.' Then Mama told us a terrible thing. In the quarry where their research party was working they found dead bodies of women, children and old people. They were standing, now they were lying down. There were no bullet holes. Were they buried alive? They were Jews. Shhhhh! No one is allowed to know! Why not? To prevent panic.

I remembered Edik, my friend from the train. But I couldn't cry. It was very frightening. The monsters! I couldn't sleep all night.

20 March 1945

We arrived in Mariupol today. We left Baba to sit on our things and went straight to the market. I have never seen one like it in my life, it was so huge and noisy! Everyone has to scream to be able to hear each other. There aren't so many counters. The ones there were had milk, sour cream, cottage cheese, dried fruit, jam pies and fish … There are so many different kinds of fish here: smoked, salted, fresh. Fishermen sell it. They have the freshest. We bought a huge fresh fish. The streets in Mariupol are leafy, but most of the houses are in ruins. The accommodation we've been given is outside town, in a workers' village. We live in the biggest room in a three-room flat. Our room is huge. It fits three iron beds in it, easy. And there is a balcony, too, but it doesn't have any railings so Mama won't let me go out on it. We have a table and two chairs. Mama sat down straight away and started writing in her diary. So I did too.

21 March 1945

Today I joined Year 3 at the girls' school. The boys' school is in the same building but has a separate entrance. We share the playground. I like the school, it's a proper one, the desks are proper school desks. I sat down at mine – my first ever. A nice girl sits next to me, Valya Malikova. I went to visit her yesterday. She lives in the same block as us, on the fourth floor. Their windows face the sea. We sat down together to do our history homework but we couldn't stop looking at the sea. There was a sunset. So beautiful! I got the urge to travel.

*Hundreds of miles to the north, as the Western Allies and the Soviets closed
in on her home city of Berlin, Lieselotte remained in Droyssig. With her
family in Berlin caught in what Hitler declared to be 'a fortress city', to be
defended to the end, and American troops rapidly approaching Droyssig,
Lieselotte wondered what to do next.*

3 April 1945

7.45 (in the morning) in bed. There was a meeting yesterday and Dix
announced that all the girls who could get home should leave the
school. Elise said right away that getting to Berlin was out of the question, she heard that all points of entry were blocked. So I asked Elise
if I could also make a call. After ten minutes I got through and said
that I was coming home. Mummy was against it, she said that I had
to realize I would be going to a city on the front line, possibly to my
death. But if I really wanted to then I should come. Mummy thinks I
am much safer here, even if the Americans come, because it is just a
small village; maybe she's right. I told Elise that my mother was happy
for me to come home. So she said I could. At goodnight time Miss D.
said she was surprised that my parents were letting me travel. I have
never felt so confused. What should I do? I so want to go. Mummy
might need me and I might be able to help her. I will only take one
suitcase and my monkey with me then if we have to run from the
Russians I'll be able to help carry other things. I don't think she would
try to get away if she was on her own; perhaps I can persuade her, give
her courage. She is always very anxious and so is Aunt Lotte. If only I
knew it was the right thing to do to leave tomorrow. Everyone here
says I'm mad to go to Berlin, it's only a question of time before the
Russians arrive.

I have never had to make such an important decision by myself. Until now there have always been other people to make important decisions for me. It is so, so hard. I don't think I can do it!

Where will I be this time tomorrow?

12 April 1945

Now I am at home [in Berlin] I'm sure I was right to come. The Americans have already overrun most of Thüringen.

The journey home was terrible. I didn't get here until eleven at night, after a twenty-hour journey. I am happy I got out in time. It is important for families to be together at times like this. Unfortunately Daddy isn't with us, he is a soldier digging trenches in Riesa. Bertel is with the Volkssturm [German territorial army] and is meant to go into action in Friedrichshagen [east of Berlin].

The wood around here is full of trenches. All the trees have been cut down, all the streets have tank traps and you can hardly get through anywhere. People call them laughter traps – when the Russian tanks capture Berlin they will stop in front of them and laugh for a couple of hours until their bellies hurt, and then drive across them in two minutes flat. There are guns on Dahlewitzer Chaussee. Bertel is being trained to use a bazooka; apparently girls are being taught how to use them too. They are meant to be a match for any tank.

I am glad I'm here now, though it's not always very pleasant. There are usually two four-hour blackouts every day as there's not enough electricity and you have to run into the bunker every night when the air-raid sirens go off.

It is amazing how openly and insolently people express their opinions now and they are mostly against the Nazis. No one is afraid to speak out any more despite the domination of the Gestapo. No one dare inform on anyone now because they think that if they do, later on the Russians or the Americans will have them hanged.

I don't understand why my people didn't rise up against the tyranny of the government a long time ago. Was it out of fear of the SS? Or is the German population made up of cowards? I think it is. Perhaps fear of the bombing has made people more stubborn. Now everyone wants the hated Nazis to go, except for a few fanatics who are for the chop when the Nazis are defeated. I'm sure they'll all be hung. I am so glad I never got involved in politics.

People think the Americans and the Russians will take Berlin. This can't go on much longer. Let them be damned, the whole Nazi brood, those war criminals and murderers of Jews. What have they done to my country? They have destroyed it, and us too, and everything we once loved. How could they have brought so much death, suffering and misery to our people? Millions of young Germans have died for them. Dear Frau L. sacrificed her husband for them.

But I can't believe this is the end of Germany, even if it's the end of us.

CHAPTER TWELVE

The Final Months of the War
March–September 1945

'The War is Over'

Hachiro Sasaki shortly before his final mission.

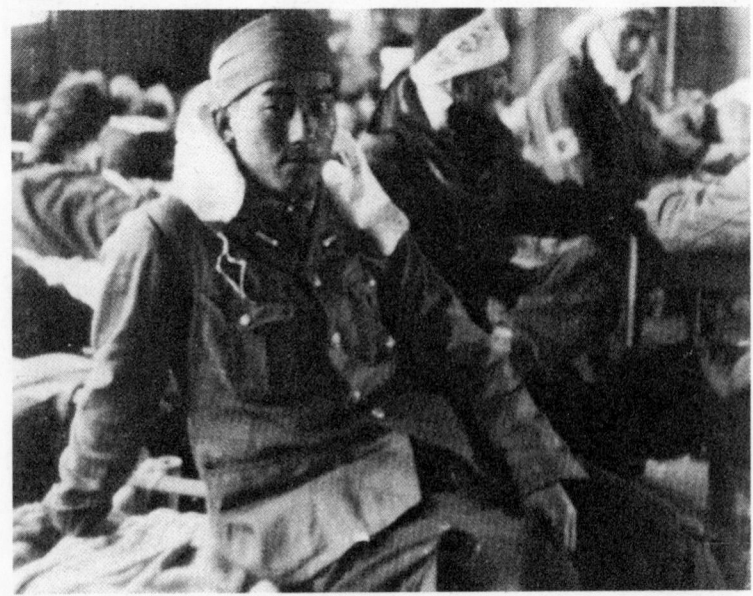

*A*t a meeting held in February 1945 at the Black Sea resort of Yalta, Stalin once again assured Roosevelt and Churchill of his commitment to free elections in a post-war Eastern Europe. While the issue of who would take Berlin itself remained unresolved, an undeclared race was on between Western troops and their Soviet allies to reach the capital. In the spring of 1945, as Anglo-American troops prepared to cross the Rhine in the west, and Soviet forces approached Berlin from the east, German commanders ordered their embittered soldiers, together with thousands of underage members of the Hitler Youth and remnants of pro-Nazi foreign divisions, to fight to the end. Refusing to accept even the possibility of defeat, Hitler threatened to unleash another 'top-secret' weapon.

While work on creating the German atom bomb was nowhere near completion, Manhattan Project scientists in the United States were close to testing their device and were certain the bomb would be ready in July, August or September of 1945.

That spring, fierce fighting had broken out in and around the tiny volcanic island of Iwo Jima, the first Japanese home island to be occupied by American forces. The US Air Force managed to establish a narrow strip of its land as a runway for their latest B-29 bombers and were able to start regular air raids on the Japanese mainland. Though this was not the first time Japan had been bombed, the proximity and capacity of the US aircraft ensured the raids were more consistent and devastating than ever before. Japanese civilians were ordered to learn hand-to-hand combat, emulate the kamikaze code of 'certain death, certain kill', and prepare for mass suicide, but there was little they could do against the relentless incendiary attacks from the sky.

In the Pacific, across Europe and in America, the young diarists who survived to see the last months of the war now either hoped for victorious peace, fought to the bitter end, or prepared to face defeat. While Micheline Singer's diary for this period is sadly missing, and Vasily Baranov along with Herbert Veigel stopped writing earlier in the war, Brian Poole, David Kogan, Hachiro Sasaki, Klaus Granzow, Lieselotte G., Mikiko Kato and Elvira Filippovich continued to record their thoughts and experiences in the final months of the war.

On 9 March 1945, sixteen-year-old Japanese teenager Mikiko Kato saw US bombers flying over her coastal home town of Haramachi, 200 miles north of Tokyo. That day an estimated 130,000 people were killed in Japan's capital city in the single most destructive bombing raid of the entire war. Though details of Tokyo's devastation didn't emerge until later, the next morning Mikiko described what she saw in her own town.

10 March 1945

There was a B-29 raid last night. No bombs were dropped, but we spent over an hour in the bunker while the bombers roared above us. They sounded just like our planes. You couldn't tell the difference. Soon the sky in the south went all red. We heard the town of Taira was burned to the ground.

The B-29s annoyed me even more than the Grummans [US planes]. I heard some of them are flown by women. They flew above, as if they'd come over just to mock me. They made me sick, I felt violated. They're close enough to send in the B-29s. We can no longer relax at night.

13 March 1945

People have started sending stuff to safe places. Mother has been in the storage place with Grandmother to sort out our things. We never thought we'd see the B-29s here, but here they are. They might land near us. Could they? It's making me anxious. We used to say we'd never see enemy planes, then came the Grummans. We said we'd never see the B-29s, so we'd be all right at night. Then the other night they flew over us, looking down at us in the middle of the night. We're expecting the enemy to come by land next. Mother suggests I go to a safe place in Yamagata, but who wants to go there?! I'd sooner die than be evacuated. I might be useless, but I won't get in anyone's way when the time comes. I should be able to put out a fire or two. I don't want to be writing to the soldiers that I've been evacuated. No way. But if the enemy does invade, I'll go. I don't mind being killed by a bomb, it's nothing out of the ordinary for us, born in wartime. But if there's a land invasion and they take me hostage and rape me, I couldn't stand that. I'd rather take poison, or go to Yamagata.

8 April 1945

I was asked to look after some of the newly arrived trainee pilots today. Oh how sweet and lively they are! The boys in the year above were nice too, but not as nice as this lot. They all want to join the air force too, but they're so green.

12 April 1945

[Trainee pilot] Kawana and some other students have gone home on leave. I gave Kawana a fan with the sun and cherry blossoms painted on it. I didn't want everyone to see it, but he waved the fan from the moving train. I was really embarrassed.

The sirens stopped for a while but then went off again in the afternoon. We saw B-29s, about ten at a time, flying over from the north coast, five or six times. They made me angry, but this time I had time to look at them properly and they looked better built than our planes. They were impressive.

13 April 1945

Another air raid today, only one plane this time, probably inspecting yesterday's damage. 'Inspecting the damage'? How infuriating to think of it like that, to see it from the enemy point of view.

I've just heard on the news that 'rotten Roos' [nickname for President Roosevelt] has died suddenly. I screamed. It felt so good. It doesn't mean we can now win the war, of course, but it's great news, so exciting.

This is Mikiko's last diary entry. Years later, recalling her decision to stop writing, Mikiko felt she 'had no more room' left, not just in her notebook, but also in her mind. Amidst continuous air raids and the arrival of countless new trainee pilots to prepare for suicide missions, she had 'begun to think she no longer cared'.

That very day, former Tokyo University student Hachiro Sasaki, now a twenty-two-year old Special Attack pilot, wrote his final letters home from an air base near Okinawa.

13 April 1945

Hirasawa, my friend,

Here I am at this air base in a southern country. The cherry blossom is in full bloom. The fighter planes have been leaving non-stop since yesterday. They will never return. We haven't been given our orders yet, but we must be ready at all times. So I'm grabbing this chance to write to you. I slept really well last night. The sun was setting beyond the blossoming pink renge fields. The freshly cut lawn at the school where we are stationed reminds me of all the early summer days me and you spent together, and of all the walks I used to take with my older brother. The scent of the air at twilight. It filled me with all kinds of emotions. I have a photo of him and me together, and a lock of your hair, which I'm taking with me. There goes another plane. We'll get the order any minute. We'll attack with everything we've got. This is a man's true calling. I am lost for words.

Your friend, Hachiro Sasaki

Hachiro also wrote to his family, but that letter no longer exists. Years later his younger brother Taizo recalled: 'It was a simple letter. It said that the time to carry out his true wishes had come, he asked for forgiveness for the impiety of dying before his parents, he was deeply sorry for confronting his father and wanted to apologise as many times as necessary'. A fellow pilot remembered seeing a different version of that letter.

13 April 1945

Father, farewell,

I was not able to repay you for your fatherly kindness. Tomorrow I am going to die for Japan. Father, I won't ever see you again, but I shall be by you, forever and ever. I loved you very much. I never dared to talk back to you, but I also never told you that I loved you. Let me say this to you now, because this is my last chance. I love you, Father. While I was growing up, you never allowed yourself to show your affection towards me; but I know you were always watching me with love in your heart.

Yours, Hachiro

The next day, Hachiro Sasaki died in a suicide attack on a US warship.

In the early hours of 16 April 1945, sixty German suicide planes crashed into bridges over the Oder in East Germany as 3,000 Soviet tanks began to cross the river as part of the Red Army's final assault on Berlin. Four days later, sixteen-year-old Berliner Lieselotte G. described her first encounter with the Russians in Friedrichshagen, on the capital's eastern outskirts.

22 April 1945

The Russians are here!

It all happened unbelievably quickly. Hitler is finished. We will never have to say 'Heil Hitler' again!

It was shocking to see real Russians right in front of us, with their machine guns and bayonets, their chests criss-crossed with ammunition belts. Of course, we know everything about the Soviets from the government propaganda! They're all meant to be murderers and rapists, but they all behaved pretty decently and did nothing to us, even though we were shaking with fear. They arrested soldiers and searched men for weapons.

At last, freedom from the Nazis! Last night we put a white flag out of our window and went to bed, but there was no peace. The sky was full of German planes attacking Soviet supply lines, and Russian artillery firing non-stop. We are so used to the noise by now that we've become quite indifferent to it. Now we sit waiting for the Russian soldiers to come searching and looting. They do a lot of that, apparently.

A few days later, twenty-two-year-old technician Brian Poole, now stationed at RAF Rivenhall airfield in Essex, shared his latest thoughts with Trudie Lach, a close friend after six years of correspondence.

24 April 1945

Dear Trudie,

By now you will have had your birthday and all the celebration will be over. Our life is creeping away much too fast, Trudie, it doesn't seem but yesterday that I was looking around for your 21st birthday present. I wonder what we would both have been doing now – if there hadn't been a war?

I suppose the most thrilling news is the Russian penetration into the Berlin suburbs. I think they deserve that privilege because they have suffered so much at the hands of the Germans. I suppose you have seen pictures in the newspapers of these revolting and disgusting murder camps that have been overrun by Allied troops. Despite the fact that we have been told of these things since 1937 it seemed unbelievable, but now we realize what despicable swine the Hun are. The whole German popu-lace are to blame for all these things, they must have known what was going on inside these places. They must all suffer for these things until they are fit to take their place alongside the respectable nations of the world.

The weather now is typically British, beautifully warm one day and quite cold and windy the next. I'm quite brown now, in fact the skin is peeling off my neck. It isn't painful so I'm not worried. We could do with a little rain now – something good from the sky instead of rockets. I am glad they stopped now.

Well Trudie the old brain box is empty for the present so I'll say cheerio, keep well and please remember me to your folks.

Love,

Brian

Just a few days after her first encounter with the Russian soldiers, Lieselotte described the final days of the battle for Berlin.

29 April 1945

We never ever imagined we would ever see a day like last Sunday! Our flat was badly hit when German planes bombed Friedrichshagen. As plaster rained down from our ceiling, I thought my time was finally up. We had to leave our flat in a mess and spend the night at our neighbours' place. When darkness fell, the Russians arrived, a whole squad of them. They feasted on the food in our flat while we sat in the cellar, shaking.

We've been hearing endless stories of how the Russians drag women out of cellars to rape them, fourteen-year-old girls and eighty-one-year-old women even, sometimes eight times in a row. So we stay in the cellar all day long and bolt the door whenever we hear a Russian come into the house.

Hundreds of people killed themselves in our district last Sunday. Our pastor had shot himself, his wife and his daughter, because the Russians broke into their cellar and started doing it with his girl. Frau H. shot both of her sons, then slit her daughter's wrists and then her own. They both survived. Our teacher Miss K. hanged herself because she was a Nazi. The local branch leader 'S.' shot himself and Frau N. took poison. It's lucky the gas is off, otherwise even more people would have killed themselves; we might have too. I was so confused! I saw no way out, I thought a Russian would take me too. I would have had an abortion, I don't want to bring a Russian child into the world.

Last Friday our new mayor gave a speech in the market place. He is a former Communist who spent the Hitler years in Moscow. The first thing he said was that from now on we were all Communists! So we just changed overnight. One day everyone's a Nazi, the next day we're Communist. From brown skin to red. It's ridiculous. Everyone wants to join the Communist Party now, but it's hard if you weren't a member before. It was interesting to listen to ordinary people talking amongst themselves. They were criticizing Hitler, but some of them were critical of Bolshevism too. I will keep well away from all that party nonsense. The only thing I might be is a Social Democrat, like my parents.

That day, as US forces liberated concentration camp survivors at Dachau and Soviet troops entered Ravensbruck, Hitler composed his final will and testament, and prepared to marry Eva Braun.

Four days later, with Berlin captured by the Red Army, sixteen-year-old German soldier Klaus Granzow was fighting at Luttowitz, 40 miles east of Dresden.

3 May 1945

We are under continuous shelling. We are firing in the direction of Radibor, 2–3km from here. There are some cavalry regiments fighting on our side near here, wild Cossacks with their little horses and Vlassovite units. They ride like the devil on their warhorses; when they pass by we can see the tension on their faces. They're in a bad situation. They are dead if they fall into Russian hands, but still they behave with dignity and pride. We are not allowed to talk to them, give them anything or go near them at all. The artillery fire was heaviest in their part of the wood. All the trees were flattened, there were dead horses with bloated bellies all around and corpses of fallen Germans, or Cossacks, it was impossible to tell them apart.

Damn this war! Damn it!

5 May 1945

At our last position we still managed to live quite well, in terms of food I mean, because we slaughtered a sheep and a pig. There's already an armistice in the west, it's all coming to an end and the weirdest rumours are going around. People say the Americans are going to release all their prisoners, rearm them and throw them at the Bolsheviks, to kick them out of Germany. Our home must be liberated again at some point. Some are hoping there'll be another attack, but most of us are just waiting for it to be over. Everyone says they would carry on fighting if they could join the Americans against the Russians, for however long the war lasts.

We are surrounded again, the Russians have trapped us in what must be a huge circle reaching almost as far as the old Western Front.

So much has happened in the last few days. Hitler is dead. People say he was shot. Stalin is meant to be dead too. What to believe? Everything is falling apart.

And we were brought up to believe in a National Socialist Greater Germany, which no longer exists.

My greater belief is in Christianity. But if that were to fall apart too, what then?

That day, Brian wrote to Trudie from RAF Rivenhall.

5 May 1945

Dear Trudie,

Any day now I suppose it can happen. I suppose we will take it all for granted as with the lifting of the black-out and the cessation of aerial bombardment. Not very important things to you perhaps, but very important for us here. Life will be so unreal for quite a while. I suppose soon I myself and the other men of my age will be sent out to the Far East. Once we get our equipment shifted I can't see Japan lasting more than 18 months. All the older men are anticipating early release but I myself don't think I'll get out until late 1946 or early 1947. One of the penalties for being young I suppose.

I saw the atrocity films from Buchenwald. It is impossible for me to describe the scenes. Those who were still alive wandered around like Zombies or rather their bones did. Life meant nothing to them at all. I hope this film is shown in America. It is disgusting but very necessary to show it to everyone.

I don't know if I told you but I won a radio a few weeks ago. Now I have a 3-valve portable. But of course I can't take it out of the billet unless I am posted.

How are you these days? You must be plodding along OK. At least I hope so. Please give my regards to your people. Cheerio for now.

Love,

Brian

Four days later, Klaus Granzow made another diary entry, from Bohemia in Czechoslovakia, annexed by Germany as part of Sudetenland in 1938.

9 May 1945

3 a.m. The war is over. Our commander just told us. There is an armistice in the east now, too. We have lost the war. Everyone is pinning their hopes on the Americans. We are going to try to get through to the West. We are leaving the rocket launchers behind and will bury sixteen rounds of ammunition nearby.

We have ditched everything else: gas masks, shooters and all the rest of the junk. We don't want to have equipment on us in case we're captured by the Russians. Some people have got themselves civilian clothes already. I've got a leather outfit I picked up at the naval depot, so I'm going to wear that. But where can we disappear to? We don't know which places the Russians have taken, or where we can get across to the west.

11 p.m. South of Tetschen-Bodenbach. What a day. I am shattered. But I can't sleep. I will never forget today as long as I live. We had a plan: to get to the Elbe on foot and then find a boat and sail to Hamburg overnight.

We lost the rest of our platoon pretty quickly. After 20 kilometres we met up with some guys from the other unit. They found some damaged lorries in a wood and managed to create a real work of art – a working lorry out of a pile of junk. We whizzed along over tree roots and rocks until we got caught in a ditch, and the lorry turned over but luckily no one was hurt.

At Böhmisch-Leipa. We came across a man with a horse and cart. He didn't say a word, I think he was Czech, but he let us get in. There was complete chaos when we got into town! The Czech guy stopped his cart and gestured that we should run. He pointed to the north, then under his arm, then made a sign as if slitting his throat. We knew what he meant: the Czechs were looking for SS soldiers. Their blood groups are tattooed under their arm; anyone with a tattoo is killed on the spot. We ran off – lucky they didn't force me to join the SS at my Armed Readiness Camp!

We reached the Elbe. There wasn't a boat in sight, just thousands of soldiers looking for one. Some made rafts, others swam for it. Many drowned. There was complete chaos, everyone wanted to get to the west.

Then a ferry arrived. It filled up instantly. That was my chance. Those of us standing on the bank swam to the boat. I have no idea how I managed to get on. I found some strength in my arms, then I was pushed and pulled until I was on deck. I hardly had time to wring out my wet clothes before we reached the other side.

And now I have to go on alone, northwards, towards Dresden! I met my first Russian, just before Tetschen. I thought to myself, this is it, but he ran towards me in his filthy uniform, gun slung over his shoulder, and embraced me. He was no older than me, and he just kept laughing and shouting: 'The war's over! The war's over!' And then off he went, shouting 'I'm going home!', waving goodbye with both arms.

That Russian guy was right: we should all be allowed to go wherever we want. No one should take us prisoner, they should just let every soldier go home!

Home! Can I dare to think I'll get home? I need some sleep first. I am lying down in a barn, resting. I will carry on tomorrow. Dear God, please help me get home.

Just over a week since the Red Army takeover of Berlin, sixteen-year-old Berliner Lieselotte G. was despairing at her fate, humiliated by having to follow the Soviet orders.

9 May 1945

Why has God turned us into slaves? It is enough to break your heart. What has happened to the German people? I don't think I can survive this, but God's ways are mysterious. He chooses our fate; if we do survive, these pages will be an eternal reminder of our humiliation.

From 7.45 in the morning until 6 or 7 in the evening we have to do hard labour, carrying stones. It's bullying, pure and simple. There are overseers who never think we're working fast enough. I am not used to physical labour, it's hot and we don't get anything to eat. We get half a kilo of meat a week and 1,000g of bread. So you can eat three (dry) slices a day. A few days ago the Russians filmed us women working hard. I was so disgusted by their smiling faces, taking obvious pleasure from watching German women tormented like this, forced to work and sweat. Where is our freedom? Is it only in you, dear God? But you don't allow suicide!

And tomorrow is Ascension Day.

The Russians are planning a huge firework display. Victory celebrations.

Having managed to get back across the Elbe, Klaus Granzow kept going west.

10 May 1945

I am in Dresden again, the third time in weeks. It's a nightmare. Everyone is living in fear. The Russians are celebrating their victory by running after women and girls. A family took me in, because their son is the same age as me. They gave me a bed for the night and some food. They even let me have a wash! The woman said: 'Other mothers will treat my son like this too, I know they will!'

But how did I get to Dresden so quickly? It was midday and getting very hot when we suddenly came across a Russian checkpoint. A commissar pulled me down off the lorry and took my leather jacket off me. I was in shock, but the Russian laughed and gave me his canvas coat in exchange. We were allowed to continue our journey. As soon as I was back in the lorry, I quickly turned my leather trousers inside out. If they got stolen too, I'd have to show up at home in my underpants.

In the end I walked to Dresden alongside a young man in a striped concentration camp uniform. He told me some horrific things which I found hard to believe. He was just skin and bone. Women offered him clothing but he said he felt safer in his prisoner's outfit. All he wanted to do was to get to Berlin.

But where do I go now?

Still far away from her home in Moscow, ten-year-old Elvira Filippovich
described victory celebrations in the Ukrainian town of Mariupol with her
mother, Baba and their neighbours.

10 May 1945

The war ended yesterday. The loudspeakers in the street were screaming the news but inside our flat there was quiet crying: Vera held a death
telegram in her hands. Masha hasn't had a death telegram, or any kind
of letter, for four months. My Baba was crying, too, then she started to
have a go at Mummy: 'Time to go home, back to our place!' And my
mummy was saying: 'But we won't be allowed to go back there! It's been
taken! By an NKVD officer!' But Baba won't give up: 'We could live in
the corridor. What about Vladik? Where's he going to go?' Vladik is
Mummy's brother, he's been missing since the spring of 1942. He is probably dead. Most of the volunteers died then. But Baba is trying to
persuade Mummy that her dear Vladik is alive, she can feel it in her heart.
Mummy finally managed to calm Baba down. She said she has told our
neighbours where we are in case Vladik comes back.

   In the evening, the neighbours and some other women came into our
flat, one by one. Their faces were smeared with tears and they looked
guilty as they tried to persuade Baba to 'read the cards'. Baba laid out
the cards and persuaded them all, one after the other, that their loved
one was 'alive', or will 'come back'. The neighbours calmed down after
that and brought us sweets. We made tea and started congratulating each
other about the end of the war. Then they all sang songs and started
crying again.

Elvira's uncle Vladik never returned, just one of an estimated 27 million Soviet citizens to have died in the war.

In Britain, Brian shared frank details of his VE Day celebrations with his Trudie.

12 May 1945

Dear Trudie,

It's all over now and we are so back to normal, I sometimes forget that the war with Germany has come to an end. I'm a little on tenterhooks too because if I am to go out to South East Asia Command I'd sooner go now instead of beating around here. Now the future doesn't seem so terrifying, because we can see a clear way to complete victory.

I know you will tell me how VE Day was celebrated in Miami. I'll tell you what I did (if you are not ashamed of me!). I had made up my mind to go to church previously but decided to celebrate with a certain amount of restraint as the war wasn't really over. But as I went with the boys, the drink began to flow in what could be called a torrent. You couldn't help but notice that all the cares of nearly six years of war, the fear of imminent death were all being cast aside and a new spirit was in the air. By the time we were all very merry we ran into some friends. A woman whom we met in a canteen that we frequent and her husband (please note!) invited us to their home. The party grew hot and furious. We drank, danced and sang, drank still more and then lit a big bonfire in the street and danced round it until we were dizzy. Afterwards they took us to their friends, where the same process continued. When you realize, Trudie, I don't drink a lot and never touch spirits but I had beer, whisky, gin, sherry, cocktails and champagne that night, so by midnight I was well under the weather. By 1.30 a.m. I went out flat on my face, consequently causing them to put me to bed. The next I knew, I was being awakened at 9 a.m. with tea and many aspirins. I couldn't face breakfast as my head was like lead. Later I was informed that I had been making violent love to one of the chap's wives (a woman aged thirty-four with two children). I had to blush and everyone else laughed their heads off. I'm not ashamed of all the drink I had because it was a special occasion, wasn't it Trudie? Say yes please!

Glad you sent the snaps at last. I think they are perfectly wizard. I like the one with the built-up hairstyle and the high-necked frock. There's something quite remarkable about the expression on your face, so business-like, efficient and, if I may say, so very, very beautiful. I don't know why you are complaining about your figure – take it from me, it's superb. You dress so smartly, Trudie, I'd give a year's pay just to be seen out with you!

P.S. Those earrings are very becoming.

Well, I am away to London tomorrow for a forty-eight-hour pass. I'll tell you what I did next week. Cheerio for the time being.

Love,

Brian

In Berlin, Lieselotte G. adjusted to her first peaceful spring in six years.

11 May 1945

It is Her Birthday tomorrow. It smells of lilac again, like every other year. I have been picking tulips in the garden, just like I did last year, on the day I had my last lesson with her. How much has changed since then! Her husband and father are dead. Germany has fallen, conquered. And yet I still love her just the same as before. Perhaps it is no longer Frau L. herself I love, perhaps she is the embodiment of an idea, the idea of all that is beautiful, good, noble and true in this world. We have heard rumours of peace, but no one knows anything for certain any more. We used to have to try so hard to even imagine what peace would be like. Peace! After six years!

17 May 1945

Little R. told me today that almost all Hitler Youth boys from the Bann 120 group have been killed in the fight for Berlin, most of them on Heer Street. That's where Bertel was. I can't believe it. But Frau L. didn't believe it either and look! O, Bertel! So many soldiers dodged it, ran away, but Bertel was too enthusiastic for that. And what for? For Hitler? For Germany? Poor boy! You were so messed up, did you really have to pay for it with your blood? Why now, when everyone knows it's a lost cause, that nothing can save us? O Bertel! I never really knew you. You never opened up. I don't really know what drove you to your death. Should I be angry with you for your blind fanaticism, or respect the fact that you were so patriotic? Did you choose to die rather than bear the shame of slavery? Could you not see that Hitler had turned us into slaves too? Or were you only bound to Hitler by the oath you were forced to take? Couldn't you have done something more useful for Germany, our holy Fatherland, than die a pointless death? I think that Germany will be free and beautiful again. Perhaps our grandchildren will live to see that day.

It is all so terrible, and the worst thing is that I begin to realize, more and more, how bad and small-minded I am.

Lieselotte's brother, Bertel, did survive the war, as did Lieselotte and Klaus Granzow. Two months later, in July 1945, Lieselotte's home went to the Soviet sphere of influence as part of the post-war settlement agreed at Potsdam. Klaus's family farm in Pomerania would go to Poland, his family forced to resettle further west with millions of other Germans.

In Potsdam that July, as Western leaders discussed news of the successful atom bomb test, Churchill felt there was finally a real possibility of an 'end of the war in one or two violent shocks'. On 24 July 1945, President Truman wrote in his diary that 'the bomb was to be used between now and 10 August'.

At the end of that fateful July, at an annual summer camp for Jewish teenagers in upstate New York, David Kogan celebrated his sixteenth birthday.

29 July 1945

Today I'm entering my seventeenth year.

The campers sang: 'Let us bring peace to David on [his] birthday.' Of course it was tactless of me to come out in my dirty clothes waiting for the singers to finish. The management made cake in my honour, which was served at a party with some milk and cookies. I was introduced to an interesting custom prevailing in Jewish Palestine. Was placed on a chair and held on tight while four strong boys lifted me up sixteen times. It's a great thrill. One feels as if he is flying in space.

31 July 1945

Today is one of the landmarks in my life, for on this day I took my first shave. We went up to the guest house, where I carefully watched Larry shave himself, and after he finished, I began to lather up my face. Just then Bob, the camp chauffeur, came in and warned me against the move with the wise expression of a man of twenty-five – but it was to no avail. During the whole evening my face felt drawn taut-dry and uncomfortable, but it was an experience I shall never forget.

On 6 August 1945, a specially adapted B-29 bomber dropped an atom bomb on the Japanese city of Hiroshima. A second atom bomb was dropped on the city of Nagasaki three days later.

14 August 1945

Since the entrance of the atom bomb into our collection of arms in the war between the United States and Japan, there have been eager questions on the lips of millions: 'How long?' Finally, after supper today, we heard the news. THE WAR IS OVER. I cheered – but my cheers were empty, for I had no stake in the war. Then later in the evening, as I sat, or laid in bed, I thought of what the words VICTORY and PEACE mean. I realized that for the first time since 1935 all the leading and lesser nations of the world were at peace and were not trying to butcher each other. I realized that free peoples had triumphed over aggressor-led peoples – God's Moral Law prevailed. I realized that there was a lot of HOPE for a better world in the minds of men – perhaps more hope than after 1919. I hope we can achieve peace and prosperity all over the world.

16 August 1945

Last evening was declared 'Victory Night' and was very beautiful indeed. The songs which led America victorious in five wars, songs such as God Bless America, America, Over There, When Johnny Comes Marching Home Again, were sung alongside the ancient and modern Hebrew songs of peace, such as Sholom Aleichem and others. After prayers and speeches the evening concluded with the songs of the Victorious Nations.

Today was my day off and Mary and I hitched to Lehighton. Hitching is fun – the open air – seeing the country – having conversations with different people. One feels as free as the wind, and learns an awful lot that isn't in the books.

With Japan's capitulation, the war was finally over, a war which had claimed the lives of well over 50 million people across all continents, the vast majority of them civilians.

In Britain, Brian Poole wrote to Trudie Lach, expressing his thoughts on the future.

20 August 1945

Dear Trudie,

After all the dilly-dallying it has happened at last. As it came as an anticlimax people were not aroused to the same pitch as they were on VE Day. I think they are being quite cheeky, don't you? The Jap is living up to his name by being very shady and snake-like in his replies and actions but I know MacArthur is the man to deal with them. I can't imagine him giving them any opportunity to double-cross the Allies.

Now we can look forward to a period of progress towards a brighter future. If America, Russia and ourselves can keep together I see no reason whatsoever why there should not be everlasting peace. If we fail to do this the world will be in turmoil in less than no time. Let us all then realize our responsibility to the world. I think it is a well-known fact that with our new government we will have a more straightforward foreign policy, more honest and more suitable to a world needing guidance.

What on earth are tuna croquettes? I have a hazy idea that tuna is a big fish you catch in tropical waters.

In reply to your question, I see no reason why you shouldn't go on building skyscrapers because one stupid airman flew into the Empire State Building. Skyscrapers have stood up to the elements, they have solved a problem concerning limited ground space, so airmen of the future must know the area where these buildings are situated and consequently fly above them. So spoke Poole!

Love,

Brian

Six years to the day since Germany invaded Poland, New Yorker David Kogan added one further entry to his diary.

1 September 1945

As I write this at the end of the day, I am listening to the actual broadcast of the surrender of Japan to General MacArthur and representatives of the United Nations. They are describing it like a baseball game. I only hope they don't play the game of war any more.

Epilogue

*W*hen, in September 1939, his home town of Ostrów was annexed into the Third Reich, sixteen-year-old Edward Niesobski decided to join the resistance. As a member of the outlawed Polish Scouts, Edward defied the German ban on all Polish language and cultural activities and set up an illegal school for young scouts in a nearby forest. Using stolen radios and equipment, he trained the children in survival techniques, signal codes and weapons handling. Edward was elected local scout leader and in time joined the Polish Home Army as a courier, transporting arms and documentation between Polish districts annexed into the Third Reich and the rest of occupied Poland. Though Edward kept a diary throughout this time, he was unable to write about his underground activities for fear of compromising himself and those around him. Twice arrested and imprisoned, on 19 July 1944 Edward was executed by a German firing squad at the Žabików concentration camp. His father, two younger brothers and aunt were also executed as members of the resistance. Edward was posthumously awarded a Silver Cross for his contribution to the underground struggle of the Polish Scouts during the Second World War.

When Dawid Sierakowiak died in Łódź ghetto in August 1943 he had just turned nineteen. His diaries were discovered, after the Russians liberated the city in January 1945, by Wacław Szkudlarek, a Polish gentile and the original occupant of the flat which became the Sierakowiak family's ghetto home. Szkudlarek found five notebooks beside a stove, the missing ones presumed burnt by someone stoking the fire over the winter. The first two notebooks were published in Poland in 1960 in a volume *edited by Lucjan Dobroszycki, a contemporary of Dawid's who survived the ghetto.*

Leading Aircraftman Brian Poole was demobbed from the RAF in October 1946 and went on to become a secondary school geography teacher in Nottingham, where he met his future wife, Joyce. They married in 1953, had two daughters and settled in Shropshire. Trudie Lach married a lawyer and settled in Florida. Though she and Brian continued to write to each other after the war, they never met. Joyce, grateful for Trudie's support of Brian over the years, offered to buy her husband a ticket to meet Trudie in person, but he declined. The penpals continued corresponding until Brian's death in 1981 at the age of fifty-six. On Trudie's death, Brian's letters were returned to England and are now preserved at the Imperial War Museum. Trudie's letters to Brian have never been traced.

After the war Micheline Singer worked as an interpreter with the US Army, going to Bavaria as a lieutenant with the voluntary Women's Auxiliary Corps, becoming, as she put it, one of the occupying forces herself. Micheline and her future husband, Dutchman Maurice Bood, worked for the European Recovery Program ('Marshall Plan') in Munich, Heidelberg and Mannheim. While in Germany, Micheline tracked down the officer who had let her off after discovering her fake pass and sent him some food parcels. Micheline and her husband settled in Paris and had a son. Micheline went on to become a writer and journalist; her many novels remain unpublished. She was working on a biography of her relative, Louise Colet, writer, feminist muse and Flaubert's lover, when she died after a long illness in 1980 at the age of fifty-four.

Herbert Veigel returned to Germany from the Russian front and spent the last two years of the war training young recruits. He was promoted to lieutenant before the battle for Berlin, in which he was wounded just as the war ended. Dressed in civilian clothes, he pretended to be a French forced *labourer and went to a succession of hospitals, eventually ending up in a Red Army hospital in Warsaw. While he was still recovering, a Russian doctor ushered in one of his 'fellow countrymen', a French Jewish survivor from Auschwitz. She did not give him away. It took Herbert until 1956 to trace her. By then Herbert had trained as a dentist, married, had three children and was living near where he grew up in the Black Forest. Being able to thank her, Herbert later said, was one of the greatest moments of his life. Herbert was well into his seventies when he rediscovered his wartime letters. His mother had given them to her brother just before the Allied raid on Heilbronn in December 1944 in which she and Herbert's father were killed. Herbert died in 2008 aged eighty-six.*

More than thirty years after parting with her older brother Yura Ryabinkin, Leningrad siege survivor Ira, now Irina Ivanovna, read a magazine article quoting extracts from his diary. She had spent years after the war trying to find her brother and had no idea that he had kept a diary. She rushed to the magazine's office to ask if they knew anything of his whereabouts, but all the journalist could tell her was that local children had found his diary – a badly damaged exercise book – and used it in a school display commemorating the siege of Leningrad.

New Yorker David Kogan continued to keep his diary after the war, recording thoughts on American politics, religion and the state of the world, and detailing his exploits at school and numerous attempts at dating. On finishing school top of his year, he gained a scholarship to study at Cornell University. With a promising future ahead, David considered careers as a journalist and a lawyer, but fell ill soon after graduation. After months of different treatments, David was diagnosed with lymphoma and died in March 1951, aged just twenty-one.

When Hachiro Sasaki's family received notification of his death in April 1945, accompanied by a medal and a small amount of money, Hachiro's father went out to the local shop and spent all the money on a large bottle of sake. He returned to drink it in silence at home and never worked again. Hachiro's mother supported the family for the rest of her life, taking in lodgers and selling ties to make ends meet. Hachiro's name remained unmentionable until after his father's death. Neither a memorial service nor a funeral was ever held for Hachiro, but years later his younger brother Taizo Sasaki, now Emeritus Professor of Physics at the University of Tokyo, published Hachiro's diary in his memory.

Soviet partisan Ina Konstantinova was buried in the forest where she died, covering her group's retreat with submachine-gun fire. In 1949 her remains were exhumed and transferred to a cemetery in her home town of Kashin. Her parents' small wooden house became a museum dedicated to Ina's memory, her room preserved as she left it the day she ran away to join the partisans. After the war, streets and regional Young Pioneer groups were named after Ina who, together with thousands of other youngsters who fought in the war, was hailed as an example of bravery and selfless dedication to subsequent generations of Soviet children.

Klaus Granzow was interned in a Russian POW camp when the war ended, and was discharged suffering from tuberculosis three months later. He arrived back at his family farm in Mützenow in Russian-occupied Pomerania just before his eighteenth birthday. His whole family survived the war. For a time they continued to farm their land, which the Soviets turned into a collective farm, but they left for West Germany in 1948 when the area was handed over to Polish control. Klaus settled in Hamburg where he became the well-known actor and writer he had always dreamt of being. Years after the end of the war Klaus retrieved his diary which he had left with Hanni, the daughter of the family with whom he was billeted, in Hainichen in 1945. Klaus died in 1986 at the age of fifty-eight.

Vasily Baranov stopped writing his diary in January 1944, but managed to conceal it through numerous searches and rescue it when his barrack was set on fire during an air raid. Struggling to survive on meagre rations and anything else he could procure, he continued to work as a forced labourer at aircraft factories in East Germany. On 17 April 1945, Vasily was liberated by US troops, and in September was repatriated to his home village of Merinovka in southern Russia. Soon after his return, Vasily got in touch with Olga Karpechko, a young girl he had fallen in love with before they were both conscripted to work in Germany in 1943 and with whom he had managed to stay in contact. They were married soon after. Both worked at a local collective farm near Merinovka. Vasily later trained as a music teacher and worked at a Briansk music school until his retirement. To this day Vasily, Olga and their children live in Briansk.

Lieselotte G. gave her diary to two historians who were researching personal narratives of life in Berlin during the Second World War. Lieselotte had not looked at her diary since the war and on rereading it in later life was surprised at the 'stupid things' she had written in it. She went on to become an active Social Democrat, like her parents.

After Warsaw was liberated in January 1945, the Przybylska family returned to the city for a few days to hold a funeral for their beloved Wanda. After the war Jadwiga could not bear to speak about the period of the uprising, the memory of her sister dying in her arms was always too painful. Any open talk of the Warsaw uprising was forbidden in Poland until the 1960s, the participants presented as enemies of the Soviet communist system and enemies of the 'true Polish patriots'. Jadwiga didn't even tell her son, Tomasz, about the uprising, afraid that he would talk at school and get them all into trouble. Eventually, when Tomasz was fourteen, the same age as Wanda, Jadwiga gave him her diary to read.

The two Jewish women hidden by the Przybylskas in their flat survived the war and remained in Warsaw. Friends later told Yad Vashem (the Holocaust Martyrs' and Heroes' Remembrance Authority) about the family's brave actions, for which Jadwiga, then the only surviving family member, was honoured as one of the 'Righteous Among the Nations'.

A former inhabitant of the Łódź ghetto, Avraham Benkel, found the journal of the anonymous boy diarist when he returned to Łódź in July 1945. Benkel's own house was in ruins and he came across the diary, written in the end pages and margins of the novel Les Vrais Riches, *in the abandoned building next to his own. He kept it for twenty-five years before giving it to Yad Vashem.*

Japanese teenager Mikiko Kato continued to look after Special Attack pilots until July 1945 when, with the prospect of Allied landings, she was sent away for safety to a remote mountain village. Before she left Mikiko befriended trainee pilot Michiyasu Yamaki, a young student from Taiwan. Days before Michiyasu's scheduled final flight from an air base in Manchuria, news came of the Japanese surrender. Though Michiyasu went back to his base as ordered, two of his fellow pilots crashed their planes in a double suicide pact, unable to bear the shame of returning home defeated. In 1952, Michiyasu and Mikiko were married. The couple ran a pharmacy in Haramachi until their retirement. Mikiko Yamaki turned eighty in March 2009.

Elvira Filippovich remained in the Ukraine until leaving school in 1952. Though she came top of her year, she agreed to forsake her 'Gold Medal for School Achievement', and thereby an automatic place at any university of her choice, in favour of a classmate orphaned by Stalin's Purges. He would have had little hope of going to university, whereas Elvira felt she could choose whatever path she wanted. Returning to Moscow eleven years after she had left, on the eve of the war, Elvira considered becoming a journalist, a doctor or a physicist, but chose to train as a vet. It had been her grandmother's reasoning that Elvira should choose a secure profession with direct access to food, so she might never go hungry again. During her studies, Elvira fell in love with and married a fellow student from the Czech Republic. On graduating, she and Ivo left Russia to work on a Czech farm with their young daughter, Liena. Later, the family returned to the Soviet Union to develop the 'Virgin Lands' of Kazakhstan. After completing a PhD, and contributing dozens of academic articles, Elvira retains a passion for writing; she continues to write short stories and keeps a diary, to this day.

Acknowledgements

*W*e owe great thanks to a number of people who have encouraged and guided us, often beyond their remit: Jonathan Lewis and Martin Hitchcock for their unwavering support; Natasha Fairweather, our agent at AP Watt and a constant source of encouragement; and to the team at HarperCollins Publishers, without whom this book would not be the book it is now: our editors Claire Kingston and Louise Stanley, Denise Bates, Kirstie Addis, Susanna Abbott and Katherine Patrick, and our copy editor Katie Johnson.

The following people have through their own works or in person brought individual diaries to our attention or provided us with information, for which we are greatly indebted: Martin Gilbert; Richard J. Evans; Alexandra Zapruder; Alan Adelson; Kamil Turowski; Michael H. Kater; Nicholas Stargardt; Daniil Granin and Ales Adamovich; Laurel Holliday; Ingrid Hammer and Susanne zur Nieden; Kazimiera J. Cottam; Pavel Polian; Richard Vinen; Emiko Ohnuki-Tierney; Witold Banach; Andrzej Drzycimski; Joan Beddington.

We have been helped greatly by the staff of the British Library where we spent much of our research time, the Imperial War Museum's Department of Documents, the United States Holocaust Memorial Museum, the Emanuel Ringelblum Jewish Historical Institute and Yad Vashem, the Holocaust Martyrs' and Heroes' Remembrance Authority, who went out of their way to be of assistance.

For their patience, astute comments and encouragement on reading early drafts of the manuscript we are grateful to Paul Bernays, Natasha

Fairweather, Martin Hitchcock, Will Jacob, Jonathan Lewis, John and Tamsin Slyce.

We are extremely grateful to Kishi Yamamoto, Małgorzata Chrobak, Klara and Wanda Kemp-Welch, for their excellent translations and to Stephen Sharkey for his subtle polishing of the translations. On a personal note, huge thanks to Ben, Eleanor, Joel, Lukas, Paul, Tristan, Will and Zig who have been a constant source of support, and distraction.

One of the greatest pleasures in producing this book has been to come into contact with the surviving diary writers and the relatives of those who died. They have answered endless questions, provided photographs and helped immeasurably in increasing our understanding of the accounts: our great thanks to Elvira Filippovich, Tatiana Semionova, Mikiko Yamaki, Thomas and Ilona Veigel, Jadwiga, Tomasz and Andrew Wolf, Waltraud and Norbert Schlichting, Maurice Hendrik Bood, Christophe Bood, Nicole Singer, Joyce Poole, Professor Taizo Sasaki, Jan Kahn and Dorothy Miller.

Finally, we are deeply indebted to the sixteen young people whose remarkable accounts form the basis of this book.

Permission to reproduce extracts and photographs:

Grateful acknowledgement is made for permission to reproduce extracts from the following copyrighted works (all of which are listed in full in the Bibliography):

Extracts from the diary of the Anonymous Boy with permission from Yad Vashem, The Holocaust Martyrs' and Heroes' Remembrance Authority, and from Alexandra Zapruder. Extracts from Vasily Baranov, *Dnevnik Ostarbeitera* [*Diary of an Ostarbeiter*], with permission from Pavel Polian;

translated by Svetlana Palmer. Extracts from Micheline Bood (née Singer) *Les Années Doubles: Journal d'une Lycéene sous l'occupation* [*The Double Years: Diary of a Schoolgirl under Occupation*] with permission from Maurice Bood; translated by Sarah Wallis. Extracts from the diary of Elvira Filippovich: *Ot pionerki do chelnoka pensionerki* [*From a Young Pioneer to an Old Age Pensioner*], with permission from the author; translated by Svetlana Palmer. Extracts from the diary of Lieselotte G. from *Sehr selten habe ich geweint: Briefe und Tagebücher Aus dem Zweiten Weltkrieg von Menschen aus Berlin,* with permission from the editors, Ingrid Hammer and Susanne zur Nieden; translated by Sarah Wallis. Extracts from Klaus Granzow's *Tagebuch eines Hitlerjungen 1943–1945* [*Diary of a Hitler Youth*] with permission from Waltraud Schlichting; translated by Sarah Wallis. Extracts from *The Diary of David S. Kogan,* edited, with an introduction by Meyer Levin, Beechhurst Press Inc., New York, 1955, with permission from the widow of Meyer Levin, Tereska Torres. Extracts from the diary of Ina Konstantinova: *Defending Leningrad: Women Behind Enemy Lines,* with permission from the editor, Kazimiera J. Cottam PhD. Extracts from the diary of Edward Niesobski: *Dziennik harcerza i 'Szarotki' (1939–1944)* [*Diary of a Scout and His Girlfriend*] with permission from Andrzej Drzycimski; translated by Małgorzata Chrobak and Svetlana Palmer. Extracts from the unpublished papers of Brian Poole with permission from the Trustees of the Imperial War Museum, Department of Documents, and Joyce Poole. Extracts from the diary of Wanda Przybylska with permission from Jadwiga Wolf; translated by Sarah Wallis. Extracts from Yura Ryabinkin's diary published in *Blokadnaya Kniga* [*A Book of the Siege*] by Daniil Granin and Ales Adamovich; translated by Svetlana Palmer. Extracts from Hachiro Sasaki, *Seishun no Isho: Seimei ni Kaete, Kono Nikki, Ai* [*A Testament of Youth: Diary and Love, in the Absence of Life*], used by permission from Taizo

Sasaki; translated by Kishi Yamamoto. Extracts from *The Diary of Dawid Sierakowiak*, notebooks 2 and 4 from the archives of the Emanuel Ringelblum Jewish Historical Institute in Warsaw and from notebooks 1, 3 and 5 from the archives of the United States Holocaust Memorial Museum; translated by Klara and Wanda Kemp-Welch. Extracts from Herbert Veigel, *Christbäume [Flares]*, with permission from Thomas Veigel; translated by Sarah Wallis. Extracts from Mikiko Yamaki (Kato), *Inochi – A Diary of a Girl in War*, with permission from the author; translated by Kishi Yamamoto. Letters of Kukimoto Nobuhide by permission from his brother, Mr Kukimoto; translated by Kishi Yamamoto.

Photographs are reproduced by kind permission of the following archives and individuals:

Yad Vashem, Holocaust Martyrs' and Heroes' Remembrance Authority (pages from the Diary of the Anonymous Boy); Pavel Polian (Vasily Baranov); Maurice Bood (Micheline Singer/Bood); Elvira Filippovich; Ingrid Hammer and Suzanne zur Nieden (Lieselotte G.); Waltraud Schlichting (Klaus Granzow); Andrzej Drzycimski (Edward Niesobski); The Trustees of the Imperial War Museum and Joyce Poole (Brian Poole); Jadwiga Wolf (Wanda Przybylska); Taizo Sasaki; United States Holocaust Memorial Museum (Dawid Sierakowiak); Thomas Veigel (Herbert Veigel); Mikiko Yamaki; Mr Kukimoto.

Cover photograph © David Seymour/Magnum Photos

Bibliography

Diaries and Letters:

ANONYMOUS BOY

Łódź Ghetto: Inside a Community Under Siege, compiled and edited by Alan Adelson and Robert Lapides, Penguin, New York, 1991 (extracts); complete diary published as *Les Vrais Riches Notizen am Rande: ein Tagebuch aus dem Ghetto Łódź,* edited by Hanno Loewy and Andrzej Bodek *(Mai bis August 1944),* Reclam, Leipzig, 1997; extracts published in Alexandra Zapruder, *Salvaged Pages,* translated by Dana Keren, Yale University Press, New Haven, CT, 2004

VASILY BARANOV

Dnevnik Ostarbeitera, edited and introduced by Pavell Polian; *Znaniye* Literary Magazine, Issue 5/1995, Moscow, 1995; P. Polian and N. Pobol, *Nam Zapretili Bely Svet …,* Rosspen, Moscow, 2005

ELVIRA FILIPPOVICH

Elvira Filippovich, *Ot pionerki do chelnoka pensionerki,* Saturn, Podolsk, 2000

LIESELOTTE G.

Ingrid Hammer and Susanne zur Nieden (eds), *Sehr selten habe ich geweint: Briefe und Tagebücher aus dem Zweiten Weltkrieg von Menschen aus Berlin,* Schweizer Verlagshaus, Zürich, 1992

KLAUS GRANZOW

Tagebuch eines Hitlerjungen 1943–1945, Carl Schünemann Verlag, Bremen, 1965

MIKIKO KATO

Inochi – A Diary of a Girl in War, Hakuteisha Inc., Tokyo, 1996

DAVID KOGAN

The Diary of David S. Kogan, edited, with an introduction by Meyer Levin, Beechhurst Press Inc., New York, 1955

INA KONSTANTINOVA

Devushka iz Kashina, Molodaya Gvardiya, Moscow, 1947; *Devushka iz Kashina: Dnevnik i Pis'ma, I. Konstantinova, Vospomminaniya i Ocherki o Ney*, Moskovskiy Rabochiy Publishing House, Moscow, 1974; *La Jeune Fille de Kachine*, edited and translated into French by Elsa Triolet, Les Éditeurs Français Réunis, 1950; *Defending Leningrad: Women Behind Enemy Lines*, edited and translated by Kazimiera J. Cottam Phd, Focus Publishing, Newburyport, MA 1998

EDWARD NIESOBSKI

Edward Niesobski and Jadwiga Pfeiferówna, *Dziennik harcerza i 'Szarotki'* (1939–44), Zaklad Narodowy im Ossolińskich-Wydawnictwo Wroclaw, Poland, 1986

BRIAN POOLE

Unpublished correspondence, Department of Documents, Imperial War Museum, London

WANDA PRZYBYLSKA

Cząstka mego Serca, Cytelnik, Warsaw, 1969; *Una Parte del mio Cuore*, translated by Carlo Angli and Remo Pedace, Sandron, Firenze, 1963; *Journal de Wanda*, edited and translated by Zofia Bobowicz, editions Cana, Paris, 1981; *Ein Teil Meines Herzens*, translated by Lucie Ranft and Renate Weiss, Donat-Verlag, Bremen, 2006

YURA RYABINKIN

Extracts published in *Blokadnaya Kniga* by Daniil Granin and Ales Adamovich, Sovetsky Pisatel, Moscow, 1979

HACHIRO SASAKI

Seishun no Isho: *Seimei ni Kaete, Kono Nikki, Ai*, edited by Fujishiro Hajime, Showa Shuppan, 1981

DAWID SIERAKOWIAK

The Diary of Dawid Sierakowiak: Five Notebooks from the Łódź Ghetto, edited by Alan Adelson, translated by Kamil Turowski, Bloomsbury, London, 1996; *Dziennik Dawida Sierakowiaka*, edited by Lucjan Dobroszycki, Iskry, Warsaw, 1960 (Notebooks 2 and 4); Notebooks 1, 3 and 5, Art and Artifacts Archive, the United States Holocaust Memorial Museum

MICHELINE SINGER

Micheline Bood, *Les Années Doubles*: *Journal d'une Lycéene sous l'occupation*, Robert Laffont, Paris, 1974

HERBERT VEIGEL
Christbäume, Dietz Verlag, Berlin, 1991

Reference:

Adelson, Alan, and Robert Lapides (eds), *Łódź Ghetto: Inside a Community under Siege,* Penguin, New York, 1991

Aldrich, Richard J., *Witness to War: Diaries of the Second World War in Europe and the Middle East,* Doubleday, London, 2004

Ambrose, Stephen E., *Handbook on German Military Forces,* Introduction, Louisiana State University Press, Baton Rouge and London, 1990

Axell, Albert and Hideaki Kase, *Kamikaze: Japan's Suicide Gods,* Longman, London, 2002

Banach, Witold, *Ostrów pod znakiem pegaza Wydawnictwo Poznańskie,* Poznań – Ostrów Wielkopolski, 2005

Barnard, Christopher, *Language, Ideology, and Japanese History Textbooks,* Routledge Curzon, London and New York, 2003

Beevor, Antony and Artemis Cooper, *Paris after the Liberation: 1944–1949,* Penguin, London, 1994

Beevor, Antony, *Berlin: the Downfall,* Viking, London, 2002

——*Stalingrad,* Viking, London, 1998

Berger, Joseph and Dorothy, *Small Voices, A Grownup's Treasury of Selections from the Diaries, Journals and Notebooks of Young Children,* Paul S. Eriksson, Inc., New York, 1966

Breloer, Heinrich (ed.), *Mein Tagebuch, Geschichten vom Überleben, 1939–47,* Verlagsgesellschaft Schulfernsehen, Cologne, 1984

Browning, Christopher, *The Origins of the Final Solution,* Heinemann, London, 2004

Daniels, Gordon, 'Japanese Domestic Radio and Cinema Propaganda, 1937–1945: an Overview', in *Film and Radio Propaganda in World War II*, edited by K. R. M. Short, Croom Helm, London and Canberra, 1983

Davies, Norman, *Rising '44: The Battle for Warsaw*, Macmillan, London, 2003

Dobroszycki, Lucjan (ed.), *The Chronicle of the Łódź Ghetto 1941–44*, translated by Richard Lourie, Joachim Neugroschel and others, Yale University Press, New Haven and London, 1984

Duménil, Anne, Nicolas Beaupré and Christian Ingrao, *1914–1945: L'ère de la Guerre, Nazisme, Occupations, Pratiques Génocides, Tome 2, 1939–45*, Agnès Vienot, Paris, 2004

Earhart, David C., *Certain Victory, Images of World War II in the Japanese Media*, M. E. Sharpe Inc., New York and London, 2008

Ehrenburg, Ilya, *Lyidi, Gody, Zhizn*, Khudozhestvennaya Literatura, Moscow, 1967

Evans, Richard J., *The Third Reich at War*, Penguin, London, 2008

Fifty Years of Japanese Broadcasting, edited by History Compilation Room, Radio & TV Culture Research Institute, Nippon Hoso Kyokai, Japan NHK, Tokyo, 1977

Filipovich, Zlata and Melanie Challenger, *Stolen Voices: Young People's War Diaries, From World War I to Iraq*, Penguin, London, 2006

Fussell, Paul, *Wartime: Understanding and Behaviour in the Second World War*, Oxford University Press, New York and Oxford, 1989

Gilbert, Martin, *Second World War*, New Edition, Phoenix Press, London, 2000

Goodwin, Doris Kearns, *No Ordinary Time, Franklin and Eleanor Roosevelt: The Home Front in World War II*, Simon & Schuster, New York and London, 1994

Haste, Cate, *Nazi Women,* Channel 4 Books, London, 2001

Herf, Jeffrey, *The Jewish Enemy: Nazi Propaganda during World War II and the Holocaust,* The Belknap Press of Harvard University Press, Cambridge, MA, 2006

Hilberg, Raul, *The Destruction of the European Jews,* Yale University Press, New Haven, CT, 2003

Holliday, Laurel, *Children's Wartime Diaries: Secret Writings from the Holocaust and World War II,* Pocket Books, Simon & Schuster, New York, 1995

Horwitz, Gordon J., *Ghettostadt: Łódź and the Making of a Nazi City,* Harvard University Press, Cambridge, MA, 2008

Kater, Michael H., *Hitler Youth,* Harvard University Press, Cambridge, MA, 2004

Keegan, John, *The Second World War,* Hutchinson, London, 1989

Knopp, Guido, *Hitler's Children,* translated by Angus McGeoch, Sutton Publishing, Stroud, 2002

Lewis, Jonathan and Ben Steele, *Hell in the Pacific: from Pearl Harbor to Hiroshima and Beyond,* Channel 4 Books, London, 2001

Lingeman, Richard R., *Don't You Know There's a War On? The American Home Front 1941–45,* G. P. Putnams, New York, 1976

Lomagin, N. A., *V tiskakh goloda. Blokada Leningrada v dokumentach germanskikh spetssluzb i NKVD,* Evropeiskii Dom, St Petersburg, 2000

Longmate, Norman, *How We Lived Then: A History of Everyday Life in the Second World War,* Hutchinson, London, 1971

Nikitin V. A., ed., *Neizvestnaya Blokada: Leningrad 1941–44,* Limbus Press, St Petersburg, 2002

Ohnuki-Tierney, Emiko, *Kamikaze, Cherry Blossoms, and Nationalisms: The Militarization of Aesthetics in Japanese History,* The University of Chicago Press, Chicago and London, 2002

Ohnuki-Tierney, Emiko, *Kamikaze Diaries, Reflections of Japanese Student Soldiers*, University of Chicago Press, Chicago and London, 2006

Overy, Richard, *Russia's War*, Allen Lane, London, 1998

Paulsson, Dr G. Steve, *The Holocaust*, Imperial War Museum, London, 2000

Polian, Pavel, *Zhertvy Dvukh Diktatur*, Rosspen, Moscow 2002

Pryce-Jones, David, *Paris in the Third Reich 1940–44*, Holt, Rinehart & Winston, New York, 1981

Stargardt, Nicholas, *Witnesses of War: Children's Lives under the Nazis*, Jonathan Cape, London, 2005

Tuttle, William M., *Daddy's Gone to War: The Second World War in the Lives of America's Children*, Oxford University Press, New York and Oxford, 1993

Vinen, Richard, *The Unfree French: Life under the Occupation*, Allen Lane, London, 2006

Ward, Geoffrey C. and Ken Burns, *The War: An Intimate History 1941–1945*, Alfred A. Knopf, New York, 2007

Yamanouchi, Midori and Joseph L. Quinn SJ (trans.), *Listen to the Voices from the Sea (Kike Wadatsumi no Koe)*, University of Scranton Press, Scranton, PA, 2000

Yamashita, Samuel Hideo, *Leaves from an Autumn of Emergencies, Selections from the Wartime Diaries of Ordinary Japanese*, University of Hawaii Press, Honolulu, 2005

Zapruder, Alexandra, *Salvaged Pages: Young Writers' Diaries of the Holocaust*, Yale University Press, New Haven, CT, 2004

Index of Diarists' Entries and Letters

THE
RELIC GUILD

EDWARD COX

Copyright © Edward Cox 2014
All rights reserved

The right of Edward Cox to be identified as the author
of this work has been asserted by him in accordance with
the Copyright, Designs and Patents Act 1988.

First published in Great Britain in 2014
by Gollancz
An imprint of the Orion Publishing Group
Carmelite House, 50 Victoria Embankment,
London EC4Y 0DZ
An Hachette UK Company

This edition published in Great Britain in 2015
by Gollancz

1 3 5 7 9 10 8 6 4 2

A CIP catalogue record for this book
is available from the British Library.

ISBN 978 1 473 20031 9

Typeset by Deltatype Ltd, Birkenhead, Merseyside

Printed in Great Britain by Clays Ltd, St Ives plc

The Orion Publishing Group's policy is to use papers
that are natural, renewable and recyclable products and
made from wood grown in sustainable forests. The logging
and manufacturing processes are expected to conform to
the environmental regulations of the country of origin.

www.orionbooks.co.uk
www.gollancz.co.uk